TEACHING ACCELERATED AND COREQUISITE COMPOSITION

TEACHING ACCELERATED AND COREQUISITE COMPOSITION

EDITED BY
DAVID STARKEY

UTAH STATE UNIVERSITY PRESS
Logan

© 2023 by University Press of Colorado

Published by Utah State University Press
An imprint of University Press of Colorado
1580 North Logan Street, Suite 660
PMB 39883
Denver, Colorado 80203-1942

All rights reserved

 The University Press of Colorado is a proud member of the Association of University Presses.

The University Press of Colorado is a cooperative publishing enterprise supported, in part, by Adams State University, Colorado State University, Fort Lewis College, Metropolitan State University of Denver, University of Alaska Fairbanks, University of Colorado, University of Denver, University of Northern Colorado, University of Wyoming, Utah State University, and Western Colorado University.

ISBN: 978-1-64642-476-4 (hardcover)
ISBN: 978-1-64642-477-1 (paperback)
ISBN: 978-1-64642-478-8 (ebook)
https://doi.org/10.7330/9781646424788

Library of Congress Cataloging-in-Publication Data

Names: Starkey, David, 1962– editor.
Title: Teaching accelerated and corequisite composition / edited by David Starkey.
Description: Logan : Utah State University Press, [2023] | Includes bibliographical references and index.
Identifiers: LCCN 2023023486 (print) | LCCN 2023023487 (ebook) | ISBN 9781646424764 (hardcover) | ISBN 9781646424771 (paperback) | ISBN 9781646424788 (ebook)
Subjects: LCSH: English language—Rhetoric—Study and teaching (Higher)—United States. | English language—Remedial teaching—United States.
Classification: LCC PE1405.U6 T38 2023 (print) | LCC PE1405.U6 (ebook) | DDC 808/.0420711—dc23/eng/20230731
LC record available at https://lccn.loc.gov/2023023486
LC ebook record available at https://lccn.loc.gov/2023023487

Cover illustration © Natalypaint/Shutterstock; background © Alvaro German Vilela/Shutterstock

CONTENTS

List of Tables   vii

Introduction: A Sea Change
  David Starkey   3

PART I: CURRICULAR DESIGN

1. Developing a Successful Accelerated Composition Program
  David Starkey   17

2. Establishing a Corequisite Writing Model in a Postremedial Two-Year College
  Meridith Leo   45

3. Inching toward Equity: Graduated Choice in the Corequisite Classroom
  Lesley Broder   65

4. ALP Instructors' Experiences Teaching across Modes during the COVID-19 Pandemic
  Carrie Aldrich and Sarah Prielipp   80

5. Reflective Practices in Teaching for Transfer
  Melissa Favara and Jill Darley-Vanis   99

PART II: ASSESSMENT

6. Labor-Based Grading to Reduce Anxiety, Improve Flexibility, and Recast Instructor-Student Relationships
  Mark Blaauw-Hara   121

7. Finding the "Right" Amount of Rigor in the Research Paper
  Melissa Long   135

PART III: READING

8. Integrating Reading and Writing: A Four-Step Process
   Peter Adams   161

9. Tea with a Friend: Teaching Challenging Reading in the Corequisite Classroom
   Jami Blaauw-Hara   175

10. More Than Busywork: Journals as a Method of Success in First-Year Composition and Corequisite Courses
    Gregory Ramírez   190

PART IV: NONCOGNITIVE LEARNING

11. Accelerating Success: Noncognitive Learning in Composition Courses
    Margaret Nelson Rodriguez   207

12. Revisiting Dweck's Growth Mindset in the First-Year Corequisite Classroom
    Charlee Sterling   231

PART V: FACULTY DEVELOPMENT

13. Corequisite Composition Courses: A Need for Institutionalizing Professional Development for Programmatic Success
    Haleh Azimi and Elsbeth Mantler   251

Index   273
About the Authors   277

TABLES

6.1. Labor-based course grading rubric   130
11.1. EPCC graduation rates   209
13.1. Below credit and acceleration pre-IRW   255
13.2. Acceleration with IRW   255

TEACHING ACCELERATED AND COREQUISITE COMPOSITION

Introduction
A SEA CHANGE

David Starkey

A SEA CHANGE

Ten years ago, accelerated, or corequisite, composition was something of a fringe movement in college composition studies. Granted, its core principle was straightforward. Students enrolled in developmental English courses were leaving college at a far higher rate than they were completing their first-year composition (FYC) courses. Two-year college students were especially hard hit. In California, "70% of incoming students [were] required to enroll in one or more remedial courses" (Henson and Hern 2014, 1). Yet a study done at Butte College (a community college in rural northern California) found that "only 50% of students who began one level below college in writing in Fall 2010 completed college English within two years. For students who began two levels below college in writing, that number dropped to 27%. Among students starting three to four levels below college, just 18% completed college English within four years" (7). Not surprisingly, attrition rates like these meant only a small percentage of entering community college students were reaching transfer level, and even fewer of those went on to graduate from four-year institutions (Molloy 2018). However, when all students, no matter what their "assessment level," were given the opportunity to enroll in college-level English courses, pass rates for FYC classes increased significantly. At Chabot College, for instance, pass rates increased from a low of 28 percent among nonaccelerating students to a high of 57 percent among accelerating students, while at Las Positas College, the numbers rose from a low of 35 percent among nonaccelerating students to a high of 68 percent among accelerating students (Eagan and Hern n.d.).

Surprisingly perhaps, when one considers the evidence in support of acceleration, there was no sudden mass migration to this new approach to teaching. Indeed, skeptics were legion. Many instructors wondered whether they were doing students any favors by moving them deeper into their college careers with underdeveloped writing skills. And if "standards" were being lowered in order to accommodate students who would otherwise have accessed one or more levels below college, wasn't that essentially another form of grade inflation? Moreover, even granting the numbers like those reported from Chabot and Las Positas Colleges, didn't that mean 32 percent to 43 percent of accelerating students were still failing? What about that population? Who could they turn to if there was no remediation? Finally, faculty teaching in stand-alone developmental education programs—there were twelve in the California Community College system in 2012—felt their very existence as professionals was being threatened, and with good reason, as time has shown. (As we'll see at the end of the introduction, even now, not everyone is convinced acceleration is the *only* way to go.)

Nevertheless, by the autumn of 2021, when the essays for this collection were being completed, the situation had altered dramatically. According to Michelle Clark (2021), a senior executive at Macmillan Learning, fully 50 percent of instructors in the publisher's market were "teaching in some kind of corequisite model." That sea change in the prevalence of acceleration, which was often mandated by legislation, meant that—sometimes literally overnight—faculty who had been teaching one way for decades had to rethink their entire pedagogy. While both the Community College of Baltimore County's accelerated learning program and the California Acceleration Project continue to generate and collate important teaching resources, to date there is no print collection of articles focusing on classroom pedagogy in accelerated composition classrooms. It's not that ALP and CAP don't guide instructors in productive directions—the Community College Research Center (CCRC) at Teachers College of Columbia University and the California Community College's Research and Planning Group (RP) also deserve mention—but the relative paucity of scholarship on acceleration outside these few go-to sites and a scattering of very recent journal publications mean every new resource is a valuable one. Indeed, this book's original title—*Just in Time*—was borrowed from a widespread practice in corequisite composition of waiting to teach a skill until just before it is necessary for a learner to complete an assignment. We have arrived at that moment, and the emphasis throughout is on classroom practice and pedagogy.

This pragmatism can be partly explained by the fact that nearly all the contributors are current or former community college English instructors. Two-year college teacher-scholars are, as Patrick Sullivan (2020) notes in *16 Teachers Teaching: Two-Year College Perspectives*, "very rare in our profession" (3). One of the reasons for this rarity is that scholarship among community college faculty is not often valued or rewarded by administrators, including department chairs. Sadly, some colleges openly discourage scholarship, believing it distracts faculty from their teaching. Fortunately, one of the other main challenges *Teaching Accelerated and Corequisite Composition* contributors faced—writing their chapters while teaching up to five sections of composition—is also a source of their expertise. The work here is the result of hard-won hours, days, weeks, and years in classrooms both face to face and virtual. Readers who have come looking for high-flown theories with no application to real-world composition have come to the wrong place. However, if they are seeking cogently argued, experienced-based essays on real-world teaching, they will not be disappointed.

A BRIEF HISTORY OF ACCELERATED COMPOSITION

By most accounts, the story of accelerated composition starts in the early 1990s with Peter Adams, coordinator of the writing program at what is now the Community College of Baltimore County. Adams realized that while success rates for students enrolled in developmental composition classes might initially look acceptable, on closer examination it became clear only a small percentage of these students were moving through the entire composition sequence, and even fewer students were actually transferring to four-year colleges. After analyzing the data, Adams came to believe having to complete a remedial writing course was simply too much of a burden for the majority of CCBC students. Rather than preparing them for the college-level composition course in their future, remediation ultimately waylaid students. Indeed, many students who assessed into developmental composition courses didn't enroll in those classes at all.

In 2009, Adams—along with Sarah Gearhart, Robert Miller and Anne Roberts—published "The Accelerated Learning Program: Throwing Open the Gates" in the *Journal of Basic Writing*. That pivotal article outlined the history of basic writing in the United States and the "very low success rates for developmental programs nationwide" (55). Adams and his coauthors lauded the value of "mainstreaming" developmental writers, arguing that when "students placed into basic writing are allowed to go immediately into first-year composition, their sense that they are excluded from the real college, that they are stigmatized as weak writers, and that they may not be 'college material' is greatly reduced" (60).

The article ends with a number of recommendations about how best to design an accelerated learning program, most of which have become staples of accelerated learning communities across the country. Among those recommendations are cohort learning (small groups of students taking multiple courses together with the same instructor); small class size and heterogeneous grouping (eight basic writers mainstreamed into a college-level class of twenty); attention to behavioral issues and life problems; and contextual learning (students aren't *preparing* to write for college; they *are* writing for college).

The same year "The Accelerated Learning Program" was published, the Bill and Melinda Gates Foundation—a longtime advocate of K–12 developmental education—formed Complete College America. The mission statement of CCA (2009) echoes the concerns of the Baltimore professors: "We've made progress in giving students from all backgrounds access to college—but we haven't finished the all-important job of helping them achieve a degree." Among Complete College America's recommendations are "guided pathways to success." Features of the pathways model include clear, complete, and coherent programs of study; guiding students very early toward "meta-majors," that is, broad areas of study from which they can choose their specific major; a series of milestone courses that track the student's progress; and "intrusive, just-in-time advising" focusing on "students most in need of services."

The growing belief in the efficacy of acceleration was in part based on research conducted at the City University of New York's Graduate Center and at the Community College Research Center at Teachers College of Columbia University. The CCRC's Thomas Bailey and two colleagues—Shanna Smith Jaggars and Davis Jenkins—summed up much of the research arguing for guided pathways and accelerated learning in their 2015 book *Redesigning America's Community Colleges: A Clearer Path to Student Success.* They point out that many students "are confused by a plethora of poorly explained program, transfer, and career options; moreover, on closer scrutiny many programs do not clearly lead to the further education and employment outcomes they are advertised to help students achieve" (2). To improve outcomes, the authors suggest "creating more clearly structured, educationally coherent program pathways that lead to students' end goals" (3). In short, it is no longer enough simply to "open the gate" to all students; we must find a way to guide them to the end of the path: graduation and a career.

Not surprisingly, considering its origins in the Community College of Baltimore County and among early adopting colleagues at Kingsborough Community College in Brooklyn, accelerated learning has taken particular hold in community colleges, where it is, unfortunately, sometimes easy for students to get lost in the shuffle. In California, home to more community colleges than any other state, Katie Hern, cofounder (with Myra Snell) of the California Acceleration Project (2015), has been instrumental in transforming approaches to college remediation. Citing several studies, Hern notes that "placement tests are weak predictors of students' performance in college." She argues that "placement is destiny. When students are assessed 'not college ready,' the treatment prescribed—layers of remedial coursework—leaves them less likely to reach their goals."

Because underrepresented students heavily populate developmental composition courses, accelerated learning has attracted the interest of advocates for student equity. In *America's Unmet Promise: The Imperative for Equity in Higher Education*, Witham et al. (2015) call for a creation of "equity by design," in which "equitable practice and policies . . . accommodate differences in the contexts of students' learning." An equity-based approach does not treat all students the same. Instead, it recognizes "differences in students' aspirations, life circumstances, ways of engaging in learning and participating in college, and identities as learners and students" and makes appropriate adaptations for those differences (8).

Advocates of accelerated learning have also found inspiration in the work of neuroscientists who have demonstrated—as Stephanie Liou at Stanford's Huntington's Outreach Project (2010) explains—that "the brain continues to reorganize itself by forming new neural connections throughout life. This phenomenon, called neuroplasticity, allows the neurons in the brain to . . . adjust their activity in response to new situations or changes in their environment."

Carol Dweck, a psychology professor at Stanford, has done much to popularize these ideas through her work on fixed versus growth mindsets, and her ideas are frequently referenced in this collection. In "Brainology: Transforming Students' Motivation to Learn" (2008), she points out, "Stereotypes are typically fixed-mindset labels. They imply that the trait or ability in question is fixed and that some groups have it and others don't. Much of the harm that stereotypes do comes from the fixed-mindset message they send." In contrast, Dweck looks to the potential of growth mindset, which, "while not denying that performance differences might exist, portrays abilities as acquirable and sends a particularly encouraging message to students who have been negatively stereotyped—one that they respond to with renewed motivation and engagement."

In part because accelerated learning has strong research foundations, it continues to become more widespread. Tennessee was an early adopter, eliminating not only college remediation but, in 2018, all tuition and fees required to earn an associate's degree. Florida allows students to skip developmental classes if they choose, and Texas has been steadily increasing the percentage of developmental composition students required to enroll in corequisites in all public colleges and universities.

Other states have made similar moves, with perhaps the biggest change coming in California, where Assembly Bill 705 went into full effect in the fall of 2019. AB705 prohibits "a community college district or college from requiring students to enroll in remedial English or mathematics coursework that lengthens their time to complete a degree unless placement research that includes consideration of high school grade point average and coursework shows that those students are highly unlikely to succeed in transfer-level coursework" (Seymour-Campbell 2017). A lively debate has ensued about how we can know whether a student is "highly unlikely" to succeed in a college-level class (more about this below), but in the meantime, California community college faculty—like their colleagues throughout the country—have been energetically revising their curricula, applying their considerable knowledge, energy, and experience in an effort to make acceleration work. *Teaching Accelerated and Corequisite Composition* aims to be part of that vigorous exchange of ideas and information about reformed classroom practice.

Teaching Accelerated and Corequisite Composition

Teaching Accelerated and Corequisite Composition is divided into five parts, with the first and longest section of the book taking a deep dive into one of the central questions of teaching corequisite composition: To what extent do we need to alter our curricular design? My own chapter, "Developing a Successful Accelerated Composition Program," takes a big-picture look at issues likely to arise when building a new curriculum and how those challenges might be faced. Meridith Leo's "Establishing a Corequisite Writing Model in a Postremedial Two-Year College" examines some of the same challenges through the lens of her own experience helping to create such a program at Suffolk County Community College. In "Inching toward Equity: Graduated Choice in the Composition Classroom," Lesley Broder focuses on ways to engage accelerating students, specifically those enrolled in online asynchronous courses. Carrie Aldrich and Sarah Prielipp continue the conversation about teaching ALP online—specifically, during the pandemic—with a detailed study of the experiences of several of their colleagues at the University of Alaska Anchorage. The final chapter of the first section, Melissa Favara and Jill Varley-Danis's "Reflective Practices in Teaching for Transfer," investigates the complex and creative challenges of teaching accelerating students transferable concepts and transferable skills.

The book's second section focuses on assessment, another crucial issue for instructors and their students transitioning to accelerated learning. With so many students who might once have been deemed underprepared enrolled in college-level writing courses, how can we fairly evaluate their progress and build on the strengths they bring to the class? Mark Blaauw-Hara's solution is to recast the instructor-student relationship through labor-based grading, in which students agree on a contract with their instructor stipulating how much work they will do that semester and "receive credit for doing that hard work." In "Finding the 'Right' Amount of Rigor," Melissa Long argues we should not burden our students with undue expectations. Instead, instructors of research-based writing should "assess the student's ability to demonstrate research, critical thinking, and competent writing," keeping "our focus on [those] threshold concepts" and not "letting other factors seep into our assessments."

Section 3 looks at the pivotal, yet often overlooked, role reading plays in the writing process. In his chapter, Peter Adams, arguably the most important ALP theorist, turns his attention to IRW. "Integrating Reading and Writing: A Four Step Process" provides "a brief history of integrated reading and writing, explain[s] the sources of its difficulty of implementation, and suggest[s] solutions to those difficulties." Jami Blaauw-Hara's "Tea with a Friend: Teaching Challenging Reading in the Corequisite Classroom" focuses on teaching metacognition as the basis for "mindfully incorporating challenging reading with supportive classroom strategies." And Gregory Ramírez's "More Than Busywork: Journals as a Method of Success in First-Year Composition and Corequisite Courses" discusses the benefits of various types of reading journals, including their documented connection to increased student pass rates.

The fourth section covers noncognitive learning, an area of study that has been associated with accelerated learning from its very beginnings. Margaret Nelson Rodriguez's comprehensive "Accelerating Success: Noncognitive Learning in Composition Courses" argues for the importance of contextualization as a key to accelerated teaching "because it provides the framework for the developmental course to be purposeful and meaningful to students" and "also bridges content learned in a semester to future courses and to life." In "Revisiting Dweck's Mindset

Theory in the First-Year Corequisite Classroom," Charlee Sterling investigates Carol Dweck's work on fixed and growth mindset. Sterling acknowledges that while "racial bias, poverty, or learning differences" might be obstacles "no amount of effort can overcome," the work of the Stanford psychologist remains critical to helping students bolster their noncognitive skills.

The book concludes with a chapter by the current codirectors of the Community College of Baltimore County's accelerated learning program, Haleh Azimi and Elsbeth Mantler. "Corequisite Composition Courses: A Need for Institutionalizing Professional Development for Programmatic Success," which draws on their backgrounds in two different but related disciplines, academic literacy and English, and emphasizes the need for ongoing training for ALP faculty.

Together, these thirteen chapters provide the fullest discussion to date of accelerated and corequisite composition. While there is some inevitable overlap and disagreement in the conversation, the authors' varying perspectives on how to foster student success only enrich the overall exchange.

AGAINST EITHER/OR

Attentive readers of *Teaching Accelerated and Corequisite Composition* will notice a subthread running through the collection: not all college English instructors exposed to accelerated learning have embraced the movement. Some professors have likened acceleration to an unstoppable tidal wave generated at least as much by college administrators hoping to cut costs as it is by professors wanting their students to thrive. Despite statistics showing underrepresented students succeeding at higher rates than those who are tracked through developmental courses, these doubters worry that students are being rushed through their college education, that they don't have time to change their minds (and majors) and make life's inevitable mistakes.

Many advocates of accelerated composition would bristle at this skepticism. Hern (2020) of the California Acceleration Project, states flatly, "If we can't identify a group of students that does better starting in a remedial course, remedial courses should not be on the table" (4). Kathy Molloy, the founder of the acceleration program at Santa Barbara City College, agrees: "The data is clear—a significantly higher number of students complete the college-level class when they go directly into that course than if they attempt the basic writing sequence. And those marginalized students who placed into basic writing classes at disproportionately higher levels are experiencing the biggest gains in terms of completion rates" (Molloy and Starkey 2021, 7).

And yet dismissing the concerns of those with questions about acceleration short-circuits a potentially productive conversation about student learning. Despite all the data supporting acceleration, do we as educators truly want to create a situation in which no student has recourse to remediation, even if they actively seek it out? However persuasive the argument for corequisite composition, there is some evidence to suggest not *all* remediation thwarts student progress. Florence Xiaotao Ran and Yuxin Lin (2019), for instance, found that corequisite remediation in thirteen community colleges affiliated with the Tennessee Board of Regents was, indeed, generally quite successful, but they were concerned about the fate of students entering the course from more than one level below college readiness:

> It is unclear how corequisite remediation affects students who score further below cutoff and presumably have greater academic needs. Some evidence suggests that students with lower levels of academic preparation benefit from an intensive focus on building basic academic skills, either in prerequisite remedial sequences or in programs delaying college matriculation, such as CUNY Start. It is thus important for future research to examine how corequisite reforms affect the students who are the most academically vulnerable.

Perhaps the most eloquent defense of retaining remedial education was written by Suh et al. (2021), members of the National Organization for Student Success's Equity, Access, and Inclusion Network. In "Clarifying Terms and Reestablishing Ourselves within Justice: A Response to Critiques of Developmental Education as Anti-Equity," the authors note, "While equality references equal treatment, equity requires the acknowledgment of unequal starting points and the provision of varied resources or opportunities in order to produce fair outcomes" (4). They conclude,

> Institutional change is not as simple as eliminating standalone developmental classes to place students directly into college-level courses. Rather, this work requires (1) acknowledging how educational institutions often reproduce oppression, (2) striving to dismantle systemic oppression, and (3) engaging in constant self-reflection on our own socialization and assumptions. (6)

However, the distinction between acceleration and developmental education may not be as hard and fast as it sometimes seems. In her chapter in this collection, Broder recalls reading a passage in the Community College Resource Center's analysis of acceleration noting that "ALP's primary innovation is structural rather than instructional." Broder remarks, "This brief descriptor stayed with me as I established faculty development sessions or brainstormed ways to set up my class. It is the *structure* that is different, but the *instruction* is the same." She concludes, "When we talk about best practices for ALP, we're really considering best practices for teaching; no matter what their level, our corequisite students *are* our composition students."

Indeed, while the contributors to *Teaching Accelerated and Corequisite Composition* specifically address their insights to instructors of accelerated composition, much of what they have written will be useful to anyone teaching college composition, including our colleagues devoting their talents to pre-college-level courses. After all, the movement toward acceleration literally began in the *Journal of Basic Writing* when Adams and his fellow instructors at CCBC drew on their passion for helping developing writers. As Adams (2020) eloquently states in another article,

> Developmental education is the focal point for the American Dream. It is the most democratic segment of higher education. It is filled with students who are the first generation in their families to go to college; students who are not sure that they belong in college; students who lead very stressful lives; and, students full of hope that they will be able to improve their situation in life. (19)

Despite all the obstacles facing our students, and ourselves, it is our job, our *mission*, to help them towards their goals. Corequisite composition is a powerful tool for equity and inclusion, but it is even more powerful when it reaches out to and makes use of the wisdom of *everyone* who cares about student success.

REFERENCES

Adams, Peter, Sarah Gearhart, Robert Miller, and Anne Roberts. 2009. "The Accelerated Learning Program: Throwing Open the Gates." *Journal of Basic Writing* 28 (2): 50–69.

Adams, Peter. 2020. "Giving Hope to the American Dream: Implementing a Corequisite Model of Developmental Writing." *Composition Studies* 48 (2): 19–34.

Bailey, Thomas, Shanna Smith Jaggars, and Davis Jenkins. 2015. *Redesigning America's Community Colleges: A Clearer Path to Student Success*. Cambridge, MA: Harvard University Press.

Clark, Michelle. 2021. "Hello Sales Team! Introducing *Hello, Writer*." Presentation at the Macmillan National Sales Meeting, December 16. docs.google.com/presentation/d/1V83IYtMRGREhgheRZ7xjMsYPr15SuZ3DDS152nqCU5Q/edit#slide=id.g10703ad9208_0_470.

Complete College America. 2009. "Overview." linkedin.com/company/complete-college-america/about/.

Dweck, Carol. 2008. "Brainology." National Association of Independent Schools, Winter. www.nais.org/magazine/independent-school/winter-2008/brainology/.

Eagan, Catherine, and Katie Hern. n.d. "15+ Years of Accelerated Reading and Writing: Chabot and Las Positas Community Colleges." Presentation at the 5th Annual Conference on Accelerated Developmental Education, Baltimore. Last revised July 17, 2013. alp-deved.org/2013/08/15-years-of-accelerated-reading-and-writing/.

Henson, Leslie, and Katie Hern. 2014. "Let Them In: Increasing Access, Completion, and Equity in College English." *California Acceleration Project.* accelerationproject.org/Portals/0/Documents/let-them-in-final.pdf?ver=2016-09-29-124642-623.

Hern, Katie. 2015. "Some College Students More Prepared Than Placement Tests Indicate." *EdSource*, November 12. edsource.org/2015/some-college-students-more-prepared-than-placement-tests-indicate/90418.

Hern, Katie. 2020. "Disrupting the Deficit Narrative about Early AB 705 Data." *CAPacity Gazette* July: 4–5. https://accelerationproject.org/wp-content/uploads/documents/Cap_Gazette_2020_Jul_Web.pdf.

Liou, Stephanie. 2010. "Neuroplasticity." HOPES: *Huntington's Outreach Project for Education at Stanford*, June 26. hopes.stanford.edu/neuroplasticity/.

Molloy, Kathy. 2018. "SBCC Express to Success." California State University, San Bernardino. Accessed December 15, 2021. www.csusb.edu/sites/default/files/SBCC%20Express%20to%20Success%20-%20Kathy%20Molloy.pdf.

Molloy, Kathy, and David Starkey. 2021. "Leaning into Acceleration: A Conversation Between Kathy Molloy and David Starkey." *Writing on the Edge* 31 (1/2): 1–10.

Ran, Florence Xiaotao, and Yuxin Lin. 2019. "The Effects of Corequisite Remediation: Evidence from a Statewide Reform in Tennessee." CCRC Working Paper 115, *Community College Research Center, Teachers College, Columbia University*, NY, November. ccrc.tc.columbia.edu/media/k2/attachments/effects-corequisite-remediation-tennessee.pdf.

"Remediation: Higher Education's Bridge to Nowhere." 2012. *Complete College America.* completecollege.org/wp-content/uploads/2017/11/CCA-Remediation-final.pdf.

Seymour-Campbell Student Success Act of 2012: Matriculation: Assessment, AB 705. 2017. California State Legislature. https://openstates.org/ca/bills/20172018/AB705/.

Suh, Emily, S. Owens, Ekateryna O'Meara, and Leanna Hall. 2021. "Clarifying Terms and Reestablishing Ourselves within Justice: A Response to Critiques of Developmental Education as Anti-Equity." *National Organization for Student Success.* www.researchgate.net/publication/352392755_Clarifying_Terms_and_Reestablishing_Ourselves_within_Justice_A_Response_to_Critiques_of_Developmental_Education_as_Anti-Equity.

Sullivan, Patrick. 2020. "Introduction: Democracy's Unfinished Business." In *16 Teachers Teaching: Two-Year College Perspectives*, edited by Patrick Sullivan, 3–33. Logan: Utah State University Press.

Witham, Keith, Lindsey Malcom-Piqueux, Alicia C. Dowd, and Estela Mara Bensimon. 2015. *America's Unmet Promise: The Imperative for Equity in Higher Education.* Washington, DC: Association of American Colleges and Universities.

PART I

Curricular Design

1
DEVELOPING A SUCCESSFUL ACCELERATED COMPOSITION PROGRAM

David Starkey

What are the essential elements of a successful accelerated composition program? Clearly, there can be no single answer to that complex question, but I believe it is important to address it at the outset of *Teaching Accelerated and Corequisite Composition*, before my co-contributors offer their more granular investigations of many of the specific elements I discuss. This chapter, therefore, takes a big-picture approach. While it is primarily intended for faculty—and administrators—who are just beginning to develop an accelerated composition program, it should also provide useful reminders of some of the field's most effective practices for departments whose programs are already established.

The chapter is divided into three sections: (1) discussions of some of the necessary preparations for convening accelerated classes; (2) recommendations for what to do when classes are in session; and (3) suggestions for important follow-up work after the semester is over. The material covered could easily have become the subject of a book-length work, so I have done my best to zero in on what I believe are the most important elements in a successful program. In addition to my research, and plenty of conversations with fellow instructors of accelerated composition, my recommendations are, above all, based on my experience teaching in Santa Barbara City College's nationally honored Express to Success program, founded and directed by Kathy Molloy.

ESP received the California Community Colleges 2012 Chancellor's Award for Best Practices in Student Equity, and the program's prominence was a crucial factor in SBCC winning the Aspen Institute's 2013 Prize for Community College Excellence. The Express to Success program generated overwhelming data showing it was helping propel enrolled students toward higher course-completion rates. In spring 2017, for instance, 70.4 percent of students assessing one course below college level completed the one-semester accelerated college-level course offered through ESP. By contrast, after a full year, only 28.2 percent of students starting at the developing level who were not enrolled in accelerated composition had completed the college-level course: a 42.2 percent difference (Molloy 2018, 13). Then-SBCC president Lori Gaskin called ESP "synergistic" and "transformational," praising "the integration of effective teaching practices, structured pathways, curricular compression, group-based learning experiences, peer-based connections, and interventions and support services that keep students focused, grounded, and linked together" (Galvan 2012). Express to Success was a program that truly lived up to its name.

Ironically, ESP was discontinued in fall 2019 when California Assembly Bill 705 took effect, effectively making all math and English departments in the California Community Colleges system accelerating programs. The resulting confusion, with some colleges embracing the opportunity to implement acceleration, and others doing as little as they legally could ("Invalid Placement" 2021), is one of the inspirations for this chapter. I wanted to gather in one place the best advice I could find for developing a coherent program, one that is equitable and far-seeing and that places students' best interests at its core. While I frequently reference my home state, and the work done at the Community College of Baltimore County, the recommendations offered here are meant to be applicable to colleges across the country.

BEFORE THE SEMESTER BEGINS

Understand the Rationale for Acceleration and Keep
Abreast of the Latest Developments

The ESP data shared above, showing accelerating students succeeding at an astonishingly high rate, varies from institution to institution, of course, but it is nearly always remarkable, especially when it is accompanied by institutional will and financial resources. In July 2020, the year after AB 705 went into effect, the California Acceleration Project reported that in first-semester composition courses, "the average one-term completion rate has doubled, increasing from 32 percent to 65 percent across the 12 colleges examined. And at one college—Porterville—completion is almost six times higher" (Hern 2020). In an article for *Capitol Weekly* on March 18, 2021, Andrew Nickens, vice president of legislative affairs for the Student Senate for California Community Colleges, sums up the rationale for acceleration quite clearly: "Getting stuck in remedial classes predicts academic failure. Students must pay for the classes but don't earn any credits towards a bachelor's degree. And over a decade of research shows that starting in a remedial class makes them less likely to earn a degree."

At its best, therefore, acceleration ensures that countless college students who would have dropped out due to the financial, emotional, and physical stress of slogging through unnecessary classes are instead completing college-level coursework in English and math, and—though somewhat less successfully ("Through the Gate," n.d.)—also completing the coursework necessary to earn a bachelor's degree.

Perhaps most important, as Leslie Henson and Katie Hern (2014) argue,

> increasing student access to college-level English can be a powerful lever for reducing equity gaps among under-represented students of color. While all students saw greater completion after the policy change, students of color saw the greatest completion gains, narrowing the gap between their completion and white students' completion. This is likely because, under standardized placement testing, students of color are much more likely to be classified as "underprepared" and denied access to college English. In short, because students of color were more disadvantaged by the previous policy, they had more to gain from the change. (14)

Indeed, because the data are so convincing, proponents of acceleration have long contended that when it comes to student success, the onus of proof should be on those who are *not* implementing acceleration rather than those who are.

Nevertheless, developing an accelerated composition program can be a complex and fraught endeavor, so it makes sense to take advantage of the know-how of those who have already accomplished the task. For those just beginning, it might be helpful to begin by reviewing *Teaching Accelerated and Corequisite Composition*'s introduction, which sketches out a timeline of the development of accelerated composition. The first extended discussion of the topic, "The Accelerated Learning Program: Throwing Open the Gates" by Adams et al., which was published in 2009, is essential reading (and available online through the Education Resources Information Center). In 2020, Adams took a second look at acceleration with an equally reasonable and pragmatic article: "Giving Hope to the American Dream: Implementing a Corequisite Model of Developmental Writing." The Community College of Baltimore County, where Adams and several other contributors to this volume teach, hosts the accelerated learning program website (alp-deved.org), where the basics of ALP are explained and all presentations for the group's annual meeting—the Conference on Acceleration in Developmental Education (CADE)—are housed.

An even more robust collection of history and news can be found at the website of the California Acceleration Project (accelerationproject.org), which is led by Katie Hern in English and Myra Snell in math. CAP is a powerhouse of information about and promotion for acceleration, with an active Publications page touting the movement's latest accomplishments and combating doubters with reams of data.

Finally, a similar wealth of data can be found on the website of the California Community Colleges system's Research Planning Group (rpgroup.org). The RP Group is a "a non-profit, non-partisan team" of administrators, staff and faculty "working together with a shared and resolute goal: to increase the success of California Community Colleges and beyond" ("Who We Are," n.d.). The RP Group researches more than just accelerated learning, but its findings are, in addition to always being supported by extensive data, succinct, often illustrated, and written in administrative- and legislative-friendly language. It's a good place to turn for an intelligent summing up of acceleration's core values.

Secure Funding

Once a college has decided to adopt an accelerated composition model—or that decision has been made for the college—it is vital to ensure sufficient funding is secured to ensure the program continues beyond its initial phase. While acceleration has delivered spectacular results, properly implemented, it can be expensive. Watching the sudden dissolution of my college's Express to Success program because of budget cuts was a distressing experience, one that could have been avoided with a long-term administrative commitment to the program.

As Peter Adams (2020) points out, "Too often, the state mandates . . . require implementation of a corequisite model by a certain date but provide few or no resources to support that implementation. . . . As a result, some schools are implementing corequisite models that are not robust enough to produce the dramatic improvements in success rates we all hope for" (26–27). Obviously, budgets shift with the prevailing economic winds, but that is all the more reason to secure dedicated funding for an educational approach proven to be so successful.

The budget battle for community colleges begins by documenting just how few remediating students in the intuition are transferring to four-year colleges, and ultimately graduating, in comparison with those who are accelerating. Nothing says success like seeing our students accomplish their goals, and highlighting individual acceleration success stories, with details and images, can make those narratives all the more powerful to those who control the purse strings.

Collaborate with Math

It's no coincidence English and math are working together in acceleration throughout the country. There is power in numbers. (And our math colleagues are *really* good at making acceleration success rates visible to the larger campus.) Especially in community colleges, these are typically the two largest departments. Most, or all, of a college's students enroll in an English or math class, which means the great majority of students stand to benefit from acceleration, another important rationale for ensuring its funding is adequate and uninterrupted.

Meeting on a regular basis, English and math faculty can exchange ideas and problem solve together. Granted, the two disciplines will inevitably approach acceleration through different avenues. According to one study (Bahr et al. 2019), "A higher GPA is necessary to signal readiness for college-level coursework in math than is necessary to signal readiness for college-level coursework in English" (201). However, despite any disciplinary or pedagogical variations that may arise, collaboration between the two departments guarantees acceleration will have a powerful voice on campus.

Rethink Course Design with Acceleration in Mind

One of the most consistent complaints of faculty thrust into accelerated composition courses is that they are unprepared for the sudden mix of developing and college-level writers. These instructors are remembering past semesters, when students were sorted—too often by computer programs like ACCUPLACER—into categories that were often myopic at best and inequitable at worst but that did ensure *most* of the students entering the class had a similar skill set.

Acceleration rejects that model outright and requires a corresponding—sometimes quite painful—recalibration of faculty attitudes towards student preparedness. The necessary adjustment may require time, and encouragement from faculty already teaching accelerated courses, but once instructors have a clearer idea of their new student population and the goals of their new course, they will need guidance to develop curriculum that benefits these students, that tells them they belong.

Of course, an effective instructor finds many ways to make students feel welcome, from the first day's greeting to the parting on the final day. These affective behaviors are important and will receive more attention below, but from a course-design perspective, instructors can help students feel at home even before they arrive in the classroom by carefully planning the semester so each activity scaffolds up to the next in a manner that it is equitable, clear, relevant and reflective.

Melissa Ko's "Course Design Equity and Inclusion Rubric" (2021), available at Stanford's Teaching Commons, offers one helpful method of evaluating course content. The rubric features categories such as "Personal Connections and Relevance," "Transparency of Content," "Diversity of Perspectives" and "Diversity of Media" that remind instructors—especially those who have been teaching for a while—to take a fresh look at not only what material they are assigning but also how they expect students to respond to it. Moreover, as Asao Inoue (2015) points out, "Addressing and negotiating one element [of a writing assignment], say . . . part of a rubric, means you are addressing others, such as power relations and the ecological places where students problematize their existential writing assessment situations" (284). Ideally, the rubric is "an articulation of something other than standards, such as a set of dimensions worth exploring and questioning, a starting point, not end point" (285).

Accelerating students are diverse not just in their learning backgrounds and styles but in every conceivable way. In "Moving Beyond Disability 2.0 in Composition Studies" (Wood et al. 2014), the authors stress the importance of "accessible course design and emphasize a dynamic, recursive, and continual approach to inclusion rather than mere troubleshooting." These instructors remind us that "disability's presence, like the presence of students with race, class, or gender differences, is not a 'problem' but rather an opportunity to rethink our practices in teaching writing" (148). Suggestions for new prompts and new methods of assessment can be found on the ALP, CAP, and RP websites, as well on the websites of individual colleges such as the Rochester Institute of Technology (n.d.).

Naturally, the course homepage and syllabus should be easy to navigate. Instructors not only model clear writing for their students in these documents, they also ensure expectations are clear and concrete. And it is in the syllabus and weekly schedule that instructors demonstrate—by assigning diverse authors and content creators in varied genres—that they honor a range of ways of expressing ideas and opinions. Of course, students cannot succeed unless their basic needs are met. Even the most dedicated student necessarily prioritizes the problem of locating shelter and food over a problem-solution essay. The class homepage, therefore, should also link to campus resources, and reminders about those services should appear throughout the semester.

While English instructors may take for granted the significance of their own field of study, the discipline's relevance may not be immediately apparent to a student planning to study chemistry or computer science. It's vital, therefore, early and often to connect the value of effective written and spoken communication to success across the curriculum. In a study of college students from nonmajor sections of biology, psychology, and English, researchers found students feel an increased sense of belonging to the course in which they are enrolled when they perceive "academic tasks are interesting, important, and useful" (Freeman, Anderman and Jensen 2007, 205).

While we will never be able to fully see the world through the eyes of our students, *trying* to imagine what various groups are facing as they enter the class on that first day, while actively searching for our own biases, will go a long way towards ensuring our course design supports the goals, and challenges, of acceleration.

Insist on a Corequisite Course.

The terms *accelerated composition* and *corequisite composition* are often used interchangeably, but I've avoided that usage because many accelerated programs do not mandate that developing students enroll in a support course. Indeed, in "Giving Hope to the American Dream" (2020), Adams identifies four widely used approaches to the idea of additional support, only one of which employs a corequisite that specifically reinforces the material being taught in the college-level composition course:

1. the *Fast Track or Stretch Model*, which "comprises developmental students only";
2. the *Studio Model*, in which developmental students "are mixed with an equal or greater number of college-level students" and also enroll "in a one-hour studio course with students from a variety of other courses requiring writing";
3. the *Tutoring Model*, in which "all students are enrolled in a credit level course," but developmental students are offered additional support in the writing center;
4. the *Accelerated Learning (ALP) Model*, in which ten developmental students "join an equal or larger number of college-ready students in a 3-hour per week ALP section of the credit-level course. The students who are not yet college ready also register for an ALP developmental

section for an additional 3 hours per week. At some schools, the support class meets for fewer than three hours per week. At other schools the support class is taught by a different instructor." (27–29)

Examined from a purely bottom-line perspective, the tutoring model is clearly the most appealing, although as Adams (2020) points out, "Many schools report a lack of student visits to the computer lab or Writing Center if such visits are not required" (28). If, as Adams et al. (2009) argue, the ALP model is so effective in part because the college-level course includes both developing and college-level students, the fast-track model essentially rejects that premise by eliminating the traditional college-level students altogether. The studio model does provide students with the opportunity to work on their writing outside the college-level English course, but the material does not reinforce the specific instruction students receive in their composition class.

Only the ALP model, which, not incidentally, was adopted by SBCC's ESP program, ensures developing students spend time in the classroom with their college-level peers *and* receive instruction connected to their college-level English class. While the corequisite does have its challenges—keeping restless students on task in a computer lab isn't easy—it does provide students with the opportunity to try out what they are learning in the college-level class. Students who are working on their essay drafts can ask questions of their instructors that might have flummoxed them—and halted their progress—if they were writing on their own. Moreover, in the corequisite, composition issues from the global (thesis and organization) to the very local (where to put the parentheses in an MLA citation) can be discussed in as much detail as students require.

While one objection to the corequisite in my department was that it shouldn't be mandatory because it might interfere with students' full lives and myriad responsibilities, the counterargument, which I endorsed, was that students wouldn't attend the support course unless it was mandatory. That turned out to be the case after the passage of AB 705; voluntary corequisite courses were underenrolled, with many of them eventually cancelled. After a few semesters, they were no longer offered at all. That was a shame: the California Acceleration Project's mantra of "high challenge, high support classrooms" is rendered almost meaningless without the second half of the equation.

Foster Student Awareness of and Buy-In to Acceleration

The transition from teaching in the Express to Success program for the last time, in spring 2019, to the first semester of AB 705, in fall

2019, when all composition students were accelerating, was—for me, at least—a stark one. Before enrolling, ESP students signed a contract committing to the extra time that would be required to accelerate from one course below college-level (where they had assessed) to successfully completing the college-level course in a single semester. The contract even asked students to pledge they would work fewer than nineteen hours a week at their jobs during the semester they were accelerating.

Looking back from a distance of several years, that contract seems outdated and fraught with possible inequities. Was it fair to ask an economically struggling student to limit their work hours when that lack of additional pay might cause housing and food insecurity? Moreover, the data, as we have seen, support the mainstreaming of *all* students, no matter what their current skill set is. Doing so ensures the highest percentage of "throughput," the percentage of students who successfully complete transfer-level courses in a predetermined timeframe. As acceleration demonstrates, when students placed in classes one or more course levels below college are given the opportunity to escape the "leaky pipeline," many do leave college.

And yet I continue to believe a key element of ESP's resounding success was alerting developing students to the fact that they were making a conscious decision to enroll in an accelerating class. In the semester after AB 705 resulted in the elimination of the ESP program at SBCC, not a single student ever mentioned any awareness that there had once been an assessment system for first-semester composition. And, of course, as entering first-year students, why in the world would they have that piece of information?

From one perspective, of course, that's ideal. Everyone appears to begin the class on an equal footing, and obviously we don't want to shame students by pointing out, on the first day, that some of them are more accomplished academic writers than others. However, we do students a grave disservice if we do not make them aware of the support they may need to succeed. If, for instance, a student would benefit from enrolling in a corequisite, but they are unaware of its existence, or we are forbidden to recommend the course, or the course is not being offered, their chances of passing the course diminish considerably. It's worthwhile, therefore, to spend time throughout the semester, but especially at the beginning, explaining what acceleration is and why it is in place. Early ungraded writing assessment can alert both instructor and students to the need for support services, assuming they are available.

DURING THE SEMESTER
Always Be Mindful of Equity

The need for a keener awareness of how instructor biases play out in the classroom, discussed in the previous section is, obviously, even more important during the semester itself. As Ibram X. Kendi (2019) points out, no one is "colorblind," and everyone must actively and continuously combat their own inherent and often unrecognized prejudices. In Kendi's words, "To be antiracist is a radical choice . . . requiring a radical reorientation of our consciousness" (23).

From course design to classroom discussion to essay prompts and writing assessment, in *Teaching Men of Color in the Community College*, J. Luke Wood, Frank Harris III, and Khalid White (2015) argue that "faculty members must embrace an internal locus of control, believing that they possess the capacity to advance men of color and other disadvantaged student groups" (73). The authors make a number of specific suggestions for reaching out to previously disenfranchised students: teaching relevant content, building in critical reflection and "metacognitive moments," providing collaborative experiential learning activities like community-based service and attending music or cultural events, careful and ongoing performance monitoring, and early interventions when necessary. The classroom described in *Teaching Men of Color* is a site attuned to student needs and interests, one in which the instructor is ever vigilant and always flexible.

Build Community

Again, ensuring a sense of belonging and inclusion are baked into the course design and syllabus is an important first step, but that won't matter if the classroom itself is not a place where students feel at home. Building a sense of belonging starts on the first day, of course, with icebreakers that not only begin the process of introducing students to one another and their instructor but also allow students to share their worries about the class, the obstacles they face, and the solutions they envision to help them successfully complete the course. Maithreyi Gopalan and Shannon Brady (2020) recommend creating an environment "that helps students feel connected to each other, to faculty and staff, and to the institution." Among their suggestions for fostering this sense of belonging is foregrounding the idea that "certain kinds of challenges in the transition to college . . . are common, shared by many students from diverse backgrounds, and likely to abate over time. Such thoughtful outreach seems to be especially powerful for Black, Latinx, Native, and first-generation students."

Sean Garrity's strategies (2020) for building community in community college classrooms, where most or all students may live off campus, include making extensive use of small-group activities, awarding extra credit for attending campus events, and asking students to learn about and report on campus resources. As Garrity points out, "Some other faculty members may view these kinds of activities and assignments as a waste of time, someone else's responsibility at the college, or antithetical to rigorous college writing instruction. But as first-year composition instructors, we are often one of the first points of contact for students at the community college—students who are anxious, overwhelmed, fearful and often feeling alone without their tight-knit high school friend group around them."

We employed all these approaches in the Express to Success program. In addition, each semester, students who had previously passed the course spoke to those just setting out on their journey. They provided advice and encouragement and offered pragmatic responses to pressing issues during Q&As. Four- or five-person "study-buddy" groups helped those who were confused or had missed assignments to catch up. Indeed, the courses took on some of the more positive aspects of self-help sessions (see the section on growth mindset below), and there was a kind of celebratory aspect for each accomplishment—a favorite song played on YouTube after a particularly demanding lesson, or a pizza party after turning in the research paper. We tried to create the sort of environment an instructor's "student self" would be keen to be part of.

Foster Growth Mindset, Grit, and Other Noncognitive Skills

Building community requires building student self-esteem. Dennis Lawrence (2000) contends that "a person's self-esteem is dependent on the relationship between their *self-image* and their ideal self" (1). Essentially, the discrepancy between self-image, a person's realistic view of their own strengths and weaknesses, and ideal self, the person they would like to become, either moves the person towards closing the gap between self-image and ideal self, or it results in a significant level of frustration: "We say that people who have low self-esteem lack confidence in themselves so that they are reluctant to take risks either personally or in the learning of a new skill, e.g., reading. They will be so aware of their inadequacies, both as people and in their skills, that they will avoid situations they perceive as likely to cause them further unpleasant feelings" (4–5). A strong accelerated composition program helps students bridge the gap between self-image and their ideal self, and it does so by insisting the gap is not only *okay*, it's actually *necessary* for growth to take place.

Foster Growth Mindset

The mindset described by Lawrence is the very one Stanford psychologist Carol Dweck addresses in her book *Mindset: The New Psychology of Success* (2006). In that groundbreaking volume, Dweck contrasts "fixed" and "growth" mindsets. A fixed mindset assumes "your qualities are carved in stone" (10). You are who you are, and no matter what you do, you're never *really* going to change. In contrast, growth mindset "is based on the belief that your basic qualities are things you can cultivate through your efforts. Although people may differ in every which way—in their initial talents and aptitudes, interests, or temperament—everyone can change and grow through application and experience" (7). As Dweck points out, having a growth mindset doesn't just mean being "flexible or open-minded." Instead, students with a growth mindset, to quote from Dweck's article "Brainology" (2008), "believe that intelligence is a potential that can be realized through learning. As a result, confronting challenges, profiting from mistakes, and persevering in the face of setbacks become ways of getting smarter."

Moving towards a growth mindset is an active and ongoing process. Dweck argues in a *Harvard Business Review* article (2016) that "it's critical to reward not just effort but learning and progress, and to emphasize the processes that yield these things, such as seeking help from others, trying new strategies, and capitalizing on setbacks to move forward effectively." Moreover, institutions, as well as individuals, must "continually reinforce growth mindset values with concrete policies." Ultimately, she claims, we are all "a mixture of fixed and growth mindsets, and that mixture continually evolves with experience." In short, "A 'pure' growth mindset doesn't exist."

The act of writing is full of challenges, course corrections, and constant minor victories and defeats—a veritable laboratory for creating a growth mindset. Consequently, college composition classes are particularly valuable sites for encouraging students to confront their setbacks head-on so they can unpack them and strategize ways to effectively address similar challenges the next time they arise. In fact, it's possible to cultivate a growth mindset in everything we do in our writing courses: from class discussions in which equitable participation is paramount, to essay prompts that encourage growth-mindset qualities like experimentation and introspection, to assessment and evaluation on written work that emphasizes constructive criticism and praise for risk-taking.

Foster Grit

However talented the faculty teaching accelerated composition classes may be, most students must dedicate themselves to the hard work it takes to become stronger writers. As I frequently told my ESP students, if you want to successfully complete two courses in the time most students take to finish one, you may well have to double the amount of time and effort you put into the class.

Fortunately for many students, once the initial fear of going faster than normal wears off, the exhilaration of moving quickly can actually be quite energizing. Still, accelerated learning isn't just about speed; it's also about determination. The work of University of Pennsylvania psychology professor Angela Duckworth often, and rightly, finds its way into accelerated composition courses. In *Grit: The Power and Passion of Persistence* (2016) and in her widely viewed TED Talk (2013), which inspired the book, Duckworth defines grit as the "passion and perseverance for very long-term goals. Grit is having stamina. Grit is sticking with your future, day in, day out, not just for the week, not just for the month, but for years, and working really hard to make that future a reality. Grit is living life like it's a marathon, not a sprint."

Accelerated composition courses require students to both work fast *and* demonstrate a superior level of determination. Again, it's worth repeatedly reminding students that because the class will demand so much from them, they will need to set aside extra time to do the work. One aspect of grit is knowing *which* activities deserve passion and persistence, and even those students who must work to help support themselves and their families during the course of the semester must place school at or near the top of their priorities list.

Foster Other Noncognitive Skills.

Both growth mindset and grit require adaptability, which is one of the most useful habits of mind a student can adopt. In addition to flexibility, the Council of Writing Program Administrators recommend seven other habits of mind in the *Framework for Success in Postsecondary Writing* (2011): curiosity, openness, engagement, creativity, persistence, responsibility, and metacognition. They argue that "students who develop these habits of mind approach learning from an active stance" and that the habits "help students succeed in a variety of fields and disciplines," as well as "inside and outside school" (4).

Other important noncognitive skills students should learn include managing time effectively, being aware of and adhering to classroom etiquette, and monitoring and managing physical and emotional health. Because the members of a thriving classroom community are aware of one another as human beings, the affective dimension of the class often comes to the forefront in an accelerating course. Indeed, professor Stephanie Kratz (2016) claims, "Getting to know students and their emotions is as important to the success of an accelerated developmental English course as the curriculum itself." (For a fuller investigation of this topic, see Margaret Nelson Rodriguez's chapter 11 in this collection, "Accelerating Success: Noncognitive Learning in Composition Courses.")

The Research and Planning Group established the framework below "to serve as the foundation for [their] exploration of what California community college students say they need to succeed" ("Six Factors Framework," n.d.). The success factor definitions echo Dweck's contention that an academic community isn't simply a feel-good group where every emotion is indulged. Certainly, students want to be valued, nurtured and connected with other students. But they also expect to demonstrate grit and shoulder some responsibility for their own educations, to be directed, focused, and engaged. These factors, listed below, are interconnected, with success in one area fostering success in the others:

Directed: students have a goal and know how to achieve it.
Focused: students stay on track—keeping their eyes on the prize.
Nurtured: students feel somebody wants and helps them to succeed.
Engaged: students actively participate in class and extracurricular activities.
Connected: students feel like they are part of the college community.
Valued: students' skills, talents, abilities and experiences are recognized; they have opportunities to contribute on campus and feel their contributions are appreciated.

Make Attendance Matter

"Class Attendance in College: A Meta-Analytic Review of the Relationship of Class Attendance with Grades and Student Characteristics" (Credé, Roch, and Kieszczynka 2010) confirms that positive attendance is most useful for students who are on the border between passing and failing, the very students who may face the most challenges accelerating. Therefore, while we should make allowances for the many issues that may arise in a first-year student's life—from childcare to health concerns to transportation mishaps—maintaining an attendance policy is important, and there should be consequences—clear and proportionate, to be sure—for not showing up to class.

Ultimately, though, as Mandy McGrew (2019) notes, "it behooves faculty to move beyond whether or not to require mandatory attendance and instead focus on ways we can structure our courses so that students want and need to be in class every day. Making attendance matter to our students will influence their presence in class." Among her suggestions are the following:

- Include information about how students should communicate to you about their absences.
- Share with students that you expect and want them to be in class every day.
- Design your class so students are motivated to attend and feel being in class is worthwhile.
- Communicate to students explicitly and early in the semester about the positive correlation of attendance and grades. By sharing the research on attendance with your students, you will enlighten them as to why they shouldn't skip out on class.

If the class is one both students and the instructor look forward to taking part in, the problem of attendance should significantly diminish.

Begin with Frequent Low-Stakes Reading and Writing Assignments
Any instructor who has ever tirelessly cultivated a classroom community only to see it fall apart a month or so later when the first graded essay is returned knows how deeply such assignments affect student morale. Clearly, at some point in a graded course, grading must take place, but that potentially harrowing event should be postponed until after students have begun to feel comfortable putting words and sentences and paragraphs together. The initial instructor feedback they receive should be as supportive as it is evaluative and analytical. In the words of Peter Elbow (1997), "The goal of low stakes assignments is not so much to produce excellent pieces of writing as to get students to think, learn, and understand more of the course material. Low stakes writing is often informal and tends to be graded informally. In a sense, we get to throw away the low stakes writing itself but keep the neural changes it produced in students' heads" (5). In a post to the NCTE blog *Literacy & NCTE* on September 24, 2016, Jennifer Kirsch similarly notes, "Low-stakes (i.e., non-graded) writing strengthens students' more formal writing while also discouraging them from thinking too rigidly about how

long a piece should be, and instead focusing them more on what they want to express and communicate to a reader."

In an integrated reading and writing course—that is, in an ideal accelerated composition class—instructors should take a similar approach to reading assignments. While those of us long used to tackling extensive and detailed texts may once have pictured the act of reading as a solo voyage, we now know our students generally do not benefit from this solitary experience. Instructors should begin reading instruction by creating a classroom community of readers, one "characterized by inquiry—where all are able to value and build on what they bring to the class, and where support as well as academic expectations are equally high for all students" (Schoenbach, Greenleaf, and Murphy 2012, 56). Such a class can "address longstanding educational inequalities" by "creating a sense of shared norms and safety for collaboration" (56). Naturally, collaborative reading of this sort is practiced before it is assessed, and assessed in the context for which the reading was created. (For an expanded discussion of approaches to teaching reading, see part 3 of this volume.)

Low-stakes activities teach students it's okay to take risks, to bite off more than they can chew at the moment. These activities show learning as a process, one that benefits from a growth mindset and grit. Above all, low-stakes assignments are opportunities for collaboration and community building, for developing students' sense that, at least when it comes to their accelerated composition course, they are all in this together.

Transition to More Challenging Reading and Writing Assignments

From its inception, acceleration advocates have insisted that the work their students are doing in the college-level class is in no way inferior to the work produced by nonaccelerating students. Granted, developing students may well need more support, especially early on in the semester, but once the class is fully in motion, expectations for *all* students are high.

Ideally, this transition is made easier by the many elements of a successful course that have already been discussed. An enthusiastic and well-trained faculty member offers a well-designed class supported by a corequisite section for developing students. The classroom itself is a welcoming community where students are given plenty of training in how to deal with affective and other noncognitive challenges. Writing and reading instruction is robust, but early assignments are largely low stakes and frequently ungraded.

At some point, however, many students face material that feels beyond their immediate capacity to process. At that stage, if the class is functioning well, the elements I have been discussing provide students with the confidence to grow their mindset and face the new challenge. Hern (2017) describes her reasoning for assigning accelerating students a difficult reading by theorist Paolo Freire this way:

> Before I sent students home to read Freire, I let them know that I had chosen the article *because* it was difficult. They could all read *People* magazine, but that wasn't going to help them grow as readers and become skilled with dense college-level texts. I said I knew they wouldn't understand everything but that I wanted them to read the whole thing, do the best they could, and then we'd work with it together in class. This conversation defused the reflexive shame that is often triggered when students don't understand something they've read—"I should get this, I'm in college"—and opened up the space for . . . productive persistence. Instead of withdrawing in the face of difficult material, they engaged with it more deeply. (221)

Mark Blaauw-Hara et al. (2020) found corequisite courses "do a better job at helping students quickly improve their writing skills and pass college-level writing requirements than a sequence of stand-alone developmental writing courses" (54). While students were initially cowed or flummoxed by the "writing-about-writing" readings assigned in their class, the extra time they spent in the corequisite analyzing the readings allowed them to develop "self-efficacy" and a "sense of ownership over their writing" (63). Consequently, the authors encourage "writing faculty to assign challenging, advanced reading and writing activities to developmental students, regardless of curriculum. As our findings demonstrate, such readings—and the discussions they spur in corequisite courses—can be transformative" (68).

Create and Maintain Semester-Long Connections with Counselors, Writing Support, Librarians, and Tech Support.

A crucial component of a successful accelerated composition program is ensuring students have regular access to specialized support services. In fact, aside from contact with their instructors and classmates, these may be the most important campus relationships students establish during the semester.

Make Direct Connections with Counselors

Active advising and support (Van Noy et al. 2016) helps "to convey program information to students, and [to] monitor and support students' progress through programs. Programs with active advising and student support provide targeted counseling/advising within the program, including information for undecided students, group sessions for advising, program orientations, monitoring of student progress, and supports for struggling students" (268).

A hallmark of SBCC's Express to Success program was having a dedicated academic counselor for each course section. The counselor, who came to visit during the second and ninth weeks of the semester, became the academic advisor for every student in the class. Early in the semester, the counselor ensured students were taking the correct courses for their major or pathway. Later, when students were signing up for the following semester, the counselor was able to monitor the students' progress and ensure they were continuing on in their progress towards a degree.

Cosima Celmayster (2022), my counseling partner in ESP, believes foregrounding connections between faculty and counselors reassures students of the vibrancy of a program's support system. In an email exchange with me, she wrote,

> The collaborative efforts of instructional and academic counseling faculty created a cohesive, seamless and united front of support for our SBCC students who were enrolled in ESP. Students knew that we were united in our desire to see them be successful because they saw us together in their classroom, we exchanged information back and forth about meetings we had as a team on their behalf. And I truly think that is the biggest piece of it all. We were seen as a team of support with a singular goal of creating success for the students. Though this is what we all as educators desire for our students, there was something special about them coming into the program knowing this was one of our goals as focused Instructional and Counseling Faculty and staff and then seeing our commitment to this happen during their time in the program.

In addition to academic counseling, accelerating students also benefit from ready access to personal and career counseling. Personal counselors are vitally important in crisis situations, of course, but they also help students dealing with everything from homesickness and anxiety to poor time management. And positive mental health is, not surprisingly, linked to positive educational outcomes: "Clinically distressed students who experienced a greater reduction in psychological distress during counseling experienced greater academic success over time" (Kivlighan et al. 2021, 562). A single ten-minute class visit from a friendly counselor may be all a fragile student needs to reach out for help.

And students are more motivated in their classes when they know they are working towards a specific career goal. That motivation is one of the rationales for the guided-pathways movement, and researchers have shown that "increasing the focus on career transition issues serves to promote not only academic success but also . . . students' school-to-career planning and decision making" (Shearer 2009, 53).

Provide Classroom Tutors

Another factor that accounted for ESP's success was the embedding of student tutors in both the college-level class and the corequisite. Nearly always, these students had been selected from previous accelerated courses—often from as recently as the previous semester. During their first semester as tutors, they were enrolled in a tutor-training program, and what they might have lacked in experience, they more than made up for with an ability to communicate with their peers and a first-hand knowledge of the course. One of my ESP tutors, Anna Kaavik (interview with author, November 11, 2021), believes that one of the chief advantages of having a dedicated tutor in the class was simply "how much faster the students received help. Instead of raising their hands and waiting for the professor to come around, there was another person who was just as informed who could help faster and perhaps use language that is more familiar for the student. I feel as though it is also less intimidating to ask a fellow student for help than to ask the professor."

I don't know how often I called on Anna, and her fellow ESP tutors in other classes, for help not just in answering a writing or reading question but also in quelling a budding disagreement or encouraging a student who was mentally checking out of that day's class. Students like Anna benefited financially from their work, and they often came to see themselves as experts in a field they hadn't realized they excelled in (Anna, for instance, is on track to become a CPA). Moreover, from the college's perspective, ESP student tutors, because they were still learning on the job, were a bargain compared to the more experienced tutors in the writing center.

Connect with the Campus Writing Center

Express to Success tutors worked for ESP, not the writing center, but obviously there are different approaches to bringing tutors into the writing classroom. Russell Carpenter, Scott Whiddon, and Kevin Dvorak (2014) note that "on many campuses, classroom and writing center geographies are seen as distinct, situating teaching and tutoring within different pedagogical landscapes. Classrooms are often viewed as the spaces where writing instruction takes place, while writing centers are spaces where writers receive *assistance*, not instruction. Course-embedded tutoring programs . . . attempt to bridge these distinct locations" (3).

The problem, of course, is how to scale up from a handful of select classes to a situation in which each accelerated composition course has its own writing center tutor. Financially, that might be unfeasible in many places, but that doesn't mean students can't work extensively with tutors in the writing center. The caveat, as Adams (2020) indicates above, is that unless students are *required* to meet with tutors, some of them—in my experience, unfortunately, often those most in need of help—will not do so.

Make Librarians an Integral Part of the Course

At Santa Barbara City College, during the library's open hours, assistance from a librarian is just a few keystrokes away. That access can make a world of difference to students, but the omnipresence of the chat feature associated with library search engines makes it easy to forget how important it is for students to have a specific librarian they can come to know and work with over the course of a semester. Whenever possible, I arrange with a librarian prior to the start of classes to work with my students throughout the semester. Typically, this means sending the librarian my syllabus and assignments, and students are rewarded with a course page tailored to the sort of reading, writing, and research they will be doing.

The advantages of working with a specific librarian over the course of a semester aren't for students alone. In a project that paired librarians with instructors, classroom teachers "noted that working with any other professional strengthened the quality of instruction, but that collaborating with the teacher-librarian provided even more benefits: access to resources, expertise, and connections to the broader school community" (McNee and Radmer 2017, 7).

Offer Ready Access to Technology and Technical Support

The COVID pandemic provided a poignant reminder of how reliant we have become on technology to enable learning but also how tentative our connections to that technology sometimes are. It's essential, therefore, that while instructors productively employ the digital-learning resources at hand, they make no easy assumptions about student access to or competence in the technosphere. An ACT study (Carrasco 2021) on pandemic access to technology showed "thirty-five percent of students from low-income families and 30 percent of first-generation college students had limited access to the internet. Additionally, 25 percent of students from low-income families and 18 percent of first-generation students had limited access to both technology and the internet." A large spring 2020 survey of US undergraduates confirmed these results: "Students from low-income families and . . . first-generation students had limited access to both technology and the internet" (Katz, Jordan, and Ognyanova 2021). Many of these students struggled heroically, although not always successfully, to find "workarounds for spotty internet and malfunctioning devices" in order to reach "remote learning proficiency."

In short, while technology and internet access are becoming more and more essential to college success, they are becoming more difficult to access for the very students who face the most challenges when accelerating. Even when classes are face to face, computer-assisted instruction remains an integral part of most curricula. Students need 24/7 access to a helpdesk—even if some of the technical support is provided by outside vendors—and those who cannot afford computers should have semester-long access to basic tablets or laptops like Chromebooks. Internet access, especially in rural areas, can be the biggest technological challenge for students, although there are workarounds, including providing students with maps of local hotspots, using WhatsApp rather than software that requires more bandwidth, communicating in plain rather than rich text, and offering transcripts and hard copies of all material that might be unavailable to disconnected students (Major 2020).

Consider Nontraditional Forms of Assessment

In "Basic Writing Reform as an Opportunity to Rethink First-Year Composition: New Evidence from an Accelerated Learning Program," Rachel Ihara (2020) investigates the ironic situation that, prior to acceleration on her community college campus, developmental students in many ways faced more rigorous assessment than their college-level peers. She sees acceleration as an opportunity to reimagine our assessment practices, asking,

> Should the movement to mainstream students previously classified as "developmental" result in a composition program that is more like the dissolved "basic writing" program—with both its strengths, such as faculty collaboration around assessment, and its failings, with regard to equity and access—or might it lead us to imagine alternative approaches to curriculum and assessment that retain the communal spirit of "basic writing" without it importing its more damaging elements? (101)

Specifically, Ihara argues that the success of accelerating students "might provide an impetus to explore alternative assessment practices [like contract grading] that emphasize students' persistence and labor more than their ability to produce textual products that demonstrate they have met certain abstract benchmarks" (101).

In addition to contract grading, in which students and their professors mutually agree on outcomes, accelerated composition instructors also use electronic portfolios, which allow for semester-long revision of writing. In order to provide students with more agency in the assessment process, acceleration programs have also utilized collaborative, participatory, peer and self-assessment. Inclusive assessment provides students with a range of opportunities—in and out of class, alone and in collaboration—to demonstrate their learning.

Moreover, many instructors of accelerated composition have come to question the primacy white language supremacy plays in academic writing. In July 2020, following the murder of George Floyd, the CCCC committee on Anti-Black Racism and Black Linguistic Justice, Or, Why We Cain't Breathe! published "This Ain't Another Statement! This is a <u>**DEMAND**</u> for Linguistic Justice!" (Conference 2020). Among the five demands were that "teachers stop using academic language and standard English as the accepted communicative norm, which reflects White Mainstream English!" A year later, CCCC issued the "CCCC Statement on White Language Supremacy" (Conference 2021), which concludes, "We reaffirm our commitments to linguistic diversity and to the multiple languages and linguistic histories of our students and communities and, further, affirm a commitment to the dismantling of all systems of oppression, with the understanding of the central role of WLS in the formation of unconscious and conscious biases."

Clearly, assessment of student writing is in transition, and part 2 of *Teaching Accelerated and Corequisite Composition* joins in that ongoing conversation. Whatever the outcome of this monumental transformation, many instructors probably agree that "culturally responsive assessment demonstrates that flexibility, choice and relevance . . . enable all students to choose subjects on the basis of desire to engage intellectually in the teaching and learning process" (Manathunga and MacKinnon 2001, 32).

Model the Behaviors You Want Your Students to Engage In

While this statement might seem obvious, it is worth a moment's reflection. The comments instructors make in class, online, and in course documents, and the way we treat and refer to others and ourselves, implicitly convey how we see the world. If we want our students to help build a just, peaceful, and sustainable world, we start by creating that environment, in small, in our physical and virtual classrooms.

AFTER THE SEMESTER IS OVER
Continue Faculty Development

At the end of a semester, everyone on campus is exhausted and ready for a break. This might seem like the worst possible time to convene a faculty-development meeting, but this is also the time when our impressions of what has gone right, and wrong, in our classes is as fresh as it will ever be. Even an hour's worth of discussion may prove invaluable.

Whenever that first postsemester faculty-development meeting takes place, it should be collaborative and continuing. In part 5 of *Teaching Accelerated and Corequisite Composition*, Haleh Azimi and Elsbeth Mantler discuss the need for timely and ongoing professional and faculty development and argue that the changing landscape of the field make these opportunities ever more important for faculty teaching ALP courses.

Faculty development is most useful for our students when we can see ourselves in them., Tony Maguire (2021) makes the excellent point that when remote learning is involved, "professional development should be delivered via the same Learning Management System (LMS) educators will be using to educate their students. Not only does this provide an authentic way for teachers to familiarize themselves with the platform, it also allows them to understand the digital learning platform from the perspective of their students."

Crunch the Numbers

Data collection is a major reason the California Acceleration Project was able to convince the California Legislature to mandate acceleration, as it was for the acceleration advocates in Georgia, West Virginia, Tennessee, Indiana, and Colorado before them ("Bridge Builders" 2023). What's especially striking about the many accelerated learning success stories across the country is the high "throughput," which, again, refers to the percentage of students who successfully complete transfer-level courses in a predetermined timeframe. In California, AB 705 has made the throughput directive quite clear: "Every college is required to maximize the probability that a student will enter and complete transfer-level coursework in English and math within a one year timeframe" (California, n.d.).

Equity is another key driver of administrative and legislative acceptance of accelerated education. In 2013, for instance, when ESP was running at full steam, data showed the program increased "math and English Basic Skills course completion rates by 30% and 49% respectively for Hispanic students completing two English or math classes in the same semester, compared to the number of non-ESP Hispanic students completing the same sequence of courses in one year" (Santa Barbara, n.d.).

Of course, in a statewide scaling up, as occurred in California in fall 2019, when many colleges were unprepared for acceleration, statistical disappointments can occur. However, Hern (2020) points out that even then, a close examination of institutional data may still reveal that acceleration is working: "As we assess the first year of AB 705, colleges should not revert to a myopic focus on transfer-level course success rates. Instead, we must examine our local throughput data and disaggregate it by race/ethnicity, income, disability, GPA, and other factors. If we can't identify a group of students that does better starting in a remedial course, remedial courses should not be on the table" (4).

Redesign the Composition Sequence

Often, the first-year composition sequence is divided into two parts. First-semester English, the course discussed in this chapter—let's call it English 101—focuses primarily on the basics of academic writing. The second course in the sequence—English 102—may extend instruction in academic writing, or it may focus on literature or writing across the curriculum. In another iteration, different sections of English 102 may be devoted to specific pathways or majors—writing about the social sciences, for instance, or writing for film studies.

Whatever the case, if the next course in the sequence does not consider the fact that a significant percentage of entering students are still in the process of accelerating, the same issues that created the need for acceleration will simply be postponed until a student's second semester. English 102 must make use of a similar pedagogy—one promoting community, growth mindset, grit, the movement from low-stakes to more challenging assignments, and so on—and include the same level of support—regular and equitable access to counselors, tutors, librarians, technical personnel, and so forth—as English 101. Otherwise, accelerating students will, metaphorically, find themselves slamming into a wall.

It is probably too much to ask of an already overstretched faculty to redesign their entire composition sequence when acceleration is being implemented—it certainly was at my college—but at the very least, when designing the initial course, its implications for the full sequence should have a bearing on all decisions about the first-semester course. And as soon as possible, the first year's writing classes should be integrated as closely as possible.

Make Acceleration an Integral Part of the College

Securing funding, instituting a corequisite, successfully teaching the course, collecting and disaggregating throughput data, and redesigning the composition sequence are all important steps in making acceleration a visible and fundamental part of an institution's academic life.

However, there is no denying a well-designed acceleration program may be more expensive than what is already in place. If ALP's annual Conference on Acceleration in Developmental Education and the many publications and announcements of the California Acceleration Project are relentlessly upbeat, it's not just because acceleration's basic premise is so effective, it's also because acceleration itself is always going to be in someone's crosshairs. It threatens the livelihoods of instructors of developmental English and math. It drains money from the budget, and it places English and math at the center of community college education—hardly an ideal situation for ambitious members of other departments.

Nevertheless, acceleration also makes a college look good. When more students are passing their introductory courses, more students are enrolling in drama and chemistry and political science, and more students are graduating and making their way out into the wider world, where, inevitably, many of them will extol acceleration as they remember fondly the course that helped teach them the essential skills of how to read and write and think.

REFERENCES

Adams, Peter. 2020. "Giving Hope to the American Dream: Implementing a Corequisite Model of Developmental Writing." *Composition Studies* 48 (2): 19–34.

Adams, Peter, Sarah Gearhart, Robert Miller, and Anne Roberts. 2009. "The Accelerated Learning Program: Throwing Open the Gates." *Journal of Basic Writing* 28 (2): 50–69.

Bahr, Peter Riley, Loris P. Fagioli, John Hetts, Craig Hayward, Terrence Willett, Daniel Lamoree, Mallory A. Newell, Ken Sorey, and Rachel B. Baker. 2019. "Improving Placement Accuracy in California's Community Colleges Using Multiple Measures of High School Achievement." *Community College Review* 47 (2): 178–211. https://doi.org/10.1177/0091552119840705.

Blaauw-Hara, Mark, Carrie Strand Tebeau, Dominic Borowiak, and Jami Blaauw-Hara. 2020. "Is a Writing-about-Writing Approach Appropriate for Community College Developmental Writers in a Corequisite Class?" *Composition Studies* 48 (2): 54–73.

The "Bridge Builders." 2023. Complete College America. Completecollege.org/spanningthedivide/#the-bridge-builders.

California Community Colleges, Equitable Placement. n.d. "What Is AB 705?" Accessed November 8, 2021. Assessment.cccco.edu/ab-705-implementation.

Carrasco, Maria. 2021. "First-Year Students Struggled with Online Learning Last Year." *Inside Higher Ed*, August 25. www.insidehighered.com/news/2021/08/25/first-year-students-struggled-online-learning-last-year.

Carpenter, Russell, Scott Whiddon, and Kevin Dvorak. 2014. "Revisiting and Revising Course-Embedded Tutoring Facilitated by Writing Centers." *Praxis: A Writing Center Journal* 12 (1): 3–7. www.praxisuwc.com/121journal.

Conference on College Composition and Communication. 2020. "This Ain't Another Statement! This is a DEMAND for Black Linguistic Justice!" cccc.ncte.org/cccc/demand-for-black-linguistic-justice.

Conference on College Composition and Communication. 2021. "CCCC Statement on White Language Supremacy." Cccc.ncte.org/cccc/white-language-supremacy.

Council of Writing Program Administrators, National Council of Teachers of English, National Writing Project. 2011. *Framework for Success in Postsecondary Writing*. Files.eric.ed.gov/fulltext/ED516360.pdf.

Credé Marcus, Sylvia G. Roch, Urszula M. Kieszczynka. 2010. "Class Attendance in College: A Meta-Analytic Review of the Relationship of Class Attendance with Grades and Student Characteristics." *Review of Educational Research* 80 (2): 272–95. https://doi.org/10.3102/0034654310362998.

Duckworth, Angela. 2013. "Grit: The Power of Passion and Perseverance." TED video, 6:00. www.ted.com/talks/angela_lee_duckworth_grit_the_power_of_passion_and_perseverance/c.

Duckworth, Angela. 2016. *Grit: The Power and Passion of Perseverance*. New York: Scribner.

Dweck, Carol. 2006. *Mindset: The New Psychology of Success*. New York: Ballantine.

Dweck, Carol. 2008. "Brainology." National Association of Independent Schools. www.nais.org/magazine/independent-school/winter-2008/brainology/.

Dweck, Carol. 2016. "What Having a 'Growth Mindset' Actually Means." *Harvard Business Review*, January 13. Hbr.org/2016/01/what-having-a-growth-mindset-actually-means.

Elbow, Peter. 1997. "High Stakes and Low Stakes in Assigning and Responding to Writing." *New Directions for Teaching and Learning* 69 (Spring): 5–13.

Freeman, Tierra M., Lynley H. Anderman, and Jane M. Jensen. 2007. "Sense of Belonging in College Freshmen at the Classroom and Campus Levels." *Journal of Experimental Education* 75 (3): 203–20. https://doi.org/10.3200/JEXE.75.3.203-220.

Garrity, Sean. 2020. "Community Building in the Community College Classroom." *Inside Higher Ed*, January 7. www.insidehighered.com/advice/2020/01/07/building-community-community-college-classrooms-opinion.

Gerald, Joe, and Benjamin Brady. 2019. "Time to Make Your Mandatory-Attendance Policy Optional?" *Chronicle of Higher Education*, January 13. Advance-lexis-com.sbcc.idm.oclc.orgapi/document?collection=news&id=urn:contentItem:5VGP-6WF1-DYTH-90M9-00000-00&context=1516831.

Gopalan, Maithreyi, and Shannon Brady. 2020. "Fostering College Students' Sense of Belonging Amidst COVID-19." *Penn State Social Science Research Institute*, November 4. Covid19.ssri.psu.edu/articles/fostering-college-students-sense-of-belonging-amidst-covid-19.

Henson, Leslie. 2020. "Big Gains at Strong Implementers of AB 705." *CAPacity Gazette* July: 1–3. California Acceleration Project. Accelerationproject.org/Portals/0/Documents/Cap_Gazette_2020_Jul_Web.pdf.

Henson, Leslie, and Katie Hern. 2014. "Let Them In: Increasing Access, Completion, and Equity in College English." Accelerationproject.org/Portals/0/Documents/let-them-in-final.pdf?ver=2016-09-29-124642-623.

Hern, Katie. 2017. "Unleashing Students' Capacity through Acceleration." In *Deep Reading: Teaching Reading in the Writing Classroom*, edited by Patrick Sullivan, 210–26. Urbana, IL: NCTE.

Hern, Katie. 2020. "Disrupting the Deficit Narrative about Early AB 705 Data." *CAPacity Gazette* July: 4–5. Accelerationproject.org/Portals/0Documents/Cap_Gazette_2020_Jul_Web.pdf.

Ihara, Rachel. 2020. "Basic Writing Reform as an Opportunity to Rethink First-Year Composition: New Evidence from an Accelerated Learning Program." *Journal of Basic Writing* 39 (2): 85–111.

Inoue, Asao B. 2015. *Antiracist Writing Assessment Ecologies: Teaching and Assessing Writing for a Socially Just Future.* Fort Collins, CO: WAC Clearinghouse.

"Invalid Placement Practices Widespread in CA Community College." 2021. California Acceleration Project. Accelerationproject.org/Portals/0/Documents/CAPValidation-ReportAnalysisOct2021.pdf.

Katz, Vikki S., Amy B. Jordan, and Katherine Ognyanova. 2021. "Digital Inequality, Faculty Communication, and Remote Learning Experiences During the COVID-19 Pandemic: A Survey of U.S. Undergraduates." PLOS ONE. Journals.plos.org/plosone/article?id=10.1371/journal.pone.0246641.

Kendi, Ibram X. 2019. *How to Be an Antiracist.* New York: One World.

Kivlighan, D. Martin, III, Barry A. Schreier, Chelsey Gates, Jung Eui Hong, Julie M. Corkery, Carl L. Anderson, and Paula M. Keeton. 2021. "The Role of Mental Health Counseling in College Students' Academic Success: An Interrupted Time Series Analysis." *Journal of Counseling Psychology* 68 (5): 562–70. EBSCOhost, https://doi.org/10.1037/cou0000534.

Ko, Melissa E. 2021. "Course Design Equity and Inclusion Rubric." Stanford University, Stanford Teaching Commons. teachingcommons.stanford.edu/news/course-design-equity-and-inclusion-rubric.

Kratz, Stephanie. 2016. "Learning Journals in One ALP: Making Visible Students' Voices About Writing Ability and the Non-Cognitive Context of Learning." *Basic Writing e-Journal* 14 (1). Bwe.ccny.cuny.edu/Kratz.htm.

Lawrence, Dennis. 2000. *Building Self-Esteem with Adult Learners.* Newbury Park, CA: SAGE.

Maguire, Tony. 2021. "Overcoming Remote Learning's Three Greatest Challenges." *Educator*, June 9. www.theeducatoronline.com/k12/news/overcoming-remote-learnings-three-greatest-challenges/277276.

Major, Amielle. 2020. "14 Tips for Helping Students with Limited Internet Have Distance Learning." KQED, March 24. www.kqed.org/mindshift/55608/14-tips-for-helping-students-with-limited-internet-have-distance-learning.

Manathunga, Catherine, and Dolly MacKinnon. 2001. "Socially and Culturally Responsive Assessment: Preparing Students for the New Economy." *Knowledge Demands for the New Economy*, edited by Fred Beven, Clive Kanes, and Dick Roebuck, 32–39. Samford Valley: Australian Academic Press.

Molloy, Kathy. 2018. "SBCC Express to Success." California State University, San Bernardino. Accessed December 15, 2021. www.csusb.edu/sites/default/files/SBCC%20Express%20to%20Success%20-%20Kathy%20Molloy.pdf.

McGrew, Mandy. 2019. "Make Attendance Matter." Kennesaw State University, Center for Excellence in Teaching and Learning, December 16. https://facultydevelopment.kennesaw.edu/scholarly-teaching/news-articles/make-attendance-matter.php.

McNee, Darcy, and Elaine Radmer. 2017. "Librarians and Learning: The Impact of Collaboration." *English Leadership Quarterly* 40 (1): 6–9.

"Publications." n.d. California Acceleration Project. accelerationproject.org/Publications.

Rochester Institute of Technology, Center for Teaching and Learning. n.d. "Designing Accelerated Courses." rit.edu/teaching.

Santa Barbara City College. n.d. "iPath: Pathways to Transfer Program: Improving Completion Rates, Articulation, and Student Outcomes." Last modified May 2014. www.sbcc.edu/institutionalresearch/files/inst-grants/iPathgrant.pdf.

Schoenbach, Ruth, Cynthia Greenleaf, and Lynn Murphy. 2012. *Reading for Understanding.* Hoboken, NJ: Jossey-Bass.

Shearer, Branton C. 2009. "Exploring the Relationship between Intrapersonal Intelligence and University Students' Career Confusion: Implications for Counseling,

Academic Success, and School-to-Career Transition." *Journal of Employment Counseling* 46 (2): 52–61.

"Six Factors Framework (Six Success Factors)." n.d. *RP Group.* rpgroup.org/our-projects/student-support-re-defined/successfactorsframework.

"Through the Gate Transfer Initiative." n.d. RP Group. Accessed December 2, 2021. rpgroup.org/through-the-gate.

Van Noy, Michelle, Madeline Trimble, Davis Jenkins, and Elizabeth Barnett. 2016. "Guided Pathways to Careers: Four Dimensions of Structure in Community College Career-Technical Programs." *Community College Review* 44 (4): 263–85. EBSCOhost, https://doi.org/10.1177/0091552116652939.

"Who We Are." n.d. *RP Group.* Accessed December 2, 2021. rpgroup.org/About-Us.

Wood, J. Luke, Frank Harris III, and Khalid White. 2015. *Teaching Men of Color in the Community College: A Guidebook.* San Diego: Center for Organizational Responsibility and Advancement.

Wood, Tara, Jay Dolmage, Margaret Price, and Cynthia Lewiecki-Wilson. 2014. "Moving Beyond Disability 2.0 in Composition Studies." *Composition Studies* 42 (2): 147–50.

2
ESTABLISHING A COREQUISITE WRITING MODEL IN A POSTREMEDIAL TWO-YEAR COLLEGE

Meridith Leo

On the first day of the semester when I walk into my developmental writing classes, I feel like I'm one of the students. I still like to think I can pull the look off. I sit in the back of the room and pretend to be one of them. At some point, I lean over to someone and ask if I'm in the right class to confirm I really am in the correct classroom. Then I sit with an awkward uncomfortable posture, and my nerves start to hit. I get anxious. My adrenaline starts pumping and my hands start to gently shake. That's followed by an intense warm tingling feeling that radiates throughout my body producing the sort of sweat that results from running a 5K race. I am the teacher, not the student, but I start to think about all the "stupid" things I might nervously say in my introduction of the course. Then I wonder, How did I get here?

Really, how did someone like me get into this position? Physically, I'm not the professor type. I'm covered from head to toe in tattoos, I'm vertically challenged, and people tend to think I'm a student, not a professor. I wonder if I still give off the student vibe, or if it has more to do with the tone, timbre, and cadence of my voice. Mentally I don't feel like the professor type; I suffer from an internal and deep fear I'm not smart enough and I somehow accidently came to the professional "success" or stability I have. Furthermore, I'm fearful my colleagues, or worse, my students will realize my fraudulent identity and I'll have to face the shame of that awareness. According to Pauline Clance and Suzanne Imes (1978), "Women who experience the imposter phenomenon maintain a strong belief that they are not intelligent; in fact, they are convinced that they have fooled anyone who thinks otherwise" (1). There are reasons I, and many of my "remedial" students, have these feelings. Some are linked to gender, social class, race, and/or sexual identity. For me, I'm straddling social classes and am keenly aware of

https://doi.org/10.7330/9781646424788.c002

how it impacts my thought process, teaching, goals I have for my students, and thus my psyche. These reasons, and more, are why I pretend to be a student on the first day of my classes.

I glance over at the clock and think it's not time yet; I'm not ready. Maybe I'll give the latecomers another minute. The silence in the class is intense. I really am like my students in many ways; I know they're scared, nervous, don't want to feel "stupid," and question whether they're good enough to be in college. Having had these same feelings myself led me, eventually, to implement a corequisite writing course model at Suffolk County Community College.

ON BEING A BASIC WRITER

Throughout my K–12 education, I experienced minor traumatic events that made me despise the thought of even going to college. My parents, like so many, convinced me I should attend college for one semester in order to feel things out. Even then I was in many ways the typical community college student. I went to my local community college and took a placement exam, and the outcome required that I start my first year in a noncredit developmental writing course. At the time I really didn't understand the difference between credit and noncredit courses and furthermore couldn't wrap my head around how my inability to "pass" the placement exam would directly impact my perception of education and academia for quite some time.

My recollection of the developmental writing class is a bit blurry, but I do remember a significant amount of grammar instruction that emphasized the use of what I can now characterize as a monolithic privileged discourse. Further, I had a difficult time connecting to the writing assignments because they didn't matter to me; they weren't relevant to my life or experiences. On more than one occasion the instructor belittled the opinions I had or the language I used. The instructor would say, "There's no such word as *gavone*. That's just some slang word you heard at home" (Leo 2018, 59). This pedagogical approach goes against what the writers of the revised "Student's Right to Their Own Language" were arguing for when they stated in their resolution, "By building on what students are already doing well as part of their successes in daily living, we can offer them dialect options which will increase rather than diminish their self-esteem, and by focusing on the multiple aspects of the communication process, we can be sure we are dealing with the totality of language, not merely with the superficial features of polite usage" (Committee 1974, 12). It was no surprise I didn't thrive in that "remedial" environment.

When I failed ENG 010 Developmental Writing, I dropped out of college. I felt defeated after the negative experience I had in that class and wouldn't return to college for four years. When I did return, I had to complete that same developmental writing course to *really* begin my college career. I hated the fact that I had to take the same class again, and I hated the term *developmental*; internally it impacted the way I perceived myself as a writer (Leo 2018, 59). I struggled throughout the rest of my undergraduate and part of my graduate academic career because I was labeled as a *developmental writer*. This labeling was not the first moment I felt like an outsider; it had been a consistent experience throughout my education and thus affected my return to the community college as an instructor of writing.

THE CONTACT ZONE OF A BASIC WRITER

Every time a "remedial" student enters a basic or developmental writing classroom they are asked to simultaneously invent the university within the boundaries of a contact zone. In many ways, the reasons basic writing and developmental writing courses exist is to fulfill an agenda that indoctrinates students into a privileged discourse while teaching students the boundaries of that rhetorical space. As David Bartholomae (1986) argues, we expect that students "invent the university by assembling and mimicking its language, finding some compromise between idiosyncrasy, a personal history, and the requirements of convention, the history of a discipline. They must learn to speak our language" (5). This thinking has not been entirely eliminated. For some, basic writing students need to be inducted into their academic experience but only under the framework we are willing to reveal to them. In a postremedial college, we must recreate the concept of the contact zone so students are encouraged "to negotiate the gaps and conflicts between several competing discourses," but we should also nurture individual student voices while building collaborative and caring learning communities, all while creating a virtual or physical space that exposes and celebrates differences; and if there is conflict, it should organically present itself (Harris 1995, 31). With nuances in the teaching of writing directly linked to corequisite courses, shifts are happening nationwide; however, for many years remedial writing courses at the college where I teach had a stagnant theoretical perspective I have been working to revise.

Suffolk County Community College is the largest two-year college in the State University of New York system. SCCC strategically locates itself with three campuses in different areas on Long Island in Suffolk County,

New York, and it is a commuter campus. Each of the three campuses is located in a different community, which impacts the student body and course offerings; the westerly Grant campus is located in Brentwood, a densely populated suburban area. The eastern campus is located in the rural town of Riverhead, and the largest, what is considered the main academic site, the Ammerman campus, is situated in Selden with a variety of suburban dwellings. In any given academic year, our total student population reaches twenty-five thousand, with a wide range of student ethnic and racial backgrounds; 51.3 percent of our students identify as white, we have a Hispanic population of 29.3 percent, and our self-identifying Black-African American student body is 8.1 percent. These students from diverse racial backgrounds attend multiple campuses or remain at a home campus that suits their personal and academic needs. In addition, the percentage of female attendees is 54 percent, and the male population is 46 percent. Students within the age range of eighteen to twenty-four comprise 81 percent of our population, with an adult student population over twenty-five at 19 percent (SCCC n.d.a). Traditional remedial courses have been offered on all three campuses, but because of our different student demographics and population size, each department works somewhat independently in terms of remedial writing courses.

The writing sequence at SCCC was initially designed to help students continuously develop their writing throughout several semesters. Prior to our corequisite implementation, a student might be placed into one of two remedial writing courses. ENG 09 Basic Writing or ENG 010 Developmental Writing. Both these courses were designed for students who needed to work on sentence-level writing skills along with paragraph organization and form. While the courses attempted to help struggling students, many who took these classes did not complete them in their first try. Furthermore, many of the students who placed into these courses were those from marginalized areas on Long Island where school districts are overwhelmed and underfunded. A student could either pass those remedial course(s) or place directly into ENG 101 Freshman Composition, which is the equivalent of a first-year writing course. Students in this course engage in rhetorical modes of expression while learning research skills and critical thinking, taking an in-depth look into the writing process while continuing to work on sentence-level writing. After passing the first-year composition course, students needed to take ENG 102 Introduction to Literature. While the course's content requires students to read, learn, and analyze four genres (short story, poem, novel, drama), the goal of Introduction to Literature is to assess this knowledge via written essays. Faculty that teach these courses are strongly encouraged to continue working on student writing through the writing process and collaborative peer revision; however, the class requires students to examine literary texts and summarize, analyze, and critique them, so the class functions more as a literature course than a writing one (Leo 2018, 150). This writing sequence may be similar to those at other two- and four-year colleges, and after some time we realized the initial goal of remediation was not helping our students progress to completion through the writing sequence. Something had to change.

MOVING TO POSTREMEDIAL WOKENESS

I'll never forget the moment I first learned about corequisite, accelerated learning program writing courses. I was sitting at my first Conference on Acceleration in Developmental Education (CADE) in Baltimore, Maryland. The year was 2013 and I had already been teaching noncredit remedial-level courses for some time and knew something wasn't working right. Based on my experiences, it seemed like a large group of students were being kept out of academia. I knew those students were in a position where they had to prove they belonged, and I could no longer support that inequitable process. At the 2013 CADE, I signed up for a half-day workshop that introduced me to the concept of accelerated learning program writing courses (ALP), also known as corequisite course pairing. I learned that ALP was the brainchild of Peter Adams. In his 1993 article *Basic Writing Reconsidered*, he advocates an end to "remediation" altogether and argues that "basic writing" students should not be mainstreamed directly alongside first-year composition students without appropriate support: "It is time we begin to question seriously whether segregated basic writing classrooms are the best environment for helping basic writers develop into proficient college-level writers" (24–25). Based on observations and the shifts in remediation that had been taking place, it seemed logical to discontinue a form of curricular and pedagogical approaches that were hurting students in their ability to succeed.

Initially, after learning about the corequisite model, I was skeptical, but that quickly changed after hearing about the benefits for students who took part in it: mainstreaming, acceleration, contextual learning, heterogeneous grouping, cohort learning, small class size, attention to behavioral issues, and attention to life problems (Adams et al. 2009). Learning about corequisite courses became a moment to reconsider my experiences as a developmental writer while working to examine how I approached teaching writing to "at-risk" students.

Wanting students to succeed, I was excited to hear about the possibilities the corequisite approach could offer, and I decided to take the ALP model back to my institution to talk to those who could assist me in implementing corequisite courses. My purpose in retelling and reflecting on corequisite implementation at my institution is to identify the evolutionary challenges an institution and department can have, including resistance that leads to communication irregularities, along with the emotional implications faculty face when transitioning to a post-remedial college. Furthermore, this alteration to the writing sequence forced me to rethink my own pedagogy while highlighting the change's implications for student awareness and the charge it implies for two-year colleges who continue to employ remedial writing. The corequisite revolution can succeed in the postremedial college if there is sustainable, consistent, and appropriate college-wide support. I offer suggestions for how to embed institutional change.

THE COREQUISITE RHETORICAL REALITY

After I returned from CADE, I was determined to make changes to how we approached remediation. I wanted our students to exist in a postremedial space. I borrow the term "post-remedial" from Gerri McNenny's introduction to *Mainstreaming Basic Writers: Politics and Pedagogies of Access* (McNenny and Fitzgerald 2001), where she describes the changing landscape of remediation, with states all over the nation allowing open access to disadvantaged "at-risk" student populations. McNenny states that

> whether out of absolute necessity triggered by legislative action or out of a desire to address pedagogical concerns, writing program administrators and professionals are increasingly confronted with the alternative to mainstream "at-risk" college students. That decision is further complicated by the complexities of institutional testing and placement, admissions criteria, and the ambiguous nature of criteria used to label the student populations as either "underprepared," "developmental," "inexperienced," "at risk," or "remedial." (2)

With the creation of corequisite courses, educators are attempting to move away from traditional labels that assert judgment over students' cognitive abilities. By mainstreaming students alongside writers whose abilities are similar to their own, we can work towards a shift in which a hierarchy of skills connected to courses will not exist. We should not ignore effective tools such as mainstreaming and cohort learning because they can deeply impact students in the corequisite model and have the potential to impact other integrative learning methods.

Mainstreaming in a corequisite model can have positive outcomes so long as institutional infrastructure and instructor support are present. In "The Accelerated Learning Program: Throwing Open the Gates," Peter Adams, Sarah Gearhart, Robert Miller, and Anne Roberts (2009) state, "We think the fact that the basic writers are in a class with twelve students who are stronger writers, and perhaps more accomplished students, is an important feature of ALP because these 101-level students frequently serve as role models for the basic writers" (57). In addition, this intellectual exchange bonds students to one another and creates connections that help students to feel comfortable managing the challenges of their lives as they intersect with academia. In the "Power of Academic Learning Communities," Rebecca Młynarczyk and Marcia Babbitt (2002) contend that "many of today's college students, who take a series of unrelated courses, each with a different group of classmates, perceive their educational experience as lacking in coherence or community. Learning community programs go a long way toward alleviating such problems" (74). This community building is key in the classroom but equally important among faculty and administrators who attempt to organize a corequisite model.

When I was working to implement a corequisite writing model, my biggest challenge was knowing who to speak with at my college. Consistent issues with communication across campuses, messaging within Banner and our learning-management system, and miscommunications among the registrar, advising, and placement only made matters worse. Even though Suffolk County Community College is the largest two-year college in the SUNY system, there is no college-wide writing program administrator. For institutions who want a sustainable corequisite writing model, it is important to have someone with expertise in the field who can act as a leader. Ideally, this person has the power to make decisions and implement changes in areas such as curriculum and course design and assessment procedures. Additionally, a WPA at the two-year college should work to develop community among teachers of writing at the campus and college wide. Because the college lacked leadership (WPA), I needed help to begin with the development of our writing corequisite, so I reached out to two seasoned colleagues who had a background in composition studies.

Together, we devised a plan to implement a corequisite model on the Ammerman campus at SCCC. First, we had to consider how many students might be impacted by these changes. Depending on a student's placement-exam score (in the past we used the CPT Accuplacer Sentence Level, and prepandemic we shifted to Writeplacer), they could place into a variety of either noncredit or credited writing courses. In this traditional model, at least nine hundred students each semester could be affected, and this estimate was based on only one campus; even more students would be involved depending on the other campuses' course offerings. On the Ammerman campus I opted to implement the same model the Community College of Baltimore County incorporated under the direction of Peter Adams.

After running a pilot of the corequisite model in 2015 and 2016, I worked towards concrete curriculum implementation, which was established during the spring and fall of 2017. SCCC was on its way to establishing a new writing culture, but the road to implementation would be fraught with challenges. Initially, I was successful in navigating the politics of course implementation. Multiple campus deans, our institutional effectiveness team, the campus registrar, admissions, testing, placement, and advisement partners were all on board. In part this occurred because unlike many states around the nation, New York has not been mandated by state or local policies to implement corequisite models—at least not yet. The excitement about the new corequisite model put us in a good position to design the kinds of course offerings we wanted without restraint. Beyond the benefits Adams et al. (2009) note in "The Accelerated Learning Program," some additional reasons I pushed for the inclusion of the corequisite model were suspected racial/ethnic inequities linked to unconscious course advisement and placement procedures, also known as the *cooling-out* process. Burton Clark (1960) states, "The initial move in a cooling-out process is pre-entrance testing: low scores on achievement tests lead poorly qualified students into remedial classes" (572). Much of this cooling-out process is guided by the academic advisor, as the student may continue to struggle to perform academically, resulting in probation and a return to the advisor for continued help in negotiating their academic process. Peter Bahr's (2008) study on the effects of cooling-out and academic advising on student success states that "throughout these interactions, the counselor is charged with easing from the student's grasp those academic goals that are perceived to be overambitious and substituting goals befitting the perceived capabilities of the student" (705). Because of inappropriate placement and testing procedures, some of our students at SCCC may have experienced this cooling-out process, which would have led them into noncredit remedial writing courses. The challenges in reflecting on this process or policies related to placement and testing means institutions must "define their ideas and policies as racist" (Kendi 2019, 130) and acknowledge inequities that have been endemic to college campuses since their inception. As colleges begin their early-phase implementation, they should consider how testing and advising function and determine whether those processes are equitable or divisive.

Creating a corequisite writing course may address issues of equity, but it may also lead to resistance from within a department or college at large. Internal friction can be due to lack of organizational procedures and the challenges of filling corequisite courses each semester. It is vital to work closely with academic advising and counseling centers to communicate the value of these courses and the positive impact they can have on students' academic progress. While I work hard to instill the significance of the corequisite model at SCCC, the writing culture has not shifted, in part because the college continues to offer stand-alone developmental writing courses. As a consequence, some of our advisors continue to direct students to developmental writing courses because they have been a staple course at our institution. One of the problems with this placement is that when "students perceive faculty to be remote, discouraging, or biased, they are likely to avoid interactions and to disengage from college. Warm welcome and authentic connection form the essential foundation of positive student-faculty and student-staff relationships" (Felten and Lambert 2020, 20). Therefore, the lack of in-depth advising conversations sometimes means our corequisite courses seem empty, and at times they are cancelled due to low enrollment. Furthermore, we struggled with roster issues in Banner and our LMS, and these issues still persist each semester. Because of these continued challenges, it has been difficult to unify our curriculum and course offerings across campuses, which is important for two-year colleges who have multiple campuses throughout a county or state. I was hopeful one of our sister campuses would work to adopt the corequisite model; however, to date this has not happened. In the midst of these changes, I also learned one of our sister campuses was being pushed by administration to create a course entitled ENG 100 Enhanced Freshman Composition. As I indicated in a *SUNY Developmental English Learning Community Progress Report,*

> The class was mirrored after a similar course taught at another two-year college on Long Island and is designed to help "at-risk" students who typically place into traditional developmental writing gain access to credit bearing gateway writing courses. It is different from a corequisite course pairing in that the seat limit is significantly larger, students are not

co-mingled with a separate cohort, and they meet twice a week with only one-hour tacked on to the course. This extra hour typically takes place in a computer lab and offers "supplemental support." (email to Progress Report Committee, May 13, 2019)

The Enhanced Freshman Composition course is the equivalent of our Standard Freshman Composition course, so students are not considered developmental; however, this undermining of the corequisite model, which instead should be championed, was a disturbing move and one that should be avoided.

After the implementation of the Enhanced Freshman Composition course, the English department on the Ammerman campus was nudged by administration to adopt the course, and I did so, with some reluctance. Because of the different demographics on our campuses, our new placement procedures for incoming students, and the specific student the course was geared towards, I was hesitant. The Enhanced Freshman Composition course would work well for students who place into a Freshman Composition course but fail it the first time around or students who recognize they may need the additional support and consequently self-place. I qualify this statement because I have taught Enhanced Freshman Composition, and in its current form, it does not tackle the appropriate cohort. Students who are placed into the Enhanced Freshman Composition course struggle with noncognitive issues that sometimes hinder their success. Because they do not have extended additional time with an instructor or a cohort to bond with, many do not pass the class. In addition, in conversations I had with three other colleagues who all taught Enhanced Freshman Composition, we determined many students would have been better placed into a corequisite section. As colleges across the nation determine course changes to remediation, it is vital to be consistent on multiple campuses when considering the kinds of courses that benefit a range of students. Furthermore, whether these courses are corequisite or another model, there should be a breadth of scholarship, along with appropriate qualitative and or quantitative data, to help support those changes.

Ultimately, dealing with institutions and administration who look for shortcuts can cause setbacks to the corequisite model and the national movement supporting its implementation. If an institution is attached to a combination of courses that might include supplemental support, learning communities, and corequisites within a discipline and interdisciplinarily, they should continue these courses, but not at the cost of the student's best interest. Offering a menu of course options looks "vastly different from the conventional tendency to fragment the curriculum into stand-alone courses" (Grubb 2001, 17) such as traditional developmental and basic writing courses. While I have been open minded, I identify the Enhanced Freshman Composition course as internal resistance to the corequisite model in large part because of the communication irregularities that exist college-wide at SCCC. As of now, I'm convinced that courses such as Enhanced Freshman Composition are repackaged versions of traditional developmental courses (with credit), and unless significant changes are made to these alternative courses and the students placing into them, they may not help the students we set out to reach with an equitable, nuanced writing-sequence structure.

While each campus at SCCC is enacting curricular change to help its own unique student demographic, if we shift to a postremedial learning environment, course inconsistencies can further confuse students who move between campuses and can complicate larger community messaging, leading to irregular procedures and goals. We have yet to feel the full effect of the Enhanced Freshman Composition course on the corequisite model. I caution other institutions who are pushed by their administration to create courses that are truncated or that seem inappropriate for at-risk students. Course creation and implementation are an investment of time and should not be pushed through curriculum unless thoughtful conversations and strategic planning occur.

MORE RECENT RESULTS

When the COVID-19 pandemic hit in March of 2020, we were five years into our corequisite implementation, and it's safe to say that, like many institutions, we struggled. Our prepandemic fall schedule presented a strong corequisite offering, while our spring semesters were typically a bit lighter. Throughout the pandemic academic period, our corequisite sections struggled, and many sections (remote and face to face) had to be cancelled, while our traditional developmental sections seemed to fill with students. While the pandemic hindered our progress with the corequisite courses, there were already lingering challenges with placement procedures and communication among the registrar, advising, and college-wide English departments. Because of the COVID-19 pandemic, placement testing was no longer the mechanism for student course assignment; we relied entirely on advisors informing students about the writing course options and hoped students would be guided into a course appropriate for them based on their experiences. To assist our advising and counseling office, we developed an informational flyer that could act as a reference for full- and part-time counselors as they worked with students. Moving forward, it would benefit colleges to have not only informational flyers or manuals but also a specific webpage on their college's website where students can access information related to their writing courses, including corequisite options. This kind of outreach includes students in what is happening, and during emergency situations such as a pandemic, it can act as a communication repository. If we'd had an online space to communicate with our corequisite students and offer them direct support virtually, it might have made a difference for some of them.

In the aftermath, the pandemic has shown us that students in corequisite courses desire one-on-one instruction that leads to relationships with their peers and instructor; we no longer need to hypothesize about what these students want. According to Peter Felten and Leo Lambert (2020), "The power of a culture that develops relationship-rich classrooms is inspiring, even transformational" (98). Additionally, having smaller classes can make the difference in the learning process, and on a national level we should continue to advocate for smaller class size across the board, but specifically in corequisite writing courses. With all the disruptions I had to negotiate, including the Enhanced Freshman Composition course and the pandemic, my pedagogical approaches in the corequisite courses were tested. Because of all the changes due to COVID-19, including varying modality options, I could no longer teach my corequisite students the same way I had prepandemic.

Throughout my academic maturation, I find myself constantly in search of a neoteric rhetorical pedagogy that can refine my teaching of writing. In the past I utilized place-based practices; I wanted students to develop a critical consciousness of their own identity and its relationship to the world around them. As Ira Shor (1992) notes in *Empowering Education*, "Critical consciousness, or critical transitivity, allows people to make broad connections between individual experience and social issues, between single problems and the larger social system" (127). To emphasize this approach, at times I asked students to examine their own literacy practices, perhaps compare their practices to others, and then asked them to critique a problem within the US educational system. That kind of approach evolved and led me to a cultural- and community-driven pedagogy in which I asked students to teach the class about a community they felt they were a part of. Students acted as informants, which enabled them to feel involved and also offered a moment to involve others in their unique lives and the systemic issues within their communities. This cultural wealth should be valued as a principle goal of higher education, and I will continue to work further "to foster an ethic of care among students in a way that contributes to community building" (Rhoads 1997). In my corequisite writing courses, the implications of a morphed pedagogical approach that includes place-based, cultural-, and community-driven pedagogy along with a critical expressivist, trauma-informed, and antiracist approach has proven useful.

VALUING CONNECTIONS

When I think back to my time as a student and a developmental writer, I realize what was really missing was a feeling of belonging. Initially, I didn't feel a connection to my instructors or peers, and I encountered few professors who were deeply concerned with my personal and academic well-being, but as a white cisgender woman, I have some privilege many of my peers and my students do not always experience. Ultimately the pedagogies that govern "student-faculty relationships are a primary factor in learning, belonging, and persistence" (Felten and Lambert 2020, 2). Students in corequisite writing courses thrive when they feel valued and connected, which is why it is vital to recognize that prejudiced language practices that have shaped many teaching methods at the institutional and classroom level must change. If we want students to feel a sense of belonging, they need to feel acceptance through an academic lens that is consciously aware. The position statement "This Ain't Another Statement! This is a DEMAND for Black Linguistic Justice!" presents important questions that can help guide the shifting paradigms in developmental education: "How has Black Lives Mattered in the context of language education? How has Black Lives Mattered in our research, scholarship, teaching, disciplinary discourses, graduate programs, professional organizations, and publications? How have our commitments and activism as a discipline contributed to the political freedom of Black peoples?" (Conference 2021). Institutions such as SCCC who have a mission that "promotes intellectual discovery, physical development, social and ethical awareness, and economic opportunities for all through an education that transforms lives, builds communities, and improves society" (SCCC n.d.b). Clearly, we must consider the impact traditional developmental education has on the ability for students to achieve this charge. Changes at the institutional level may make it possible to alter what happens in the classroom for marginalized students; however, as bell hooks (1994) says in *Teaching to Transgress*, "Let's face it: most of us were taught in classrooms where styles of teachings reflected the notion of a single norm of thought and experience, which we were encouraged to believe was universal" (35). If institutions are to revise policies and practices that acknowledge discriminatory approaches, instructors need to contemplate how their teaching styles might be privileging a single monolithic experience. This change may be slow to happen because "educators are poorly prepared when we actually confront diversity" (41). In some ways corequisite courses have put a brighter spotlight on discriminatory practices at the institutional and classroom level.

Over time, instructors will need to consider changes to their praxis and approaches to writing in the corequisite class. There are times an instructor will need to shift course and rework assignments because of the make-up of the class dynamic or the modality in which it is taught. Within those instructional frameworks, developing high- and low-stakes assignments, in-class or virtual workshops, collaborative group assignments, and experience with qualitative research, including observations and interviews, is valuable. The content of corequisite courses must be a fluid, flexible, and experimental process as an institution moves forward to sustain the postremedial college. In thinking about these pedagogies and theories of writing, instructors should consider what Richard Fulkerson (2005) suggests in his article "Composition at the Turn of the Twenty-First Century": "We may teach one thing, assign another, and actually expect yet a third" (680). This premise may hold true when teaching in the postremedial world, and instructors of writing should be conscious of how pedagogy interacts with assignments and thus the expectations all of us have for our students. Corequisite courses should rely on collaboration in the classroom alongside sustainable yet flexible course content and pedagogy. Over time individual institutions should reevaluate their approaches to ensure a healthy, equitable, and sustainable writing culture that helps students move through gateway writing courses by encouraging them to become excited about their academic and professional pursuits. To do this, institutions should also consider the physical and emotional implications teaching corequisite courses have on faculty.

Teachers of writing spend countless hours reading student writing and talking with students, many of whom have dealt with traumatic events in their lives. Some students in corequisite courses have experienced trauma that has impacted their learning, and discussions about this trauma can become the center for pedagogical and writing explorations; however, those approaches are not without consequence. STS, or secondary traumatic stress, is the "emotional duress that results when an individual hears about the firsthand trauma experiences of another" (Peterson 2018). I encourage students to write about things they want to resolve or emotionally process, so I read many stories related to abuse, addiction, human and sex trafficking, mental-health challenges, neglect, pain, suffering, tumultuous divorces, and difficult relationships between children and their parents. These stories stick with me and many other teachers of at-risk students. Jessica Lander, a teacher and graduate of the Harvard Graduate School of Education states, "Secondary traumatic stress is sort of the consequence of being a good teacher. If you care about students, you're probably not going to avoid it" (quoted in Walker 2019). I speak mainly to my own distress, but I have taken part in multiple conversations with full- and part-time faculty who teach our corequisite courses. Because corequisite teachers spend more time with these students, we become bonded to them, and that is when STS can spill over into the personal lives of teachers and can lead to compassion fatigue. I have experienced this fatigue with many students, and it is physically and emotionally draining. I want them to succeed so badly, and I feel such empathy for the difficulties they've had, that I stay up late worrying about the direction of these students' lives. In the same way, I also feel joy when they are happy and progressing through their courses. Jamey Gallagher, in "Setting Students Up for Success: Teaching the Accelerated Learning Program," states, "It is also personally satisfying to see students succeed" (217). This brings me to the case of a student I had in the first year of our corequisite courses.

Elizabeth Winn is a young vivacious student who has unique interests in the world around her, but when she registered for our corequisite course ENG 012 Emerging Writers Workshop, she initially struggled to acclimate to college life. In the first half of the semester, she seemed distracted and uninterested in our classes, but at midterm that all changed. Around midterm each semester, I have a sit-down with each of my corequisite students. The goal of this meeting is to check in on them and address any concerns, questions, or issues they may be having. During my midterm sit-down with Lizzy, we spoke honestly about the time and effort needed to complete both ENG 101 Freshman Composition and ENG 012 Emerging Writers Workshop, and I knew she was more than capable of completing the courses if she committed a bit more time to our work. I challenged her to dive into our course materials and encouraged her to engage in intellectual relationships with her peers. When we reconvened as a full class after these meetings, I immediately noticed a difference in Lizzy, and she impressed me with her writing and the collaborative efforts she made in both courses. She easily completed both the Freshman Composition and Emerging Writers Workshop courses and persisted with her academics by transferring to a four-year school in the SUNY system. She recently graduated with a bachelor's degree in environmental geography and a double minor in psychology and disaster studies and is looking to the next stage (Elizabeth Winn, email to author, January 27, 2020). In reflecting on her experiences in our corequisite courses, she stated,

> The ENG corequisite course was truly an effective building block for a successful academic position. Having the opportunity to share space with familiar faces in the required courses made interacting and revising a comfortable process. Instructions to share and revise peers' papers built confidence and intellect within my writing for the years to come. Having been placed in the corequisite course my first year at Suffolk was truly fundamental to the writer and student I am today.

This student and others sometimes need to be presented with an honest challenge, which I believe can ignite their intellectual prowess. There is an "intellectual payoff" and a sense of satisfaction when students see value in issues that are important to us, and thus those issues may become important to them (Gallagher 2020, 216). I have maintained relationships with other corequisite students, and whether I see them on campus or I receive an email from them, they are always excited to tell me what they're up to in their lives and within their academic pursuits. Such relationships are what Adams alludes to in that there is an increase "in bonding and attachment to the college" (Adams et al. 2009, 69). Students feel as though they belong, and when their hard work is acknowledged and valued, that acknowledgement is meaningful to them and encourages these students to continue to strive for academic excellence and hopefully even builds a sense of genuine confidence (Leo 2018, 184). Whether we worry about students' academic futures or we are exhilarated by their success, the emotional toll for faculty teaching in a corequisite model should be addressed and researched in more detail.

Student confidence may be lurking just below the surface, and when corequisite writers recognize their own abilities, they may come to realize they aren't really imposters after all. In "Rethinking the Imposter Phenomenon," Shanna Slank (2019) argues that "the question of whether IPPs [imposter-phenomenon people] have irrational talent beliefs is more complicated than the standard view suggests. I will argue that there exists a rational route to some IP beliefs, and thus that it is quite possible that many IPPs are rational" (206). Further, Slank contends that those who do not experience the imposter-phenomenon moment might lack talent and are themselves irrational (206). I don't think it fitting to distinguish between students who do or do not suffer from this phenomenon, but I believe it is relevant to consider that the questioning of self among at-risk or developmental students could be combatted in a corequisite environment with instructor and college support.

THE FUTURE OF COREQUISITE IN THE TWO-YEAR COLLEGE

Institutions must develop stronger plans to sustain the corequisite model in a post-COVID world. Many of our students at SCCC struggle with the online remote environment, which sheds an even stronger light on issues of digital literacy and the digital divide (Buzzetto-Hollywood 2018, 78). When I return fully to face-to-face instruction, I'll need to create meaningful access to technology in the hopes that students gain confidence while engaging in contextual learning within the digital world. One approach for corequisite courses is to engage in a collaborative online learning environment with international partners. SUNY offers this kind of interaction through their Collaborative Online International Learning Center, which "connects students and professors in different countries for collaborative projects and discussions as part of their coursework" (State University, n.d.). Faculty at other institutions may need to create a global network via social media or through networking at national conferences. There are many opportunities to work with colleagues across the world; it's just a matter of faculty and institutions casting out a net to incite interest. These interactions can guide students to discover meaningful relationships across disciplines while reaching out to different areas of the globe, and such interactions may help corequisite students envision opportunities they may not have considered. The SUNY COIL vision is "We believe that an educational environment that fosters shared values, mutual understanding, and critical digital literacy, and which promotes interaction across boundaries to develop leadership, collaborative problem solving and contextualized decision making, will make this vision a reality" (State University, n.d.). Layering a corequisite writing course pairing with an international interdisciplinary partner may lead to greater sustainability for the corequisite model as a whole. At least this is one direction I would like SCCC to consider, but that is dependent on who will direct the future of corequisite courses at SCCC.

Therefore, on a broader scale we must consider who the decision makers are in the framework of the postremedial college. Who has control? Who is in charge of making sound and appropriate decisions that will create equitable solutions for at-risk students? According to Derek Owens's (2001) extensive discussion on the concept of sustainability in his book *Composition and Sustainability*, "A sustainable culture cannot exist unless sustainability features prominently throughout the curriculum" (28). He further draws attention to the concept of "social traps" and borrows Robert Costanza and Herman Daly's definition, wherein "a social trap . . . (is) 'any situation in which the short-run, local reinforcements guiding individual behavior are inconsistent with the long-run, global best interest of the individual and society,' which leads to unsustainability and is something teachers and students should avoid" (quoted in Owens 2001, 29). I argue that traditional developmental writing classes have become a "social trap" and that the corequisite model is working to eliminate such a trap. Additionally, local agents and teachers of corequisite and stand-alone developmental writing should be making decisions about the future of writing courses. Creating a college corequisite task force comprised of administrators, students, and teachers who have experience with at-risk developmental populations will help open the lines of communication and promote inclusivity and transparency. This kind of advisory group can lead the postremedial college with sound, appropriate, and sustainable decision making.

We do the work we do because we care deeply for our students, and as corequisite models and changes to placement occur, we must recognize a need for participation from the entire academic community. At the fall 2019 Conference for the Center for the Analysis of Postsecondary Readiness, the president of SUNY Rockland Community College, Michael Baston (2019), stated, "There are leverage points where everyone needs to participate in order to help students become successful." If we change the existing model, that force could cause a larger systemic alteration to take place. These adjustments can become rallying moments when the whole college community recognizes that our students, especially those who have been marginalized, need a sustainable and equitable environment to successfully fulfill their academic goals and life-long dreams.

CONCLUSION

Every time I sit in one of my Emerging Writers Workshop classes, I feel I'm part of a community of writers. I feel these students are more capable of tackling the coursework than they've been given credit for. There aren't any imposters here; instead, there are students who are waiting to break through challenging academic and life experiences that have held them back. Our biggest success is our students. When I see them finding confidence and achieving their dreams, I know the hard work we do as writing instructors is paying off. We must intentionally evolve our curriculum and pedagogy to participate in the postremedial realm. Offering sustainable corequisite courses is our institutional responsibility to students who are seeking life-altering and identity-forming experiences.

REFERENCES

Adams, Peter Dow. 1993. "Basic Writing Reconsidered." *Journal of Basic Writing* 12 (1): 22–36. https://doi.org/10.37514/jbw-j.1993.12.1.03.

Adams, Peter, Sarah Gearhart, Robert Miller, and Anne Roberts. 2009. "The Accelerated Learning Program: Throwing Open the Gates." *Journal of Basic Writing* 28 (2): 50–69. https://doi.org/10.37514/jbw-.

Bahr, Peter Riley. 2008. "'Cooling Out' in the Community College: What Is the Effect of Academic Advising on Students' Chances of Success?" *Research in Higher Education* 49 (8): 704–32. https://doi.org/10.1007/s11162-008-9100-0.

Bartholomae, David. 1986. "Inventing the University." *Journal of Basic Writing* 5 (1): 4–23. https://doi.org/10.37514/jbw-j.1986.5.1.02.

Baston, Michael. 2019. "Placement, Advising, and Academic Supports in the Age of Co-Requisite Remediation." Paper presented at Conference for the Center for the Analysis of Postsecondary Readiness, New York City, November.

Buzzetto-Hollywood, Nicole. 2018. "Addressing Information Literacy and the Digital Divide in Higher Education." *Interdisciplinary Journal of e-Skills and Lifelong Learning* 14 (Spring): 77–93. https://doi.org/10.28945/4029.

Clance, Pauline Rose, and Suzanne Ament Imes. 1978. "The Imposter Phenomenon in High Achieving Women: Dynamics and Therapeutic Intervention." *Psychotherapy: Theory, Research and Practice* 15 (3): 241–47. https://doi.org/10.1037/h0086006.

Clark, Burton R. 1960. "The 'Cooling-Out' Function in Higher Education." *American Journal of Sociology* 65 (6): 569–76. https://doi.org/10.1086/222787.

Committee on CCCC Language Statement. 1974. "Student's Right to Their Own Language." *College Composition and Communication* 25 (3): 1–36.

Conference on College Composition and Communication. 2020. "This Ain't Another Statement! This is a DEMAND for Black Linguistic Justice!" cccc.ncte.org/cccc/demand-for-black-linguistic-justice.

Costanza, Robert. 1987. "Social Traps and Environmental Policy." *BioScience* 37 (6): 407–12.

Felten, Peter, and Leo M. Lambert. 2020. *Relationship Rich Education.* Baltimore: Johns Hopkins University Press.

Fulkerson, Richard. 2005. "Composition at the Turn of the Twenty-First Century." *College Composition and Communication* 56 (4): 654–87.

Gallagher, Jamey. 2020. "Setting Students Up For Success: Teaching the Accelerated Learning Program." In *16 Teachers Teaching: Two-Year College Perspectives*, edited by Patrick Sullivan, 203–20. Logan: Utah State University Press.

Grubb, W. Norton. 2001. *From Black Box to Pandora's Box: Evaluating Remedial/Developmental Education.* Community College Research Center, Teachers College, Columbia University, NY. chrome-extension://efaidnbmnnnibpcajpcglclefindmkaj/https://ccrc.tc.columbia.edu/media/k2/attachments/black-box-evaluating-remedial-education.pdf.

Harris, Joseph. 1995. "Negotiating the Contact Zone." *Journal of Basic Writing* 14 (1): 27–42. https://doi.org/10.37514/jbw-j.1995.14.1.05.

hooks, bell. 1994. *Teaching to Transgress: Education as the Practice of Freedom.* New York: Routledge.

Kendi, Ibram X. 2019. *How To Be An Antiracist.* New York: One World.

Leo, Meridith. 2018. "Integrating Emerging Writers into the Post-Remedial College: A Consideration of Accelerated Learning Programs." PhD diss., St. John's University.

McNenny, Gerri, and Sallyanne Fitzgerald. 2001. *Mainstreaming Basic Writers: Politics and Pedagogies of Access*. Mahwah, NJ: Earlbaum.

Mlynarczyk, Rebecca William, and Marcia Babbitt. 2002. "The Power of Academic Learning Communities." *Journal of Basic Writing* 21 (1): 71–89. https://doi.org/10.37514/jbw-j.2002.21.1.06.

Owens, Derek. 2001. *Composition and Sustainability: Teaching for a Threatened Generation*. Urbana, IL: NCTE.

Peterson, Sarah. 2018. "Secondary Traumatic Stress." National Child Traumatic Stress Network. https://www.nctsn.org/trauma-informed-care/secondary-traumatic-stress/.

Rhoads, Robert A. 1997. "Explorations of the Caring Self: Rethinking Student Development and Liberal Learning." Paper presented at the Annual Meeting of the American Educational Research Association, Chicago, IL, March. ttps://files.eric.ed.gov/fulltext/ED408549.pdf.

Shor, Ira.1992. *Empowering Education: Critical Teaching for Social Change*. Chicago: University of Chicago Press.

Slank, Shanna. 2019. "Rethinking the Imposter Phenomenon." *Ethical Theory and Moral Practice* 22 (1): 205–18. https://doi.org/10.1007/s10677-019-09984-8.

State University of New York. n.d. "The SUNY Coil Center." Accessed September 2, 2021. https://coil.suny.edu/about-suny-coil/.

Suffolk County Community College (SCCC). n.d.a. "Suffolk at a Glance. Welcome to Suffolk County Community College—Home of the Sharks." Accessed September 3, 2021. https://www.sunysuffolk.edu/about-suffolk/suffolk-at-a-glance.jsp.

Suffolk County Community College (SCCC). n.d.b. "Welcome to Suffolk County Community College—Home of the Sharks." State University of New York. Last modified July 7, 2022. https://www.sunysuffolk.edu/.

Suffolk County Community College (SCCC). n.d.c. "Welcome. SUNY COIL Center." Accessed September 6, 2021. https://coil.suny.edu/.

Walker, Tim. 2019. "'I Didn't Know It Had a Name': Secondary Traumatic Stress and Educators." NEA: National Education Association. https://www.nea.org/advocating-for-change/new-from-nea/i-didnt-know-it-had-name-secondary-traumatic-stress-and.

3
INCHING TOWARD EQUITY
Graduated Choice in the Corequisite Classroom

Lesley Broder

THE PATH TO COREQUISITE AT CUNY

The community college educational landscape was far different when Peter Adams visited my institution, CUNY–Kingsborough Community College in Brooklyn, in 2012. Faculty sat around crowded tables to hear about the success of the corequisite model that had just been developed at the Community College of Baltimore County. At that point, I was devoted to our program's large and thriving developmental sequence that was the centerpiece of the English department. The program offered layers of support, a string of courses many faculty believed were bridges to improve students' literacy skills before placement in credit-bearing coursework. While our local sequence was still in full gear in 2012, CUNY was in the process of catching up with national trends, coming to different conclusions about the equity implications of a long pipeline to enter first-year math and English coursework.

It would have been difficult to imagine, sitting in that meeting in 2012, that the developmental program at Kingsborough would be disbanded within a decade, with CUNY terminating all stand-alone, noncredit English classes that were not a part of the corequisite model. As part of this transition, CUNY reformed placement mechanisms by discontinuing high-stakes reading and writing placement tests and implementing a placement algorithm called the Proficiency Index (PI). The PI uses a combination of performance indicators from students' high-school work to predict whether they have a 65 percent or greater chance of earning at least a C- in first-year math and English. Students who fall outside this range are mainstreamed into credit-bearing classes but are also given additional instructional support. With the implementation of the PI, the placement options for incoming students suddenly decreased to just two: Composition I or Composition I-Accelerated

Learning Program (ALP).[1] Starting as a small pilot with just five sections and less than forty students in spring 2013, the program has grown to serve nearly four hundred students each semester, drastically reducing the number of English courses required to graduate.

Earlier developmental models at CUNY had barred students from continuing their education unless they passed two separate standardized tests. Thus, the adoption of ALP, with the removal of the gatekeeper exams and addition of supplemental instruction, is more in line with CUNY's mandate as an institution. Since its founding in 1847, CUNY's mission to offer social mobility to all corresponds to Kingsborough's own mission to provide "quality, affordable, innovative, student-centered programs of study that prepare graduates for transfer and the workforce" (CUNY, n.d.; "Kingsborough," n.d.b). Though Brooklyn is the most populous borough of New York City, Kingsborough is its sole community college, and its students make up approximately eleven thousand of the almost two hundred and twenty thousand students enrolled CUNY-wide as of fall 2022. Of the students enrolled in degree programs in fall 2021, 37.4 percent were Black, 29.1 percent white, 17.7 percent Hispanic, 15.5 percent Asian/Pacific Islander, and 0.3 percent American Indian ("Percent Enrollment by Ethnicity" 2021). Most of these students are enrolled as liberal arts or sciences majors, while the remainder are in more career-focused fields like culinary arts, criminal justice, or allied health. The student population is young for a community college, with only a fifth of the student body older than twenty-five years of age. Half work while in school, perhaps because the annual income of more than 40 percent of student households is less than $20,000 and at least 20 percent support children (Kingsborough, n.d.a.). All these students must take both Composition I and Composition II in order to graduate and their varying responsibilities off campus influence how they are able to approach their education.

THE ADOPTION OF COREQUISITE AT KINGSBOROUGH

The ALP model at Kingsborough is straightforward and mirrors many corequisite programs nationwide. Students who are deemed likely to pass place into English 1200: Composition I, a four-hour introductory

---

1. While students with low-scoring PIs are encouraged to enroll in one of two interventions—CUNY Start, a semester-long skills class, or the Immersion Program, a two-week, presemester seminar—these courses are optional, and students can skip them and enroll directly into the credit bearing Composition I-ALP, which provides additional instruction.

course in critical reading and writing. Students who could be helped by what CUNY refers to as "Light Developmental Need" coregister into special sections of Composition I, English 12A0, which include two additional hours of small-group instruction with their professor. These sessions are an extension of the class, providing time to review ideas and prepare the course portfolio. Both the ALP and non-ALP students are assessed by collaborative portfolio assessment, in which faculty exchange student writing to determine whether the criteria for Composition I have been met. If they pass, students in both English 1200 and English 12A0-ALP earn CUNY credit for Composition I, after which they must take an interdisciplinary research class, English 2400: Composition II.

The administration's rhetoric surrounding the adoption of corequisite education, and its attendant changes in placement and curriculum, was celebratory, though buy-in from faculty worried about equity has been mixed (Del Principe, Broder, and Levesque 2022, 182). Many faculty invested in the developmental sequence were dismayed it was possible to jump into credit-bearing Composition I with no prior support, fearing the shift from stand-alone remediation would water down coursework and result in higher failure rates in Composition I. Preliminary data now suggest these instructors were right to think outcomes would change, but not in the way they might have expected.

According to internal KBCC institutional data, in 2015, when the developmental sequence was still in existence, 62.3 percent of all students passed Composition I, whether in an ALP or non-ALP section; by spring 2021, when the developmental sequence ran its last few sections, the pass rate of all sections of Composition I dropped to 49.2 percent. What might interest skeptics of the new placement policy is that in this same period of spring 2015 to 2021—when pass rates in Composition I were decreasing in general—the pass rates remained the same among ALP students in these sections. Despite the ravages of the pandemic and a shifting placement policy, those who were placed into corequisite Composition I-ALP passed at a rate of 57.7 percent in spring 2015 and at a rate of 57.8 percent in spring 2021.

On the surface, it appears that the corequisite program helps students stay on track to graduate; however, inequities are revealed when examining KBCC's disaggregated outcomes for these English courses. In the last two semesters for which we have data, spring 2021 and fall 2021, while 65.6 percent of white students passed the corequisite composition class, only 41.8 percent of Black students and 41.2 percent of Hispanic students passed. Some combination of curricular factors (perhaps in the structure of the course) and external factors (like the pandemic, which made equity concerns more sharply defined) may have conspired to create this difference.

In response to growing concerns about such equity gaps, our English Department's Course Review Committee (CRC), a group that works on instructional matters critical to the composition sequence, spent several semesters revamping Composition I, coming away with a revised curriculum and course learning outcomes. As an outgrowth of this work and a move towards greater equity in course outcomes, I began to develop assignments that provide students with more autonomy over the ways they enter into and engage the course material. While scholarship on using choice as a curricular tool has yet to catch up with practice—a quick online search reveals it is a popular strategy among K–12 educators, though little scholarship has been published about it—the method is worth exploring. This essay specifically focuses on how choice boards allow instructors to differentiate instruction and empower students to decide the best ways to learn based on their academic and scheduling needs. This exploratory piece about my experience is a means to begin a conversation about encouraging students to take control of their learning.

THE EMERGENCE OF ALP NATIONWIDE AND THE NEED FOR CHOICE

For nearly a decade, I coordinated Kingsborough Community College's accelerated learning program. Since ALP's inception at Kingsborough in spring 2013, the recurrent concern of instructors, whether we had five sections or fifty, has been attrition. Repeated questions arose in end-of-term surveys and at meetings: How should nonparticipation be factored into students' grades? Should there be a punitive, automatic failure if students stop attending ALP? Should an ALP student who sporadically attends the supplemental instruction be allowed to continue in the class? Is there a way to administratively mandate attendance and participation? These questions circulate, even as the number of students who receive a noncompletion grade (for example, Withdraw) fluctuate between 9 percent and 30 percent, a huge spread that has varied over time and may result from changing guidance about what grades to assign students who are not going to pass the class.

Over the last decade, ALP models have been adopted swiftly in higher education, and their potential to allow more students to earn their degrees is promising. Initial investigation into the benefits of ALP has contributed to its adoption nationally, with results about outcomes and persistence overwhelmingly hopeful (see Adams et al. 2009, 58–59; Jaggars et al. 2015, 20). Encouraging data have also been amassed in Community College Resource Center (CCRC) reports, which documented early indicators of the efficacy of ALP (see Cho et al. 2012, 23; Edgecombe et al. 2014, 21.) My experience mirrors this research, as ALP has been of great benefit to my students, both within and outside the ALP section. The small-group members bond and form a supportive cohort, a connection that allows more risk taking in their own work. The ALP students bring this confidence into the whole-group session, as they are prepared with deeper insights and confidence. Even with anecdotal experiences like my own and the early data about the promise of corequisite models, what Shanna Jaggars, Michelle Hodara, Sung-Woo Cho, and Di Xu reported in 2015 remains relevant years later: "Despite the purported benefits of accelerated developmental education, research on the topic remains sparse" (6). Honest discussion of the challenges of and best practices for corequisite models is crucial, as state mandates restrict stand-alone developmental courses and the number of corequisite classes thereby increases.

One 2016 study that takes such an honest view, "Assessing the Accelerated Learning Program Model for Linguistically Diverse Developmental Writing Students," considered student attitudes toward ALP at another CUNY two-year school, Queensborough Community College in Bayside, New York (Anderst, Maloy, and Shahar 2016). Like the research conducted by the Community College of Baltimore County and the CCRC, they found the ALP model improved student pass rates for upper-level developmental students, both for native speakers and English-language learners, and that these students fared better than those registered in stand-alone developmental courses (13). Yet, while success was reflected in pass rates and grades, surveys showed students' own sense of satisfaction decreased over the semester. For example, while students expressed high satisfaction that course content was meaningful and appropriate at midsemester, these same students reported decreased satisfaction as the semester came to a close (23–25). Some students also seemed frustrated when comparing their writing to their peers who were not placed in the ALP program, as their own work seemed on par or even better than their non-ALP classmates' (25). The authors theorize that ALP students "are beginning to see themselves as something else besides developmental writers and are gaining a sense that their developmental class is not 'right' for them," suggesting the program turns these upper-level developmental students into "college writers" (26). This discontent is thus read in a positive light, as students' place in the academy appears to be transformed over the course of the term.

At Kingsborough, student resistance to the corequisite class is associated with nonparticipation and is rarely viewed through the optimistic lens used by our CUNY colleagues at Queensborough. When our standalone developmental program still existed, students were generally relieved to be placed into ALP, even with its additional hours, as they knew they were skipping noncredit coursework and could immediately earn credit for Composition I. This sense diminished when remediation was eliminated and their only reference point became their non-corequisite peers in the composition class. Once students realize not everyone in the whole group has supplemental instruction scheduled, the extra support can seem more punitive than beneficial. This feeling might be even stronger if they sense, like the students described at Queensborough, that their skills are no different than their non-ALP peers'. To deal with this trend, offering choice may give students a sense of control over their learning.

WHY CHOICE IS A TOOL FOR EQUITY

While offering students choices around their classwork activities might seem like a small but complicated intervention, it has the potential to make a difference for those whose performance is hindered by the outside responsibilities that make persistence in school difficult. Susan D. Blum (2020) discusses the imperative to interrogate our teaching policies and practices to promote equity in the concluding chapter of *(Un)grading*, a collection exploring the possibilities of removing standard grading practices from the classroom: "One of the greatest challenges in contemporary education is how to foster equity—not necessarily equality or uniformity—among ever more diverse student populations. Given different backgrounds, they may require different kinds of feedback—adding to the mandate that educators' educational practices occur in conversation with participating students. This mandate makes generic practices untenable. To the extent that learning in schools involves relationships, they must be remade with each new cohort" (223). Using choice to structure instruction as modeled in this essay arises from a similar movement from generic toward more flexible modes. Blum's collection suggests that though traditional assessment practices like grading seem invisible and inviolable, they forestall a more interactive approach that takes into account students' needs at the moment of instruction. Similarly, choice boards can take students' unique needs into account to create more equitable moments of class engagement.

The ungrading concept is one of many that arose just at the time when ALP and other corequisite models were developed around the United States as administrations concluded stand-alone remediation was impeding students' progress. These equity-inspired assessments attempt to provide more consistent access to course material. As Asao B. Inoue (2015) explains in a discussion of the role of labor in writing assessment, "In antiracist writing assessment ecologies, it is important to focus on labor, as we all can labor, and labor can be measured by duration, quantity, or intensity, not by so-called quality, or against a single standard. This makes for a more equitable ecology, particularly for those who may come to it with discourses or habitus other than the dominant ones" (80). The practice of offering choice adds to these conversations, as it allows even those students with unequal demands on their time the opportunity to select the modes of learning that best fit their needs.

In particular, choice boards work around material limitations that disproportionately affect marginalized students by presenting a number of paths into the course material to accommodate time constraints and current learning styles. Students who need to engage the material from various angles can complete extra assignments. Students can take advantage of conferences with the professor in the most comfortable format for them and choose the types of thinking that suit their learning, as they are the experts on what works most effectively for them. The classroom is thus reframed as a space of possibility for all, with just some upfront planning by the professor.

CHOICE BOARDS: RATIONALE AND SETUP

Just around the time students stopped viewing ALP as a time-saving measure, the pandemic disrupted in-person learning. My two overtallied ALP sections of Composition I went from being fully in person to fully asynchronous online. The learning curve for students was steep, and the sudden requirement that they take full responsibility for learning was a hard one. To help students succeed, I found it necessary to adjust my expectations about what *could* or *should* be done with the two hours of supplemental instruction, while ensuring students had the deeper experience ALP provides.

The first and most difficult leap was to reframe my notion that I could replicate the two discrete hours I would have had on campus with the asynchronous small group. Coming up with additional hours of writing assignments felt like counterproductive and excessive labor for the students and for me. Collaborative tools were already in place in the whole group, like discussion boards and online annotation tools, but the individual, personalized attention so many relied on was missing. What ALP students needed, I realized—after discussion with colleagues and much reflection—is one-on-one conferencing and time for peer review. The individualized instruction and connection to classmates help students connect in a safe context. They create a personal relationship that lets students reach out to me or their peers to help them stay afloat if life becomes difficult.

At CUNY, live meetings for asynchronous sections cannot be mandated, so building time for conferences into the curriculum required some planning. One effective and practical strategy to make these connections possible was to give students options about the way they would meet with me, and before I knew it, the idea of choice transformed the weekly workflow for the rest of the term. Each week of my ALP class is now structured within a choice board, anchored by one key activity from the whole-group work. The approach takes a cue from the popular choice-board strategy in primary and secondary classrooms, which became more widespread in remote classrooms during the pandemic.

Choice boards present students with a grid with a number of tasks to complete within a designated period. Using this method in the corequisite college classroom helps transition the supplemental hours from finite sessions in small groups at specific times to a collection of activities students can choose among at their own pace. The board can offer various ways to connect—individual appointments to meet with the professor or peers—or independent tasks that supplement the week's work. Its popularity among younger groups should not exclude it from consideration, as it provides autonomy and agency over when and how learning takes place. Choice boards work particularly well for corequisite classrooms, as they provide a visual representation of how the whole-group work fits into the small-group ALP session. We can thus empower students by ceding some control over the exact assignments they will complete while making the connections between the small and whole group clear.

Though scholarship on the efficacy of choice as a tool is limited, practical examples abound online. The examples presented below are inspired by Joli Boucher (n.d.) and innumerable teacher-shared materials highlighting the fact that what happens in practice is not always investigated and tested. The literature around choice that has been explored comes from the K–12 classroom. Patrick N. Beymer and Margareta Maria

Thomson (2015) provide a literature review that highlights how choice can give feelings of autonomy, as long as there are not too many choices. Crucially, "building an initial interest and some background knowledge on a topic before offering a choice may lead students to experience increased motivation. If students do not feel that they have some sort of expertise in a particular area, they may view choosing as undesirable and overwhelming, which may lead to an ineffective choice" (116). The scaffolding provided in the following assignments, beginning with a few choices and moving to greater complexity, leads students to this kind of competence.

After experimentation, I have found a best practice for ALP is to anchor the activities around one square that represents the work assigned to the whole class. The supplementary activities act as a constellation to the whole-group assignment, deepening understanding and providing ways to engage the week's assignments. Rather than overwhelm students with too many choices at the beginning of the semester, I start with just two options stemming from a whole-group task. Here is one example of how to structure an introductory board in asynchronous, hybrid, or even face-to-face sections of ALP:

ALP Weekly Assignment Board

Step 1: Whole-Group Work

Write me an introductory letter. This is an informal piece of writing.
To answer it completely, write at least **250 words**.
- Do you have another name/nickname you would like me to call you?
- Do you have questions about Blackboard or the flow of the class?
- What is your major? What led you to choose this major?
- What are your hobbies?
- What's your favorite book, if any? Is there anything you enjoy reading, even online?
- How comfortable are you completing online work?
- Do you have any concerns you would like to share?
- Let me know if there's anything about your learning style I should understand to help you succeed. You can also tell me about any non-school-related issues that might affect your learning and performance in this class.

The students appreciate having the flexibility to meet with me in the way that best fits their schedules. Those who work long shifts, whether overnight or during the day, often find the email option more feasible than squeezing another meeting into an already packed schedule. And once the email channel opened, they found they could easily reach out again when necessary. On the other hand, those students who really want to speak to me during a live session find the virtual Zoom check-in efficiently answers their questions and makes them more invested in the class. Beginning with just two options to fulfill their weekly work requirement sets the stage for more elaborate configurations. This grid can be customized easily to include more communication options, if, for example, you like to meet with students through texting and voice tools like Remind, Google Voice, or your own phone number. After the initial setup, this method takes no longer than traditional conferences, as long as instructors schedule boundaries ahead of time.

Once they are used to the concept of the board, I add more options for them to complete, as seen below. Layering new options over time provides more points of engagement to enrich the whole group work.

ALP Weekly Assignment Board

Step 2: ALP work

Choose one.
- Option 1: Zoom Conference
  Go to SignUp Genius and set up an appointment with me to get acquainted and talk about the semester's work.

Your name	Your appointment date/time

- Option 2: Email Conference
  Send an email to Lesley.Broder@kbcc.cuny.edu.
  In your message, describe one challenge and one success you have had in a previous English class.
  You should also tell me what your writing goals are for the semester.
  Finally, let me know if you are ever available for Zoom conferences during the term. Once I write back to you, make sure you respond to my message.

Though too many choices might feel overwhelming when presented early in the term, especially for asynchronous sections, students appreciate more choices as they become acclimated to the course and its goals. Having a variety of entry points into the shared class reading helps students develop their perspectives and prepare for more complex writing projects to come.

ALP Weekly Assignment Board

Step 1: Whole-Group Work

Post Formal Writing 2 to Blackboard by Monday at 11:59 PM. Remember to cite your sources.

Step 2: ALP Work

Choose two below.
Complete by Friday at 11:59 PM.

- Option 1: Audio Reflection
  Go to online-voice-recorder.com and record a two- to four-minute description of the strongest part of your paper and a description of the part you think needs to be revised. Feel free to read from your paper in your recording.

Your name	Link to your online voice recording

- Option 2: Zoom Conference
  Go to SignUp Genius and set up an appointment with me to conference about your essay.

Your name	Your appointment date/time

- Option 3
  Write a paragraph of 200 words (or more) on Google Docs describing the process of writing your essay. What strategies worked well? What would you do differently next time?

Your name	Link to your Google Doc

- Option 4
    Exchange your paper with your peer-review partner. Use the commenting feature of Google Docs to make 4 comments on your partner's paper based on our Assessment Criteria. Share the link below,

Your name	Link to your Google Doc

At first, I required that students complete three extra tasks, but the labor to assess this work over several sections was unsustainable. I eventually found that requiring two additional activities offers enough enrichment without making the grading difficult to maintain on my end. While one square often becomes a popular choice, students vary choices overall, breaking up the grading process from the instructor's point of view. Of course, if time allows or if the section is small, three activities can be assigned, particularly if the assessment is for completion. Students reported in end-of-term surveys that they appreciated having these options and that it allowed them to participate in a way that was most comfortable and practical for them; building up slowly, beginning with two options, ensures students are prepared for this new approach to their learning.

FUTURE PROSPECTS FOR CHOICE AND EQUITY

Students' prior educational experiences and current material needs can affect the ways they are able to engage in the work of the class. Many ALP students have outside responsibilities and financial burdens that make even coming to campus a burden. There are those who disappear for a week or two and then want to rejoin the class. Other students faithfully come to every class session and yet do not complete the work, even when they know the risks of failing. These students might be pressured to come to class by family; they might believe attendance alone will lead to passing; others are overwhelmed with work and childcare tasks. However zigzagging and irregular students' paths might be, it is helpful if our classroom can make room for all students. Hope Parisi (2020) has considered these varying paths, not all of which will lead to a passing grade:

> Regardless of passing or failing the course, all students will learn, and all students will succeed. This means understanding that progression is not linear and success in college is a varied acquisition: What happens in the classroom, what students feel they get out of it, is partly what keeps students coming back, and alongside other advocacy work, it's an area in which teacher agency has a great impact (160).

Some students are in our classrooms for the whole semester and others just make it through part of the term. Integrating choice can allow all these students to jump in and participate. The students who have the means to be efficient will have plenty of options for delving deeper into the coursework. The students who are struggling to gain footing can land somewhere when provided options to enter the course on their own terms. This is not to say providing choice will ensure each and every student passes by the end of the term. They don't. What it *does* do is give everyone a way to engage with the material along the way and, significantly, it may create opportunities for passing, or even just learning the material more deeply, for students who would not have found their way into the material without choice.

In one of the first analyses of ALP in 2010, the CCRC found the program at the Community College of Baltimore County was a more cost effective way for upper-level developmental English students to meet their required English coursework as compared to the stand-alone developmental route (Jenkins et al. 2010, 2). Within their analysis, buried amongst programmatic data, the authors make a concise but significant observation: "ALP's primary innovation is structural rather than instructional" (Jenkins et al. 2010, 6). This brief descriptor stayed with me as I established faculty-development sessions or brainstormed ways to set up my class. It is the *structure* that is different, but the *instruction* is the same. When we talk about best practices for ALP, we're really considering best practices for teaching; no matter what their level, our corequisite students *are* our composition students. While the extra hours of class time may allow for repetition, review, and a slower pace, what makes effective teaching in an ALP class will run across any section.

As we acquaint students with the extra requirements of ALP and how it will enrich their learning—framing activities with choice, and with flexibility for how the supplemental assignments can be completed—choice may be a useful tool to allow more students to persist. Community college students lead hectic lives with moving parts they are constantly trying to keep balanced. In fact, nontuition expenses like transportation or food, unexpected financial emergencies, and long working hours are enough to sabotage their ability to successfully complete coursework, outweighing even the pressures of tuition (Sharp 2021, 3). Students at two-year colleges have always juggled responsibilities outside school, and these pressures multiplied during the early years of the pandemic and will undoubtedly linger into the future. In this context, if a course does not provide flexible learning opportunities, students may be unable to participate or will just complete the minimum required, which may not be enough.

In a chapter on labor-based grading in *Race and Writing Assessment*, Inoue (2012) cautions that "the effectiveness of our grading technologies, whatever they may be, may not be evenly distributed among all students" (80). Though a perfectly equitable assignment, grading structure, or classroom routine may be impossible—given our own biases, the structural constraints of students' lives, and students' differential learning needs—we still can attempt to reach for these utopian structures. As we do, we must remember that what can be read as apathy or disengagement may sometimes be a matter of survival. When multiple learning structures are in place for students to engage in the course material, the safety net we cast to assist students is widened without diminishing instructional quality or creating unreasonable labor requirements. There are no surefire ways to guarantee students can manage our class within the contours of their lives, but to increase the likelihood of students' progress, mindful commitment on the part of the instructor may be needed to help them along.

REFERENCES

Adams, Peter, Sarah Gearhart, Robert Miller, and Anne Roberts. 2009. "The Accelerated Learning Program: Throwing Open the Gates." *Journal of Basic Writing* 28 (2): 50–69.

Anderst, Leah, Jennifer Maloy, and Jed Shahar. 2016. "Assessing the Accelerated Learning Program Model for Linguistically Diverse Developmental Writing Students." *Teaching English in the Two-Year College* 44 (1): 11–31. https://www.proquest.com/docview/1826885882?accountid=13567&pq-origsite=primo.

Beymer, Patrick N., and Margareta Maria Thomson. 2015. "Effects of Choice in the Classroom." *Support for Learning* 30 (2): 105–20. https://doi.org/10.1111/1467-9604.12086.

Blum, Susan D. 2020. "Conclusion: Not Simple But Essential." In *(Un)grading*, edited by Susan D. Blum, 219–28. Morgantown: West Virginia University Press.

Boucher, Joli. n.d. "Reading Response Choice Board." Last modified March 6, 2017. https://flippedtechcoaching.com/2017/03/06/reading-response-choice-board/.

Cho, Sung-Woo, Elizabeth Kopko, Davis Jenkins, and Shanna Smith Jaggars. 2012. "New Evidence of Success for Community College Remedial English Students: Tracking the Outcomes of Students in the Accelerated Learning Program (ALP)." *CCRC Working Paper* 53, Community College Resource Center, Teachers College, Columbia University, NY. https://ccrc.tc.columbia.edu/media/k2/attachments/ccbc-alp-student-outcomes-follow-up.pdf.

CUNY. n.d. "About CUNY: Mission." https://www.cuny.edu/about/#:~:text=The%20University's%20historic%20mission%20continues,the%20New%20York%20State%20Legislatur.

Del Principe, Annie, Lesley Broder, and Lauren Levesque. 2022. "Tracking the Racial Consequences of Placement by Probability: A Case Study at Kingsborough Community College." In *Writing Placement in Two-Year Colleges: The Pursuit of Equity in Postsecondary Education*, edited by Jessica Nastal, Mya Poe, and Christie Toth, 173–90. Fort Collins, CO: WAC Clearinghouse. https://doi.org/10.37514/PRA-B.2022.1565.2.07.

Edgecombe, Nikki, Shanna Smith Jaggars, Di Xu, and Melissa Barragan. 2014. "Accelerating the Integrated Instruction of Developmental Reading and Writing at Chabot College." *CCRC Working Paper* 71, Community College Resource Center, Teachers College, Columbia University, NY. https://ccrc.tc.columbia.edu/media/k2/attachments/accelerating-integrated-developmental-reading-and-writing-at-chabot.pdf.

Inoue, Asao B. 2012. "Grading Contracts: Assessing Their Effectiveness on Different Racial Formations." In *Race and Writing Assessment*, edited by Asao B. Inoue and Mya Poe, 79–94. New York: Peter Lang.

Inoue, Asao B. 2015. "Antiracist Writing Assessment Ecologies." In *Antiracist Writing Assessment Ecologies: Teaching and Assessing Writing for a Socially Just Future*, 77–118. Anderson, SC: Parlor.

Jaggars, Shanna Smith, Michelle Hodara, Sung-Woo Cho, and Di Xu. 2015. "Three Accelerated Developmental Education Programs." *Community College Review* 43 (1): 3–26. https://doi.org/10.1177/0091552114551752.

Jenkins, Davis, Cecilia Speroni, Clive Belfield, Shanna Smith Jaggars, and Nikki Edgecombe. 2010. "A Model for Accelerating Academic Success of Community College Remedial English Students: Is the Accelerated Learning Program (ALP) Effective and Affordable?" *CCRC Working Paper* 21, Community College Resource Center, Teachers College, Columbia University, NY. https://ccrc.tc.columbia.edu/publications/accelerating-academic-success-remedial-english.html.

Kingsborough Community College. n.d.a. "About Kingsborough Community College." https://www.kbcc.cuny.edu/aboutkcc/index.html.

Kingsborough Community College. n.d.b. "About Kingsborough Community College: Our Mission." http://catalog.kingsborough.edu/content.php?catoid=9&navoid=639.

Parisi, Hope. 2020. "Inversive Teaching." In *Sixteen Teachers Teaching: Two-Year College Perspectives*, edited by Patrick Sullivan, 152–67. Logan: Utah State University Press.

"Percent Enrollment by Ethnicity." 2021. Kingsborough Community College Office of Institutional Effectiveness. https://www.kbcc.cuny.edu/irap/documents/Enrollment-Data/2022/EnrollmentbyEthnicity.pdf.

Sharp, Naomi. 2021. "Opportunity Costs: Affording the True Costs of College in NYC." Center for an Urban Future. https://nycfuture.org/pdf/CUF_OpportunityCosts_Final.pdf.

4
ALP INSTRUCTORS' EXPERIENCES TEACHING ACROSS MODES DURING THE COVID-19 PANDEMIC

Carrie Aldrich and Sarah Prielipp

INTRODUCTION

In 2019, our department developed and implemented a corequisite accelerated learning program (ALP) course to accompany our first college-level writing requirement, WRTG A111. We designed this course for face-to-face learning and never imagined teaching it online. Until we had to.

Influenced by scholarship on antiracist pedagogy (e.g., Chavez 2021) and antiracist assessment (e.g., Inoue 2012), as well as recommendations by the National Council of Teachers of English (2015), our department recognized issues of equity in first-year writing success. Findings touting ALP success (e.g., Jaggars, Hodara, and Cho 2015; Uehling 2020) made us feel optimistic about the possibilities of shortening the writing-sequence pipeline for students while addressing issues of equity and forming stronger relationships with students. We had questions about how to best teach this class for our unique Alaskan learning context, so we designed a multiphase, mixed-methods, longitudinal study to better understand the role ALP plays in helping students succeed. This study collected data from students and instructors. In this chapter, we share data from ALP instructors to better understand their role in student success during a pandemic that pivoted all our courses online in spring 2020.

All our writing courses were offered online for AY 2020–2021, and instructors could choose their modality for AY 2021–2022. As we coded data from seven ALP instructors in spring and fall 2021, the role modality played in teaching and learning was salient across instructors' interviews and reflections. Before spring 2020, when all ALP sections met face to face, instructors mentioned community and relationship building as important aspects of the course and why they enjoyed teaching it. However, as reported by Beckie Supiano (2022) and others, they said those aspects of the course that most support student success were more challenging in the online environment.

During the coding process, our conversations with one another typically started with the struggles we faced in our own classes. Anchorage has remained a hotspot for COVID transmission since the beginning of the pandemic. Our students and colleagues have been out sick, and we have all experienced loss and intense grief. In a postsemester interview in spring 2021 about her ALP class, Martha, who has been teaching college composition for over twelve years, emphasized the importance of supporting students emotionally and preparing for big changes in higher education to extend into the future: "As far as teaching in the pandemic, you know, they say depression is up, anxiety is up among young people, so I'm trying to be as much as possible the helpful, friendly coach in the classroom. . . . I'm taking extra pains to position myself and you know, even how I dress in the classroom, just to be less intimidating. And, I guess the biggest success for me as an instructor is just that I made it through the semester myself because it was a really challenging semester."

We all want to show empathy to students, and we know their struggles are real. We also must complete our courses according to the university calendar and the parameters surrounding the classes we teach. Without time in our workloads, we've all made major changes to our courses from policies to assignments and in-class activities as we navigate multiple modalities. While quickly adapting to the shifting higher education landscape, ALP instructors at the University of Alaska Anchorage have persevered and continue to focus on student success in college-level writing regardless of modality in a global pandemic that requires constant flexibility and adaptability.

We all have different ideas about what we want our classes to look like in the future, and we're all also not sure exactly what we want them to look like because we have no way to predict the future, and the higher education landscape has changed rapidly since we implemented ALP. This uncertainty has led to students, instructors, and administrators circulating different expectations and has led us to dig into modality in our research. We recognize there are possibilities in front of us we have not considered. In this chapter, researchers and ALP instructors Carrie Aldrich and Sarah Prielipp share case studies from three participants and weave in their own experiences as well. These case studies have important implications for the future of ALP in general, particularly in this new normal taking over higher education.

ALP AT THE UNIVERSITY OF ALASKA ANCHORAGE

This study took place at the University of Alaska Anchorage (UAA), an open-access public institution serving a highly diverse community with over one 110 languages spoken in the public-school system. ALP students at UAA take WRTG 111, Writing Across Contexts, a three-credit college-level writing course required by all degree and certificate programs, along with a two-credit support course, WRTG 192, Accelerate Learning Program. Each WRTG 111 ALP class includes two sections, one for students who placed into WRTG 111 and one for students who tested below WRTG 111 and submitted a writing sample that placed them into WRTG 111 ALP. The students in our study all attended the same WRTG 111 class together, and the ALP students attended an additional two hours with the same instructor.

Before enrolling in an ALP section, students sign an agreement stating they have the time (seven to eight hours beyond their writing course), dedication, and motivation to devote to the course. Instructors in this study made efforts to emphasize relationship building, institutional knowledge, and a flexible curriculum that responds to individual student needs.

In spring 2020, our department pivoted completely online, and spring 2021 was our third semester of online learning. In fall 2021, we were wrestling with tension about how to meet students' needs, and some sections changed modality during the enrollment period. Our department offered ALP face to face, online synchronously and asynchronously, and hybrid/hyflex. Our institution initially required masking and spacing, but as of spring 2022, has never mandated a vaccine requirement for face-to-face classes. Instructors reported challenges related to modality in all approaches.

ALP SUCCESS

ALP students at our institution are mostly outperforming WRTG 111 students. From fall 2020 to fall 2021, students enrolled in WRTG 111 ALP passed at a rate of 88 percent, which is higher than students who took WRTG 111 alone (74%) and students who took WRTG 110 (67%), a pre-college-level course that is, ostensibly, easier. In postsemester interviews, instructors added depth to what the numbers show. In an interview following her spring 2021 ALP class, Martha captured the role ALP is playing in student success: "I'll be honest, what surprises me every semester is that my ALP students seem to outperform the 111 students. And then I think back and I wonder, should that be surprising? . . . I guess it shouldn't surprise me that students who are meeting, you know, four times a week instead of two, and who have access, not only to all the support you give, but to that sort of open time where they're really running the show. It really shouldn't surprise any of us that the ALP students outperform the traditional 111 students."

Sharon found signs of success in her students' reflections. In a fall 21 interview, she explained, "I asked them to think about the students they were the first day of this class, and the students they are on the last day of this class, and how they feel that they have changed and grown as writers. And almost every one of them said something along the lines of how the class and the structure of the class really helped them understand and was well organized. And the ALP students all said that they loved the extra time together and that it was really helpful to them."

ALP has been celebrated as a phenomenal success during the three years we've implemented it at UAA, which mirrors national data, and our department is constantly looking for ways to continue building our corequisite program and making it more accessible to our students.

RESEARCHERS

We are both first-generation college students with recent PhDs who do this work in order to disrupt the systemic inequalities we see in front of us every day. Our overlapping roles as teachers and researchers offer us unique access to the ALP learning context as teacher/researchers (Sunstein and Chiseri-Strater 2012). As we designed this study and collected and analyzed the data, it was important to us that this research be relevant to improving writing education for our students, our colleagues, and ourselves.

When she started her position in fall 2018, Carrie had a partial course release to research and develop a corequisite support course to accelerate our college-level writing course. In spring 2019, she piloted and conducted an initial assessment of the course. Since then, she has taught one section of WRTG 111 ALP each spring and fall, and part of her workload is devoted to researching ALP. While she prefers teaching ALP face to face, she has also taught it synchronously online and hyflex. She values this collaborative research project with Sarah, which gives them the opportunity to talk about the intersection of teaching and research and the role it can play in improving student success.

While Sarah is newer to ALP and UAA, she has been teaching courses similar to this under the guise of "developmental" courses at other institutions since she began teaching in 2005. She was excited to collaborate with Carrie on this project and to further explore how relationship building affects student success. She taught one section of WRTG 111 ALP each semester in her first year at UAA in AY 2019–2020 and also taught the course online in summer 2020. She continued to teach one section of the corequisite courses in each semester of AY 2020–2021 as synchronous online classes.

Even though we were already experienced online educators, we'd never pivoted face-to-face courses to online in the middle of the semester, and the pivot to online teaching was energy intense for both of us. Not only did we have to pivot our teaching online, but all our major professional conferences took place online, which meant that to remain on top of best practices in our field, which are changing rapidly, we needed to interact online in many facets of our careers.

DATA COLLECTION

Participants are seven instructors from the Department of Writing at the University of Alaska Anchorage who consented to participate in this study. All instructors had extensive college-teaching experience, used open-access educational materials, and discussed teaching and learning from a social justice perspective. The data for this chapter come from semistructured interviews (see appendix 4.A) that took place at the end of spring and fall semesters in 2021, as well as instructors' weekly reflections (see appendix 4.B).

DATA ANALYSIS

In the tradition of qualitative research (e.g., Creswell 2013), we analyzed interview transcripts to identify themes and patterns relative to the research questions. Data analysis involved the recursive process of reading, analyzing transcripts and reflections, member checking with participants, and debriefing with one another to enhance the credibility and trustworthiness of this research (Merriam 2009). Using the emic perspective, we talked with each other and with the instructor participants to minimize the data around themes. For this paper, we selected these three case studies from a larger pool of participants, based on attention to modality.

CASE STUDIES
Emily

As a conscientious educator, in advance of her first ALP class, Emily polled her class to ask about their modality preferences. Nobody asked her to do this, but she wanted to put her students' needs first. In their responses, students told Emily "it was invaluable to be able to be in person and ask questions," which made her think more about the benefits of being in person, even though it was difficult because of masking, distancing, and high rates of COVID transmission in our community. Many students had to miss class because they were sick, caring for others, or waiting on COVID tests after being exposed to the virus, but they were not always too sick to participate online, so she modified the course to hyflex so students could Zoom into class when it wasn't safe for them or they were not able to attend in person.

She hadn't prepared for hyflex delivery when she designed the course, so she used her laptop to bring students into the face-to-face classroom via Zoom, but she found that teaching a face-to-face class while filming herself and the class with a laptop is hard. Emily asked for a webcam, but our department did not have any to give to her, so she considered buying one out of her own pocket. In the end, she stuck to using her laptop. In her interview, she emphasized the importance of having the right technology and space for teaching.

Emily is aware that the support she gave individual students who struggled with tough life circumstances helped them make it through the class and adapt using the modality that worked for the situation. She reported a situation in which a student who had experienced a family emergency related to the pandemic had to move back to their home community in rural Alaska three weeks before the end of the semester. Emily said, "I don't think she would have gotten through this semester if she hadn't been in ALP." Emily had developed a relationship with the student in the ALP class, so she felt comfortable working with the student flexibly by distance to finish the class, but it wasn't easy, and she worked with the student up until the final deadline. The student experienced connectivity issues in her small rural community, and Emily accepted her work even when it came in late.

At the end of her interview, Emily said, "If I had known back then that so much would still be online two years in, I think I would have worked much harder to make better foundational online material so that it felt like less of a scramble still a few years in. But that's all hindsight, and I honestly don't know if I would have had the bandwidth to make things more solid with that initial pivot."

Emily also found the course had less structure than her usual teaching load. "I was surprised. I know that a couple people had mentioned this in the [ALP training] workshop [led by Peter Adams], that the students really would often dictate what they needed or wanted. And I did find that true, but the thing that surprised me about it was sometimes they just wanted to come in and talk. I mean, two of them were also in the same math class. And, you know, as we got closer to registering for courses, they just wanted to talk about other stuff happening in their academic lives to which I, you know, I figured, okay, you know, if this is what they want to use some of that space for, it seemed good." While Emily adapted to the needs of the students, she also had an important realization: "You know, it made me think, okay, so ALP is another place where maybe you can catch some of those things that might go through the bureaucratic cracks, too." For her, ALP wasn't just about supplementing writing skills; it was also a place where students could become more familiar with institutional resources and could learn to navigate the institution—key factors for student success. Furthermore, Emily found her students needed the in-person interactions to achieve that success.

Martha

With five semesters teaching ALP, Martha brings her social work background, a student-centered philosophy, and a big heart to the classroom. Martha began teaching ALP in the first semester we offered it at UAA, fall 2019, and, in addition to her MFA in creative writing, she recently completed a PhD and a TESOL certificate. Martha taught one section of our first-year composition with ALP in spring and fall of 2021 as part of her full-time teaching load. Her pedagogy is underpinned by Marxism and feminism, and she has served on a number of college and community committees focused on LGBTQ issues and supporting honors students.

Martha is a thoughtful teacher who structures her ALP course around her students' needs. She responds to students' writing for WRTG 111 and uses the ALP time to go more in depth with concepts, which she notices need more time through small groups and individual writing consultations. She keeps her course schedule fairly "loose" so she can tailor lessons to what students need. She spends a lot of time on community building, and she knows the Alaskan student population well. She waits until their third session to do full introductions "because people are sometimes still adding and dropping classes that first week. Intros usually take about half an hour, and then we get to other work. However, we end up taking the full period getting acquainted. I think the pandemic has made people really hungry for connection. I think it's okay that we devoted the whole class period to this activity because community is so important in the ALP." She is committed to knowing her students and to working with them as individuals.

This community building is what sets ALP apart from the other courses Martha teaches. With the smaller class size, she has the time to get to know her students better and to develop camaraderie that helps her students' confidence. She likes to incorporate one-on-one tutoring and writing workshops: "I'm not just conducting the orchestra, I'm sitting down with each student, looking at their drafts, and pointing things out, so it's almost like a tutoring session. And with just eleven students in the class, I can do that in one class period. I can sit down with everyone and have a good conversation with them." Unlike her other classes, which are capped at twenty-two students, ALP is capped at eleven, which means she has more workload devoted to individual students.

In spring 2021, Martha's ALP courses were fully online, but her fall 2021 course met in person, masked and socially distanced but without a vaccine mandate for our institution. Frequent internet disruptions during Zoom sessions, being locked out of institutional systems, and statewide internet outages created challenges for teaching online, but Martha and her students persisted.

She found ways to interact with students in the moment but felt she couldn't respond as meaningfully in the rhythms of the moment. She said, "I found that doing a workshop on Zoom was difficult because students wanted to share their work with me, but then we would disrupt everybody else on Zoom. I ended up using Google Docs and communicating in writing to individuals. However, I really found that I missed the classroom experience where I could sit next to students and look at their work for a bit, then move on to the next one." Even though she recognizes the difficulty of pivoting to a hyflex option, she said, "I was really thrilled with the tools that we had to work with. And I think we managed to make it work."

Martha noticed one student who never turned her camera on in the larger WRTG 111 classroom but turned on the camera when she was engaged in a small group in the ALP classroom. She said, "When they interact in small groups, something switches in their minds, and maybe they don't feel the need to hide. But that student ended up really contributing quite a bit in the small group. And I guess, if I hadn't offered that opportunity, I think the student would have had a really different semester."

Sharon

Sharon has twenty-two years of experience teaching composition, professional writing, and literature courses. With her sensitivity to students' personal challenges and wry sense of humor, Sharon highlighted the individual attention she gave to students and the positive ways they responded. Although this semester was her first time teaching ALP, she was familiar with the stretch model used at a previous institution.

Sharon chose to offer her class synchronously online, with WRTG A111 meeting once a week on Tuesdays and WRTG 192 meeting once a week on Thursdays; this schedule seemed to fill a student need. Unlike all the other ALP sections, her students were mostly Asian international students, and she had no dual-enrollment students.

Like the other instructors, Sharon centered her ALP course around doing the work for the course. She explained, "Basically, we just worked on whatever they needed to work on that week, whether it was the writing assignment or the bigger paper that was due. Sometimes it was one, sometimes it was the other. I made it really loose and open as to what we did based on what they wanted to do." She encourages all her students to revise all their papers.

Sharon structured her course in a way that helped students dig deeper into the content from WRTG A111 through activities such as practicing analyzing an advertisement alongside an analysis essay and collecting and evaluating different types of source material alongside a research essay. She said, "They seem to think about writing as a task, a chore, something that they have to prove they can do in order to jump through the hoops. And I was trying to show them that writing is something that is part of your identity, part of your selfhood, and this is a way that you can express yourself, and . . . they responded really, really well to that."

Sharon made major changes to her classes over the course of the pandemic. While she traditionally enforced strict attendance and late-work policies, she threw those policies out the window and said, "If you missed any work, go ahead and submit it. I will accept it. If you missed any of your writing assignments during the week, go ahead and give them to me. I will accept it. No grade penalties. I continued to take attendance, but I removed any point penalties from it." She believes this more flexible approach helps her give students what they need to be successful.

FINDINGS AND RECOMMENDATIONS

Modality affects teaching and learning in profound ways, including how we present content, build community, and interact with students. All the instructors showed adaptability, flexibility, and creativity in figuring things out in the moment—habits of mind we also stress with our students. But making a lesson effective for the whole group takes prethinking and preparation, and not every lesson designed for face-to-face interaction is easy to adapt to online. The following recommendations can help us develop sustaining pedagogy and foster community in ALP instruction across modalities.

Defining and Understanding Modalities

Because we have not had clear guidelines around modality, we did not use the same terms to talk about modality. Students, faculty, and advisors don't know what these terms mean or what to expect from them, and even in our interviews, different participants referred to similar teaching scenarios with different terminology. Consistent terminology, departmentally and institutionally, can help students make informed decisions and can help faculty prepare to provide students with what they need.

Asynchronous Learning

We know students benefit from the spontaneous interactions that happen when we meet with students synchronously, but the real-life context surrounding teaching and learning has sometimes prevented such interactions from happening. Based on results from this study at this point, we don't recommend a fully asynchronous ALP course. When there is no possible safe way to meet synchronously, asynchronous learning can be effective if the instructor maintains individual attention.

ALP students benefit from the relationships they develop with their instructors and the other students, and it can be more difficult to build that community, that trust, in asynchronous learning environments. For example, Carrie has found that interactive workshops in Google Docs can provide students with ways to engage meaningfully with one another without having to be in the same space or work at the same time. She has also found that accountability check-ins, which she collects using Google Forms, can help keep students focused on their writing assignments when synchronous meetings are not an option. A highly skilled teacher provides multiple opportunities for students to engage with one another. Online possibilities not captured in our study, such as virtual spaces (e.g., gaming, social media) might begin to fill the gap in belongingness in online learning.

Synchronous Learning

When she began teaching ALP in 2019, Carrie was impressed with the relationships students developed with one another. After a few informal, student-driven class periods, she watched students leave class together to have lunch. They shared stories about getting together over the weekends, texted classmates when they didn't show up, and supported one another throughout the drafting process. And it worked: a diverse group of students who wouldn't have placed into WRTG A111 based on their standardized test scores achieved a 100 percent pass rate. It is clear to her from her time teaching ALP that the relationships that form in the more intimate group are some of the most productive and rewarding parts of this curriculum and helped students form their own informal support systems to understand the hidden rules of higher education and succeed in their courses.

Online classes, particularly the synchronous Zoom sessions, were somewhat frustrating for all of us though because they made this relationship building more difficult. Sarah wrote in a weekly reflection, "They are doing okay with the work (most submitting), but they do not want to participate in our synchronous Zoom sessions. I've tried calling on people, and I'm pretty sure they aren't really there because they don't respond at all. The only participants are those who keep their cameras on." This lack of participation made it more difficult to develop relationships with students, and Sarah used this early-semester concern as a lesson about the importance of participation in college classes and how to facilitate participation in the future.

Martha echoed this struggle to engage with students in the online environment.

> My biggest learning moment in ALP was to be comfortable with silence online. In the face-to-face classroom, I learned a long time ago, it's okay to be together and be silent. Let people think. Because if you put out a question, you know, it takes them time to gather up what they might say, and then gather up the courage to say it, to look around, well, maybe someone else will raise their hand, you know, it takes time. Something about being online, especially when students aren't turning their cameras on, makes me feel that urge to rush in and talk over the silence. And so I really learned this semester, it's okay, to sit with it. And sometimes I even say little words like that, "We're just going to reflect here for a minute, just think," and then we ended up having some good discussion.

During spring 2021, when teaching ALP synchronously online, Carrie echoed the same sentiment in her weekly reflection: "I have been talking too much during the workshopping sessions. In face-to-face classes,

I feel like I'm skilled in helping to facilitate students' talk without having to do much talking myself, but in synchronous online sessions, I'm much more likely to keep talking when my questions are followed by silence."

Regardless of modality, synchronous learning has been essential to all our ALP instructors in developing relationships with our students. While online synchronous learning has created some limitations in developing strong classroom communities that underpin our in-person prepandemic ALP classes, all our participants have found ways to engage their students. For example, Sarah began utilizing fun polls in Zoom to open her classes, and she asked students to post short reflections and comments in the chat when she realized they weren't comfortable speaking up on Zoom. And Carrie even had online students connecting with one another in person: "One day, we all met online rather than face to face because I had to travel out of state to attend a conference. I was aware that Jessie and Marie—who both had their cameras on—were at different places during WRTG A111. And when we got to the ALP class, all of a sudden, Jessie and Marie were in the same place together. In the fifteen minutes between writing A111 and 192, Jessie ran over to Marie's house. I thought that was an important sign that relationship building was happening again. And when we got back to class, Marie introduced the class to her boyfriend, who was on his way to work. And we were all like, 'Bye Marie's boyfriend!' and he offered a comical goodbye in exchange. It felt like we had connected on a human level in a way that I hadn't with my students in a long time."

Face to Face

Some instructors have strong preferences about wanting to teach face to face, but without policies that make us feel safe, some are hesitant to go back. Martha shared, "I'm happy to teach face to face, I'm happy to do my share with the face-to-face classes. I know that's important, but I feel like our institution has to step up and keep us safe, too." Safety has been particularly relevant, as our administration resisted vaccine mandate requests despite a resolution requesting this preventative measure from our Faculty Senate, removed mask mandates in the middle of the spring 2022 semester, and is requiring at least 60 percent of all 2022 courses to be offered in person.

Martha shared a situation that made her feel tension between helping students and keeping herself safe: "I'm aware that one of the students I worked with most—who needed the most help—I know that she was not vaccinated because she just told me she doesn't believe in vaccines, and she's not vaccinated. Something that UAA could have done to really make my life easier is to require students who are taking face-to-face courses to show their vaccination cards. That would have made a big difference to me emotionally. My father lives with me. He's almost ninety years old, and I do not want to bring coronavirus home to my dad or my kids or any of us."

Although she finally got a good handle on Zoom and breakout rooms, Martha's reflections suggest she was glad to be back in the classroom and plans to do most of her teaching face to face in the future. Emily also expressed a desire to be back in a face-to-face environment, especially for her ALP classes:

> One thing that I was really struck by is, in ALP, we did spend a good deal of time going over the assignments. And I would field the questions from the students about the assignments, and it would take up sometimes a considerable chunk of our time together. And it really made me wonder, like I was saying, how to communicate that material online. Because the students said it was invaluable to be able to be in person and ask me those questions. And again, I don't think they would have necessarily felt comfortable asking those questions in class, although the class overall for WRTG 111 got more comfortable with doing that over the course of the semester. But then I was thinking, how do you translate that to online? Because sometimes I'll make a video explaining an assignment. But again, like I said, it'll get two views or something, you know, and you'll get essays where it's clear that students either didn't quite get it or didn't respond to the student essay models or what have you. So it made me think more about the benefits of being in person, as difficult as that is right now.

Being safer at work makes us better at our jobs, and there are clear steps our institution could take to make face-to-face learning safer for all of us, including a vaccine mandate for face-to-face classes in addition to masking, spacing, and sanitizing policies and procedures. Other possibilities for face-to-face learning not captured in our data that might make face-to-face learning safer by allowing greater distancing include meeting at a museum or open-air spaces; including campus tours or community events as part of the course; or developing curriculum that includes outdoor experiences, such as hiking, camping, or skiing, which are popular activities among faculty and students at our institution.

Hybrid and Hyflex

Other campuses are using what we call "hybrid" or "hyflex," and during the initial pivot to online learning, we all felt confused about what hybrid education means. Carrie, Sarah, and Sharon all taught hybrid courses and equated this flexibility with equity for students unable to safely make it to class. One student told Sarah, "Thank you for including us even though we're online," suggesting online students expect to receive less support.

Except for Sharon, who taught fully online, the rest of the participants dabbled in this hyflex situation and structured their courses in different ways. The data from our study highlight the importance of knowing in advance how students will arrive in our classes. Instructors and students should be able to predict what we will experience, but with hyflex, we don't know what is going to happen when we arrive in our classrooms: maybe most students will attend face to face, and maybe all of them will choose online. Facilitating group work in a hybrid/hyflex situation is really hard because it requires potentially changing lesson plans on the fly and sometimes asking students to wait while we rethink the situation.

Here in Alaska, we can expect the occasional day to be canceled because of environmental factors, and hyflex offers us the opportunity to quickly pivot to online learning. To mitigate ongoing concerns about shifting back and forth between modes, Carrie has prepared her hybrid/hyflex classes to be ready to take place fully online at any time. Sarah also prefers hybrid/hyflex formats because they allow an easy pivot to fully online for whatever reasons may arise. Since students not traditionally represented in the institution are more likely to experience situations in which they are unable to attend face to face, format became a social justice issue to Carrie, who wrote of her experiences:

> Even though I'm an experienced online educator, when I had to move my ALP class online due to the pandemic, I lost the community feeling I had worked so hard to develop, and I didn't see signs of that community developing again until fall 21. I really wanted to go back to class face to face in fall 21, but allowing students the option to participate virtually seemed like a necessary option given the pandemic context, so I offered my first hyflex section. Students could attend virtually or online. It was far from perfect. I wasn't in a classroom with a built-in webcam, so I had to film myself [using my laptop] for the students online while speaking to those physically in front of me, and that was really hard!

Emily also ended up in an unplanned hyflex situation in order to meet the needs of her students. Hyflex meant extra work for Emily, work that wasn't accommodated in her workload and that our classroom technology wasn't fully set up for either, but she saw the benefits to students, and it was important for her to make her classes as accessible to students as possible.

Hyflex also offered opportunities to develop stronger classroom communities. Carrie noticed, "I maintained more personable relationships with students who came to class a few times than the students who I never met face to face at all. For example, Luna and Imani attended the first few classes face to face and then figured out it was more convenient to attend online than take the long bus ride to campus, but our whole class maintained connection to both of them. I didn't get to know the students who attended only online well at all, but our whole class knew Luna and Imani because of the early connections we made. We told jokes back and forth that made people laugh, and they productively participated with the rest of the class." Meeting these students face to face a few times led to much stronger connections with them than with students who never attended at all.

We maintain that some mode of synchronous learning is essential to student success in ALP. Instructors shared stories of students who normally would have failed the required course due to personal situations that caused them to step away from their face-to-face classes during the semester. Through the relationships they had with these students, they were able to bring the students back to both courses and help them successfully complete the class. However, we know the more flexible the options, the more work for us. Workloads should accommodate the flexibility required of ALP instructors in hybrid and hyflex modes.

Providing Clear Policies

Our university's mission is "put students first." In order to do that, we need policies and guidelines that support teaching and learning. Unclear policies have led us to tell students, "Yes, I can Zoom you into class, no problem." It's true. Zooming a student who has the appropriate technology into a face-to-face class every once in a while isn't a big deal, but over time, and when it involves multiple students who are not equipped to engage online, it becomes a lot of work that can negatively impact the quality of the class. Policies and guidelines can help us make informed decisions about modality that can help us set boundaries for ourselves and our students and make class more productive.

We need policies that are sympathetic to students' individual crises while making our jobs as professors manageable within the parameters we are required to work in—policies that put boundaries around the modal possibilities, attendance policies, and the technologies available. Consequently, we all changed our attendance and late-work policies between 2020 and 2021. We have also had to ask students for their leniency at times. Sharon wrote,

About two thirds, maybe three quarters of the way through the semester. Because I've got a pretty strict attendance policy, I've got a pretty strict no late work policy unless you make arrangements with me in advance kind of thing. And about three quarters of the way through the semester, I just lifted those bans.

In response to the pandemic, Martha changed her attendance policy for her face-to-face class. In an interview in spring 21, she said, "I ended up changing my participation policy back when COVID first hit. I used to deduct points if students miss a class, and I revamped that to just record, you know, excused, unexcused absences and kind of see, is it a problem? Is someone missing a lot, and then they just get an overall participation grade, at the end."

CREATING ENGAGEMENT WITH TECHNOLOGY AND SPACE

Technology

Instructors must be supported in the technology they need. Whether we're teaching online or not, the expectation remains that we might be required to (re)pivot to online learning, so we must be prepared. All of us reported difficulty accessing the technology we needed to teach effectively. Sharon shared, "Quite a few of my students have really spotty internet and don't have laptops so they're taking the class on their phones. I've gotten stumped a few times trying to figure out how to set up the class so they have access to everything." Emily also experienced problems related to technology and added, "I couldn't get Zoom to work in the room that I was in. I don't know if it was my computer. Like sometimes my computer does not want to join the network there." Without access to the technology and support required for an online environment, teachers cannot effectively implement online, hybrid, or hyflex learning, and they are spending a lot of time identifying ways to make learning more accessible to students.

Physical Space

Our institutional spaces don't function in ways that align with our pedagogical beliefs. All the instructors who taught face to face asked for more thoughtful consideration of physical space and recognized the classrooms currently available to us do not align with our teaching philosophies, which emphasize student interaction. The majority of our classrooms have chairs with attached desks that can swivel up, which make it challenging for students to sit together in groups.

We need classrooms that allow us to do the kind of group work we believe in.

Martha emphasized the importance of making "the classroom community comfortable for students in order for them to come out of their shell." Physical space is important to her, and she wishes our classrooms were designed in more of a "pod approach" where students can sit together in small groups. Carrie had experience teaching in a classroom designed for interaction and student-centered activities, and she believes a similar classroom design would go a long way to supporting effective teaching and learning.

Additionally, as we mentioned in the previous technology section, our classrooms are not set up for hyflex or even having students bring their own devices to classes. In order to support ALP and flexibility, institutions must provide the tools instructors need to offer that flexibility, from classroom spaces that promote collaborative learning to technology that supports instructors' and students' needs. While some institutions may offer these types of spaces, they are often limited in availability and may even require training in order for instructors to access them.

Facilitating Professional Conversations and Development

Even though we have all worked hard on making our ALP classes better, we all reported a need for the time and space to discuss ALP with colleagues locally, at the statewide level, and at the national level, but we don't have bandwidth in our workloads for this important time. We want for ourselves what we try to make happen in our classrooms: meaningful interaction around our work. This points to a need for an ALP coordinator in our department who has time in their workload devoted to facilitating interaction among instructors and keeping us in communication with others teaching ALP around our state, as well as the national conversations surrounding ALP. In a reflection, Sharon shared her process of figuring out how to make assignments more meaningful for students:

> I think it was, for me, getting a better understanding of how to make meaningful writing assignments. Um, I think at first I was just trying to think of stuff for them to do, I was just trying to think of, well, they have to do something, you know, writing wise, on Thursdays when I'm meeting with the ALP class. So at first, I was just kind of scrambling to figure out how to keep them busy, I guess. And, and at the same time, you know, learning something about what we were doing that week. And this came from actually talking with them and fielding their questions about the writing assignments. And because I think they picked up on that a little bit, I began to realize, Oh, I could actually make these a lot more meaningful

for us as a class, not just reiterating what I talked about in lecture or what we talked about in discussion, but, you know, connecting it to things I'm actually expecting them to do and allowing them to practice it in a more meaningful way. So by the end of this semester, I think the writing assignments that I was assigning them really improved. I think they were much, much better, specific to issues that I saw that they were having.

Certainly a community of instructors sharing these experiences would help prevent other instructors from going through this process.

CONCLUSION

The pandemic has changed our profession. We keep expecting that things are going to get better and that the energy we have been putting into our classes is going to lessen, but the pandemic keeps charging on. Students have been especially needy, and finding time to devote to researching and developing professionally is more challenging than ever.

As ALP continues to grow around the nation, instructors need a variety of modalities to choose from as they tailor ALP to their own student populations. Institutions must offer modality options that meet students' needs without expecting instructors to make last-minute modal changes without the time or equipment to do so. That flexibility means we need to know what the students need, and we shouldn't all have to do what Emily did: poll our classes individually. Online teaching is more time intensive than face-to-face teaching, and that work must be considered. In order to be focused on student success and to "put students first," we must support instructors so they can do that.

APPENDIX A: SEMISTRUCTURED INTERVIEW QUESTIONS

The semistructured interview script included the following questions:

- Tell us about your experiences teaching this course this semester.
- What makes this course different from other courses you teach?
- How have you structured this course?
- Share a story about a student success this semester.
- Share a story about a learning moment for you as an instructor from this course.
- Share a story about a learning moment for your students from this course.
- What surprised you about this course?
- What would you change? What do want to do differently next time?
- What kinds of support would help you in this course?

APPENDIX B: INSTRUCTOR WEEKLY REFLECTION

The weekly reflection form asked:

- How were your classes this week?
- Share a story of success this week (student, teaching moment, class, etc.).
- Was there anything that did not go as planned? What happened? Why? What would you change about this moment?
- What support would be helpful right now?
- Do you have any other notes, comments, or observations to share here?

REFERENCES

Chavez, Felicia Rose. 2021. *The Anti-Racist Writing Workshop: How to Decolonize the Creative Classroom.* Chicago: Haymarket.

Creswell, John. 2013. *Research Design: Qualitative, Quantitative, and Mixed Methods Approaches.* 3rd ed. Thousand Oaks, CA: SAGE.

Inoue, Asao B. 2012. "Grading Contracts: Assessing Their Effectiveness on Different Racial Formations." In *Race and Writing Assessment*, edited by Asao Inoue and Mya Poe, 79–94. New York: Peter Lang.

Jaggars, Shanna, Michelle Hodara, and Sung-Woo Cho. 2015. "Three Accelerated Developmental Education Programs: Features, Student Outcomes, and Implications." *Community College Review* 43 (1): 3–26.

Merriam, Sharan. 2009. *Qualitative Research: A Guide to Design and Implementation.* San Francisco: Jossey-Bass.

National Council of Teachers of English. 2015. "TYCA White Paper on Developmental Education Reforms." CCCC Convention, TYCA Executive Committee. https://www.ncte.org/library/NCTEFiles/Resources/Journals/TETYC/0423-mar2015/TETYC0423White.pdf.

Supiano, Beckie. 2022. "The Attendance Conundrum." *Chronicle of Higher Education*, January 20. https://www.chronicle.com/article/the-attendance-conundrum.

Sunstein, Bonnie, and Elizabeth Chiseri-Strater. 2012. *FieldWorking: Reading and Writing Research.* 4th ed. Boston: Bedford/St. Martin's.

Uehling, Karen. 2020. "A Credited Support Course: Corequisite Writing Course at Boise State University." *Composition Studies* 48 (2): 143.

5
REFLECTIVE PRACTICES IN TEACHING FOR TRANSFER

Melissa Favara and Jill Darley-Vanis

An integral component of what it means to learn, thinking of the Latin *educare*, is to bring out what already resides in the learner. As seen in educational practice, however, it's only of late that we've acknowledged and moved to center reflective practice in order to facilitate the "bringing-out" process. We know if we don't provide opportunities for students to stop and analyze, consider, and reflect on their choices and experiences, true understanding and change can't move to the level of consciousness. In response, reflection has become so valuable that for many, it's as or more important than traditional writing assignments. But our field has come to value reflection and the adjustment it makes possible because of the potential for change, and this change may be most crucial for our accelerated composition students. From what we've observed by way of teaching in accelerated composition programs for the past ten years, and in keeping with reflection's recent appearance in pedagogical practice, it's likely these reflective practices have been withheld from these and all students, as reflection typically loses out to the US need to produce, to keep moving. But it's these reflective practices that have the most potential to change a learner's story: knowledge about feelings, values, motivations, and attitudes occupy space in our taxonomies for learning, and they do so because awareness and contemplation are what can change our students' stories.

But isn't the goal of reflection in composition students' awareness of writing as a portable skill, not awareness of writing as localized knowledge, meaning limited to composition as a discipline in and of itself? Chillingly, the opening lines of David Bartholomae's (1986) "Inventing the University" come to mind:

> Every time a student sits down to write for us, he has to invent the university for the occasion—invent the university, that is, or a branch of it, like History or Anthropology or Economics or English. He has to learn

https://doi.org/10.7330/9781646424788.c005

to speak our language, to speak as we do, to try on the peculiar ways of knowing, selecting, evaluating, concluding and arguing that define the discourse of our community. Or perhaps I should say the *various* discourses of our community. (4)

Writing-across-the-curriculum (WAC) and writing-in-the-disciplines (WID) programs signal the need for writing skills to transfer, but as WAC and WID courses are often taught by faculty outside composition, faculty unfamiliar with the scholarship of composition and, likely, the scholarship of transfer, the foundation for connection and portability isn't front-loaded or prioritized for the student. As a result, we fear, most students receive, without a built-for-portability pedagogy, what D. N. Perkins and Gavriel Salomon (1988) call Bo Peep pedagogy: "Let them alone and they'll come home, wagging their tails behind them" (23). Writing-about-writing (WAW) pedagogy, acknowledging all of this, is built for across-the-disciplines writing awareness, and it relies heavily on the scholarship of reflection, but it gives more energy to writing *about* the writing of others than to writing *in* the discourse communities outside traditional composition. Instead, and in response, it's writing-for-transfer (WfT) pedagogy that most successfully addresses the need for portable practice, one that synthesizes the scholarship of reflection with the scholarship of psychology and transfer.

Before reflection for transfer found its place in composition sequences, it was a consideration in the larger conversation and scholarship of how people learn. Looking back into early education theory, scholars questioned how the mind transfers knowledge from one context or situation to another. Many in the WfT conversation posit Charles Judd as a beginning: in 1908, and with the use of a physical task, Judd studied adolescent boys throwing darts at a submerged target. While some of the boys were given coaching and theories for understanding this physical act and its outcomes—in this case, the principles of optical refraction—other boys were not. Once the study conductors changed the depth of the underwater target, the boys who received the theoretical, rather abstract and reflective training performed much better in this physical task, "even though the transfer task (throwing darts) was very different from the training context (theoretical explanation of refraction)" (Barnett and Ceci 2002, 614).

Later, Perkins and Salomon (1988), the so-called "godfathers of transfer," provided the terminology to understand the conditions in which transfer is successful and in which it is not. In their *Educational Leadership* article "Teaching for Transfer," Perkins and Salomon distinguish "transfer of skill" (22) from "transfer of knowledge" (22), noting the difference, say, between a physical skill and its transfer to a new context and the more "far transfer" (22) of knowledge from one context to another. This two-pronged thought on transfer is their true focus, but they do mention the more affective transfer of "attitudes or cognitive styles" (22) as well. In this article, they consider the dearth of focus on how students transfer knowledge from one context to another, noting transfer "does not take care of itself, and conventional schooling pays little heed to the problem" (22). In the section of their article in which they ask if transfer is possible, they discuss the intentionality needed: "Rather than expecting students to achieve transfer spontaneously, one 'mediates' the needed processes of abstraction and connection making" (28).

A later development in this conversation, one that focuses on key elements for learning across the disciplines, is the scholarship of threshold concepts, those discipline-specific, often counterintuitive and hard-to-cross thresholds in any situation for learning. In order to function successfully within any discourse community, the learner must have a clear understanding of these limited but seminal concepts. This contribution comes from Jan H. F. Meyer and Ray Land (2006) in their *Overcoming Barriers to Student Understanding: Threshold Concepts and Troublesome Knowledge,* and within composition studies, for instance, genre is a threshold concept. Our students come to us not aware that writing comes in repeating and somewhat static packages, and yet it's the ability to come to identify those recurring forms, to abstract out the fundamental elements with which the student is already familiar (such as speaking to a particular audience in a particular setting with a purpose in mind), that allows the writer to transfer writing knowledge from one genre or situation to another. Essentially, both the psychology of transfer and those seminal concepts in any discipline become the foci of WfT or remix pedagogies.

In composition studies, among many others, Anne Beaufort, Elizabeth Wardle, Teresa Thonney, and colleagues Kathleen Blake Yancey, Liane Robertson, and Kara Taczak continue the conversation. What, they ask, transfers as the result of a student's learning in the current-traditional pedagogy model of composition (Beaufort 2007; Wardle 2007; Yancey, Robertson, and Taczak 2014)? What has been successful and not successful in looking at genre as the locus of most opportunity in composition theory, as the site of learning (Wardle 2009)? Next, what are the moves that transfer across all writing situations, moves that can be the focus of our energies in the teaching of composition (Thonney 2011)? And last, what can we see as the result of a long-term study, one in which students experience different types of writing pedagogies (theme-based versus expressivist versus writing instruction with an eye for transfer), in terms of the student's long-term success and portable understanding of what it means to be a writer, whether it be in academia (Yancey, Robertson, Taczak 2014), in their communities, or in their professional lives?

For our racially minoritized and all ill-served students, the stakes are high, and the need for a reformed pedagogy is urgent. From our ten years of coming to know our students' stories, we note that ALP students come to us as the recipients of a nonstandard education in one way or another. They have often been ill served by the US system or have come from a country with significantly different educational mores than those found in the US. In response, one of the beauties of WfT or remix pedagogy for accelerated students is that it starts precisely where the student is. Commencing with the familiar and resident, with what is comfortable and with the rhetoric all around them, the students begin by identifying key elements that make a familiar-to-them act of rhetoric work. In our courses, for instance, students begin with a "significant-text essay," typically choosing songs, visual art, poems, and advertisements, rhetoric they identify as significant (even if they aren't yet certain why), rhetoric that speaks to them. It is here and with the familiar that they begin the process of coming to know the threshold concepts in composition studies—critical-reading process, writing process, genre, audience, purpose, exigence, and the like—as a way to begin to think about transferable concepts and transferable skills. And at every turn, before, during, and after the writing process, the students reflect on their growing awareness of writing and its portable qualities.

Yancey, Robertson, and Taczak's seminal work, *Writing across Contexts* (2014), creates and shares the pedagogical blueprint for a course in writing transfer. In this study at their research institute, Florida State University, the authors identify the key tenets of this pedagogy and chronicle its results. *Writing across Contexts* shares their FYC transfer course, its assignment sequence, its systemic reflection, and the way students develop their own theory of writing over the course of the instruction. Teaching for transfer (TFT) or WfT is distilled even further for the needs of two-year college faculty in Sonja Andrus, Sharon Mitchler, and Howard Tinberg's (2019) "Teaching for Writing Transfer: a Practical Guide for Teachers." While we believe there are more possibilities for built-for-transfer assignment sequences than those discussed in "Teaching for Writing Transfer," the authors' work reinterprets the pillars of Yancey, Robertson, and Taczak's pedagogy in its key tenets: first, an assignment sequence committed to building a set of key rhetorical and composing terms and concepts, the threshold concepts for success in composition studies; and second, consistent, embedded, meaningful conferencing and reflection on learning, on transfer, and on projection forward to other situations the writer will encounter and draw on as a way to build on the knowledge from the composition course. On final reflection on the two-year version of the course, Andrus, Mitchler, and Tinberg write, "It's the culminating task in their learning in the course, and the beginning of their transfer journey beyond it" (86).

In our own practice, a typical assignment sequence moves the student from analysis and writing *about* writing in different genres to producing work *in* new genres, those better suited for the given message and of interest to the student. In this type of sequencing, student agency (decentering whiteness and what Asao Inoue [2015] terms the "white racial habitus" [10]) are at the fore, as students bring in their own texts as the subject of their study. Subjectivity is encouraged and made transparent in rhetorical study, and students interrogate not only their own choices in rhetorical texts but also the contexts from which they come. As such, our accelerated students control the nature of their own learning and exploration, making choices that will matter in their own fields, lives, and professional foci, but it's the careful, generalizing, and abstracting-out reflection that allows the learning to make these cognitive moves. Wrapped carefully inside each major assignment, throughout the writing process itself and as the culmination of each writing project, is reflection: students reflect on decisions they made, challenges they faced, how and when they considered and made choices about audience, and the like. They reflect on their experiences in adapting their writing in new genres, thinking carefully about the culture of remixed rhetoric in which we work and live.

Interestingly, a very recent work asks, in a new way, what is really happening when a student has the ability to move writing knowledge from one context to another? Kevin G. Smith, Kristi Girdharry, and Chris W. Gallagher (2021) argue that it may not be a direct transfer of universal concepts that is central to the learning process. They argue that it may be the disconnections, not the connections themselves, that truly facilitate portable writing knowledge. They report, "What we began to see as we followed these students over several years was not just a series of transfer episodes . . . but rather the construction of new knowledge and skills across and sometimes outside of multiple writing contexts over long periods of time. We call this integration" (6). Focusing on difference rather than similarity between rhetorical situations, they argue, the student is forever integrating, not transferring, and it is this dissonance that creates meaningful, portable writing knowledge. So in a WfT frame, they suggest, it is not transfer but adaptation and response to disconnections that makes writing knowledge resident within the student.

The piece that carries, the element that most effects a change for our accelerated students, is reflection on the writing process and an increasing awareness of the situated nature of genres within various discourse communities. Learning about the writing process, remixed for our students' needs as writers today, considers writing past (transfer in), writing current (what has been learned over the term or semester), and writing projecting forward. In this reflection in and on process, students (and a recursive curriculum) gain clarity on the key terms, those threshold concepts that they have encountered and will encounter. Without reflection, we simply can't learn. It's the reflective piece and its marriage to the scholarship of transfer that makes WfT work, providing opportunities, again and again, for the student to consider, What just happened? What did I learn, and how might those skills apply to a different situation or context?

Critics may argue that this pedagogy doesn't focus on the academic essay as current traditional pedagogies do. This is true, and in this moment, it is WfT's greatest strength. As Inoue (2015) writes, "We must understand our writing assessments as antiracist projects" (4). This pedagogy insists on student agency, portability, flexibility, knowledge of text and context, creativity. But it empowers our students, which is most true for our ALP students, as it gives them a sense of control over writing across contexts. They leave first-year composition not having learned about subject X (from a theme-based class) but about what it means to be a writer in a variety of situations. Additionally, it reenergizes our own work, giving us a renewed vision of what we do and the meaningful nature of what students can produce. The hierarchy of concerns for a faculty teaching this curriculum is much different, of course: it prioritizes genre awareness, portable reading and writing skills, and recursive, carefully crafted reflections. But this pedagogy is what our students deserve, and it is far past time. The secrets to successful writing, those insights ALP students feel have eluded them, are the core of WfT, and it's our transparency about those moves, the contexts from which they come, and new ways of being that can change the student experience.

PART 2

If WfT serves to foster students' growing self-awareness and agency as writers, the pairing with ALP in a corequisite classroom deepens that work by fostering students' agency as learners and citizens (we use the latter term advisedly, understanding its problematic nature, in the sense of people who can more confidently advocate for self and other). The nesting dolls of WfT, ALP, and Reading Apprenticeship (RA) work synergistically on at least three levels:

- WfT makes the purpose, tools, and portability of composition transparent and palpable for students, while meeting them where they are through allowing them to make choices about texts and genres.
- RA builds agency by making active reading of challenging texts, especially disciplinary reading, accessible and meaningful, dismantling the alienation and inertia many students experience when they enter by situating reading in a personal and social context
- While supporting students through 101 assignments and skill and knowledge acquisition, ALP does the crucial work of unlocking reflection and metacognition in a social setting where a small, supportive group can not only surface academic and noncognitive barriers and collaborate on overcoming them but can also collectively build familiarity with and confidence in deploying the key terms and concepts—the instruments in the WfT toolbox.

With a WfT/ALP pairing, we see the strong community building common across ALP settings, but the explicit reflective practices core to WfT pedagogy—reflecting on composition practices before, during, and after reading and writing projects and processes—can expand to fit the container of ALP and draw together the academic and the affective in exciting, powerful ways. If our ALP classroom "takes the students in the class as its starting point" (*Approaches* 2014, 32), and it is paired with WfT, which "[asks] everyone to consider the same key terms as a starting point in the class, and to think about their previous use of these concepts themselves, [so] instructors have the opportunity to bring students into the conversation about how writing works while honoring prior knowledge" (Andrus, Mitchler, and Tinberg 2019, 78), the combined power of the two pedagogies is rich with transformative possibility. In short, WfT validates students' previous academic and, more important, life experience while helping them surface ways of further developing and applying their communication skills in new ways, and the ALP setting offers opportunities for students to practice and develop their skills in a context of peers—to practice on and with their peers in a smaller, safer setting that can overwrite previously held notions of self based on less successful previous learning experiences.

The scope of work entailed in WfT is undeniably challenging, especially in a ten-week term, and especially for students who have often had traumatic learning experiences before we meet them. Here, it is worth noting our institution chose to adopt WfT as our composition pedagogy and ALP as our mode of delivery for precollege instruction after conducting exhaustive research on instructional models that foster equity in teaching and learning in direct response to institutional research that indicated our students of color, especially Black men, were completing our English courses at lower rates, especially English 101 and 098, our first-year composition course and our pre-college-level course, respectively. We sought, and seek, to increase the rates of completion across the board and eliminate the course-success and graduation-rate gaps for minoritized students. Consistent with national trends, minoritized students have long been overrepresented in our English 098, which, as a precollege class, provides an unfortunate exit point familiar in the well-known "leaky-pipe" critique of traditional remediation. Since students who come from minoritized or underserved groups are more likely to be assessed into precollege courses (Logue 2018), these students are at greater risk of not completing because of the significant hurdle precollege placement adds (Edley 2017). These students are likely to have experienced educational trauma associated with systemic racism, and there can obviously be no excellence without a greatly increased focus on equity.[1]

All students, through precisely the kind of unifying reflective practices common across WfT and ALP pedagogies, can both access and share their resilience and prior knowledge and surface their struggles productively. Ultimately, through personal and communal collective reflection that gazes both into the past and into the future, students find increased agency through vulnerability and the powerful element of the group. WfT asks students to reflect on their efforts, their strategies, their failures, their evolving understanding of the key terms, their thinking about thinking, and what they still find confusing with the understanding that reflective practice "slows student writers down, directs their focus, and provides them time to think and to become self-aware as writers" (Andrus, Mitchler, and Tinberg 2019, 78). In an ALP setting, students engage reflection collectively and with a real and well-founded expectation of immediate social support and connection.

We think in terms of each student having their own learning story—their literacy narrative, their life experience to date, and the

---

1. "About 80 percent of African Americans required to take more than one remedial class in math do not complete their math requirements within six years, compared to 67 percent of Hispanics and 61 percent of whites, according to the community college system's student-success scorecard. A recent estimate found that, among community college students, 50–60 percent of the racial disparity in degree completion is driven by decisions to place students in math remediation, according to an unpublished study by the RP Group" (Edley 2017).

place our work over the course of a term has in their story. We also recognize the class itself as having a beginning, a middle, and end—both in the arc of the whole term and within the individual class meetings.[2] At both levels, we can begin by drawing each student into the space as an authentic, multivalent self with things to learn and things to share.

On the global level of the cohort course as a whole, the most effective practice for beginning the process of establishing the safe, authentic, risk-enabling discourse of the group is grounded in the Reading Apprenticeship's model of establishing a class learning agreement (CLA), in which students surface and refine a list of the necessary conditions for a positive learning environment. The RA text *Reading for Understanding* offers an excellent exercise for this practice in which students talk through what creates comfort for them in a classroom and what teachers and student peers can do or avoid doing to foster and support learning, then gather the findings to compose a set of norms. Well known to many of us, it's an increasingly common practice because it's incredibly valuable not only as a functioning contract but as a way of immediately establishing the value of each learner and their voice in the class community (Schoenbach, Greenleaf, and Murphy 2012, 62).

We can deepen this opportunity even further by asking students to begin this process with a directed solo reflective freewrite that includes other learning contexts. If instead of asking students to focus on classroom learning, we expand the freewrite to acknowledge students have long been successfully learning—or experiencing barriers to their learning—in many venues in their lives, we can immediately signal to them that we are ready to see them as whole people and that there isn't a bright line between their academic learning and other kinds of learning. This approach sets the stage for later thinking about the ways resident habits of mind transfer both in and outside the learning journey; it makes clear this is an environment of consciousness raising about the ways concepts and moves from one communication context transfer to another. We ask students to write to a prompt for five to ten minutes: Think of a time or two you had a positive learning experience—inside or outside school, with teachers, student peers, your family, a friend, a work colleague, a supervisor, a coach, and so forth. What happened during that experience that made it possible for you to learn? It feels important to share here that in previous years we asked students to write to that prompt for five minutes and then

---

2. At our institution, the credit class in the corequisite pairing is English 101, and the cohort class is English 099; we use the language of *Approaches to Teaching ALP: A Sourcebook* (2014).

followed up with a second prompt: Now, switch gears: think of a time or times you were trying to learn something new and had a negative experience—again, inside or outside school. What happened during that experience that made it difficult or impossible for you to learn? we stopped using this prompt after learning from Em Daniels's (2022) work on trauma-informed teaching that asking students to dredge up unpleasant memories outside a therapeutic context is deeply misguided because it can retraumatize students and center the instructor as a would-be savior. Focusing instead on creating a calm, "settled" environment committed to real student agency places the emphasis on writing a new story, not reinscribing the old (29).

We advise students that they will not have to show their writing to anyone or read their whole freewrite aloud but that we will ask them to choose some themes and key ideas to share with a partner. It is always astonishing how quickly students open up to one another in the context of the pairing, inside an activity that implicitly and explicitly tells them their previous experiences and stated needs will set the rules for our work together. If, per Vincent Tinto (1997), "All effective classroom communities have three things in common: shared knowledge, shared knowing, and shared responsibility" (quoted in *Approaches* 2014, 17), this exercise is the beginning of the students knowing one another, feeling known, and asserting agency as they take responsibility for their own learning conditions. Students are typically candid in this process: they speak of unhelpful things they have experienced, like not getting adequate feedback on assignments from teachers, but they also focus on what has created positive academic learning experiences, such as working with peers who never demeaned them for asking questions. Interestingly, they also consistently talk about non-academic-setting learning experiences, like being able to learn because a manager patiently walked them through using a new cash register several times, as well as soft-skill-focused elements of the conditions for learning, like how they once improved their work and understanding in a challenging course by making space to be well rested and fed before class. When students share out, we end up with lists that look like this:

- We will provide constructive criticism.
- We will appreciate and accept constructive criticism.
- We will be kind to one another and honest so we all feel safe to make mistakes.
- We will be on time so we can get started.
- We will complete peer reviews and respond to one another in a timely way.

- We will always speak to each other with respect to create a comfortable space.
- We will be patient with each other when we need help with a concept.
- We will make sure no one's behind or struggling or being left out and work as a team
- We will be positive in class and also be willing to help each other build confidence and succeed.

The students are already engaging threshold concepts around expression and identity and reflection—*What does it look like when I'm truly learning? For which parts of that process am I responsible? What are my responsibilities to those with whom I'm learning in community? What do I want and need, and how can I ask for it?* After we distill the list, it is stationed at the top of the class website, where students have editing access to add comments or suggestions for additional items and sign their names in commitment. They are looking back at experiences that shaped them and projecting forward what kind of learning community they want to author and inhabit.

On the local level, in the class session, we can establish authentic presence and create community by beginning each session with a frank check-in based on a brief prompt-driven freewrite and share-out. As we get acquainted, prompts in the earliest weeks of the class might be *How are you today, 1–10, if 10 means you won the lottery? Briefly, why?* or *What object on your desk says the most about you right now? Why?* As the course moves toward the middle of the term, after students have established norms and begun actively working together to untangle 101 course concepts and support one another in exercising productive persistence, we move to prompts like *Write for five minutes about a success or a challenge you experienced since we last met. What keywords describe your experience?* In the share-out, we follow up shares about successes or challenges with questions about what kinds of effort went into the success or what kinds of strategies they used to overcome the challenge if they overcame it, and if they didn't overcome it, what could they try the next time they face a similar challenge? As we are working to understand and deploy the key terms of WfT in both 101 and in 099, explicitly talking about the rhetorical toolbox in both venues, in 099, students extract flexible persistence strategies from one another's share-outs, which they assemble in a persistence toolbox on a dedicated page located directly below the CLA on the course website; students get in the habit of directing themselves and peers to the list when they surface struggle and considering which tools could help with an exigent problem. In this way, students have yet more opportunities to consciously frame their communication and take turns being the one to learn and the one to share.

PERSISTENCE STRATEGIES

—Hi Writers!

This term we will be gathering strategies you all use to persist through challenges and stay in a "growth mindset" instead of a "fixed mindset." We will continue to add to this list based on what you all share in class:

> Establish routines and set aside time for your work.
> Ask for help/support from family with things like childcare to make sure you have the time you need.
> If something goes wrong, stay calm and communicate with your professors.
> Try to believe in your own ability to complete an assignment.
> Use caffeine when necessary (but not to excess!) :-).
> Ask for help from peers and your instructor early on, and don't be afraid to ask for more help as the assignment progresses.
> Don't be afraid to write a lot of messy ideas that won't make it into the final draft!

As the term proceeds and students begin to draft and revise formal written work, many students express dread about the peer-review process: "I never get good feedback—people just say it's all good or they say 'fix this' but don't say how"; "I never know what to say"; "What if they're a better writer—what can I say then?" Group generating of peer-review golden rules, like those in the letter above, can take the same pattern as the CLA—individual written reflection about helpful and unhelpful feedback experiences followed by partnered discussion and communal extraction of what the qualities of each are, leading to another toolbox. The full group share-out conversation offers a great opportunity to really establish the value every peer reviewer can bring, even when there may be a significant discrepancy in experience and confidence levels between peer partners, by/while also making numerous threshold concepts concrete for students: writing as a social and rhetorical activity, all writers having more to learn, and writing to situations through recognizable forms. Every reader can offer valuable insight via their experience as an audience member; every piece of writing can be improved; written works employ genre conventions, and the revision process involves thinking about whether an individual work meets audience expectations. At the same time, students further deepen their understanding of WfT key concepts of audience, context, and genre (students readily grasp that peer-review comments are a special category of communication with its own "rules and tools" as students work together to extract them), even negotiating the terms of a temporary discourse community. The list of peer-review golden rules lives in its own link, near the CLA and persistence strategies; we explicitly refer to it as the peer-review toolbox.

Something interesting happens when we do this activity—it seems to be a significant step in students' understanding of themselves as writers and audience members and as self-advocates. Formal reflections on the writing process that accompany the final draft of the first major assignment in 101 indicate students feel empowered, even rewarded, by their grappling with the culture of peer review: "It was exciting to find out what my audience was getting out of what I wrote"; "There was a big gap in my draft between what I meant and what I put on paper, and I got to see that"; "I learned a lot about how this assignment could be shaped from the ways other students did it"; "It helped me understand what I was doing to tell someone what I saw them doing." They come to tell a different story about themselves as givers and receivers of feedback and about the writing process, but it's very much also a story about their power to abstract from their experience and advocate for what they need—and a story about the value of their perspective as active audience members and speakers.

COMMUNITY PEER-REVIEW GOLDEN RULES

Thanks to everyone for the great ideas that came out of our first conversation about what we hope to get from peer feedback! Based on these initial small-group conversations, here is the list of things to do and not do and the areas where you have expressed interest in getting help:

DO
- be specific and point out things that are working already and things that need work: comment on what specifically makes the thing you are talking about work or not work.
- offer specific suggestions/constructive criticism on what needs more work.
- point out things that might need to be cut from the draft.
- be engaged and give your full attention to the draft as you work on it.
- comment on things like the introduction and conclusion, sentence clarity/grammar, whether the organization makes sense, whether the paragraphs are fully developed or need more.

DON'T
- be rude or harsh.
- be disengaged or inattentive.
- give vague, nonspecific praise without any constructive criticism.

Reflection on the drafting process in the credit class pairs naturally, even vitally, with reflection on persistence strategies in the cohort. In one instance, a quiet young woman of nineteen or twenty from the cohort submitted a stiff, off-topic draft for an early essay on rhetorical selves in the credit class (see Nicotra 2018). Students were instructed to consider and analyze the ways they present themselves to different audiences for different purposes; the student, we'll call her Bea, handed in a stilted draft about visual stereotypes broadly, and with it, she submitted a required "messy-draft" reflection in which she stated she didn't feel good about what she had written. She didn't have many ideas for the assignment because she had very little social life due to family issues and was struggling both on that front and with completing her work. The next day, when we opened the cohort class with the "successes and challenges" prompt, Bea shared from her freewrite that she had handed in a bad draft and why—in the context of the cohort group, she shared that her parents had had to leave the picture (she did not say why, and no one pried) and that she was responsible for raising her three younger siblings; she didn't have time to spend on hobbies or with affinity groups or socializing much with friends, though she had loved doing those things in the past.

The rest of the cohort listened attentively, then went into collective problem-solving mode and started to ask good questions: How did you used to dress for socializing with your close friends? For school? "Do you ever think about how you present yourself to your siblings?" That day, we used class time to experiment with multiple introductory strategies and revise paragraphs for sensory detail, and Bea started a new draft. Her final essay was simply impressive. She focused the new draft on the appearance and behavior choices she made to inspire her siblings' confidence that she was a competent parent and that they would all be okay and to preserve cultural and family traditions—how she rose early to do her hair and wash her face so she looked "together" to inspire confidence. She went on to describe how she arranged her hair in traditional styles and taught her siblings how to do so, and she quoted a morning cheer song she sang to her siblings each day in her native language as part of establishing in her essay how she uses expression and communication to keep her family's culture present in her parents' absence. In the reflection that accompanied her final draft, she reported, "I had to rewrite my whole draft, and I had to motivate myself to start all over, but I am still glad that I got to do this because I learned a lot from it, and I know that in the future I can write an even better essay than this one." Through personal and social reflection, she looked at past, present, and future, and she flipped the script from a self-narrative about limitations, deficits, and self-criticism to one about agency, resilience, and the rhetorical power she now knew was already resident within herself.

Again, locally, the end of each of our cohort class sessions is always an "exit-ticket" question—a rapid-fire reflection (by Post-it note in face-to-face class settings, by Zoom chat in remote classes) on what concepts students still find troublesome, or which elements of the writing process of an upcoming assignment seem especially daunting to each of them, or a similar question aimed to guide us in designing activities for the structured elements of the next class. Students pretty rapidly master the idea that candor is their friend in this circumstance when they see surfaced concerns duly centered. Globally, the credit class, via WfT practices, finds students at the end of the term drawing together their learning by articulating their own "theory of writing" grounded in the key terms: a unifying idea or ideas students can use when facing new communication situations (Andrus, Mitchler, and Tinberg 2019). Smith, Girdharry, and Gallagher (2021) find "theory of writing" to possibly be a less useful frame than "ways of thinking about writing" and point out that a rhetorical frame that exclusively looks at transfer, or what is transferable, may be missing out on a deeper learning experience. They identify this experience as "integration," a product of students identifying connections between communication situations and genres, but also identifying disconnections—instances when they need to think differently.

As cohort students contemplate the question they have been interrogating all term—What makes good writing?—we reflect in guided freewriting, then in small groups, before convening the whole cohort to respond to these questions: What habits increase my ability to do the things I want to do/complete the work I want to complete? How do I get in my own way? How do I get out of my own way? What would I say to myself on the first day of this class if I could travel back in time for just a minute? What would I remind my future self about what we did in this group? Surfacing the dissonant notes and the harmonies mirrors the connections and disconnections students can perceive in their composition study but, more significantly, in their self-aware evolution as learners and citizens—active tellers of their own stories able to recognize their own agency and the resident knowledge, skills, and habits that can enable them to authentically speak for themselves in new contexts.

It would be inaccurate to represent the WfT+ALP pairing as a panacea. Some students do not complete or do not pass with the C or higher needed to count the composition class as a successfully completed prerequisite, nearly always because life circumstances are simply too complicated or challenging and don't permit the student to be as present as they intended to be. While WfT+ALP cannot erase the presence of systemic oppression in students' lives, it can offer students opportunities to surface and interrogate language and its context critically in ways that cultivate agency.

In a recent cohort, a student we will call Drew chose, like Bea, to focus on self-presentation and cultural identity in his "rhetorical-self" essay. His analysis contrasted his own use of White Mainstream English in work settings and in the company of conservative white family members with his use of African American Vernacular English when in the company of his Black family and his friends (who are of varying racial identities but all supportive of his full range of expression). Drew was acutely aware of the potential consequences of using the "wrong" dialect for the context.

> Due to my biracial background, I grew up around two different forms of spoken English. One side of my family is a bit louder, uses more verbal contractions, unconventional sayings, a heavy dose of Ebonics which is also characterized as African American vernacular. Despite growing up around these two forms, I tend to lean towards Ebonics. Because of this, I am often very calculated in how I articulate myself at work. Yes, there is a line of thinking out there that suggests who cares what people think, just be yourself! Well, I need to care about what an interviewer thinks about me. Or, how my boss views me. I also need to be wary about what customers think about me. I tend to avoid speaking how my African American side of the family or African American friends speak in these professional situations since negative connotations are often associated with African American vernacular. Imagine if a customer had a reasonable complaint about our service or products and I spoke to them in such a way like the promotion scenario I set up earlier? I want to present how others deem as professional and competent which leads me to articulating the content of my thoughts with little to no Ebonics.

Drew came into the class a pretty accomplished writer who was especially well-served by the fact that he enjoyed the drafting and revision processes; the reflective process was newer to him, and as he engaged in solo and communal reflection in writing and in conversation, he sat with the discoveries he was making about his ability to express his thoughts and create artifacts that interrogated the linguistic elements of not only his own communication and language but also the structural elements of the world he lived in that created the contexts he navigated. He offered in his written draft reflection,

> I feel good about breaking down the aspects of the way I communicate into concepts like vernacular, cultural elements, volume, and sentence structure. I hope what I wrote is engaging while also a bit humorous as well. What I can take from this assignment is the experience of getting to talk about these nuanced ideas and put them to paper. I do think about this area of my life a lot, every day, actually.

Students were asked to include a piece of visual evidence to illustrate the key ideas of their written analysis. Drew chose as his illustrations two different photos of the NBA player LeBron James. In one picture, James stands before a microphone on a stage in a suit as a row of seated older, all-white male NBA officials applaud him. In the other, we see James relaxing in his NBA jersey, laughing and lounging with friends—clearly at ease. There were elements of agency in the essay, to be sure—Drew's use of his own critical thinking and writing skills to deconstruct and explain the limitations context placed on his expression, and his ability to consciously choose the linguistic tools and patterns he felt were not so much appropriate for his purposes as they were necessary because of biased structures, was powerful. And yet, the final notes of his essay rightfully lingered on frustration with what is: "The forms in which I communicate have purpose, and that tradeoff of authenticity for exacting outcomes I want has paid dividends. However, I do hope that I can work in an environment where I can be a little less calculated all the time, and that I can find more social circles where I can be myself."

Then something really powerful happened in the course of Drew's work. The next major assignment, a typical WfT-style analysis, asked students to create a memo about two examples of a genre of their own choosing, considering its purpose, audience, context, and what "rules and tools" the genre relies upon. The memo's audience was people who would like to become creators in the chosen genre. He chose NBA-themed podcasts hosted by current or former NBA players and focused on retired player JJ Redick's show *The Old Man and the Three* and current player Draymond Green's eponymous *The Draymond Green Show*. Consider his summary of *The Draymond Green Show*:

> Draymond is known for being a rowdy and provocative player on the court which also translates to his show. Draymond does not hold back and is far more unfiltered than most players in any context. For example, in a clip of Draymond Green Show uploaded on May 6th, 2022, a radio host appeared on the debate show First Take and essentially told Draymond to shut up and play out of spite for his provocative personality. Draymond unleashed his emotions on his podcast offering his raw reaction for fans . . . he relies on his vibrant and provocative personality and games he just played in to engage his audience.

The summary is offered in illustration of Drew's observations that this genre creates "content ecosystems" in which hosts can "be real—players often give generic and bland answers to the media, if fans wanted that, they would just watch post-game interviews." Here, we read "generic and bland" as analogous to composed for the workplace—for settings in which the speaker is subject to externally (power-structure) imposed constraints.

Drew offers as an illustration of the power of the genre a clip of Green (2022) responding to sports commentator "Mad Dog" Chris Russo's above-noted public demand that Green stop talking about politics and confine himself to the basketball court:

> I'm not sure what gives him the right to speak for America . . . we're not shocked that he would think that he has the right to speak for America . . . I'm not one to pull the race card very often because we all know the role that race played in the world that we live in . . . but that definitely had a real racist connotation, a real racist undertone, and even beyond it having a racist undertone. We don't even need to go any further than, who are you? What have you done in your life to say "America's tired of him, shut up and play . . ." Those shut up and play, shut up and dribble days are long gone. It has no place here, nor will it be tolerated . . . when I say, sincerely yours, the new media, what I mean by that is that the landscape of media is about to change . . . you will no longer be allowed to put out these false narratives . . . you will be held accountable . . . you know why? Because we're doing it now. And we speak it, and we can do it. The days of players being held accountable and you no longer being held accountable are over . . . We're not livin' with that no more. Sincerely yours, the new media.

In a class freewrite, Drew reflected,

> I believe my strongest element is how I communicate to my audience, would be player podcast hosts. I use the rhetorical concepts to basically say that this is your opportunity to be authentic, and how that engages an NBA fan audience. Why are these players conducting the show in the way they are and what outcomes does this exact. So, just unpacking a concept down to its rhetorical bones is more or less sharpening a tool I use in other areas of life. . . . [I] put together in my opinion an effective piece that discusses something that I am passionate about.

So many things are happening here because of the fusion of reflection, the portability of communication across genres and contexts, and student-led topic choice. The student, coming off a first assignment in which he expresses the desire to see more professional and personal contexts in which authenticity is possible, next makes a move to discover a genre that bakes in authenticity and speakers are themselves effectively confronting the "white racial habitus" (Inoue 2015, 10); crucially, Drew himself has brought this genre into the classroom as a subject of rhetorical study and situated himself as an authority in the narrative. His resident familiarity with and appreciation for the genre has provided firm ground for him to initiate a conversation, to sharpen his own rhetorical awareness, and to gaze forward to the genres into which he will be repurposing messages in a changing mediascape. WfT gives the writer the tools of "whatis" to participate in, to celebrate, and to construct what should be.

REFERENCES

Approaches to Teaching ALP: A Sourcebook. 2014. https://alp-deved.org/wp-content/uploads/2015/03/Combined-sourcebook.pdf.

Andrus, Sonja, Sharon Mitchler, and Howard Tinberg. 2019. "Teaching for Writing Transfer: a Practical Guide for Teachers." *Teaching English in the Two-Year College* 47 (1): 76–89.

Barnett, Susan M., and Stephen J. Ceci. 2002. "When and Where Do We Apply What We Learn? A Taxonomy for Transfer." *Psychological Bulletin* 128 (4): 612–37. https://psycnet.apa.org/record/2002-01514-006.

Bartholomae, David. 1986. "Inventing the University." *Journal of Basic Writing* 5 (1): 4–23.

Beaufort, Anne. 2007. *College Writing and Beyond: a New Framework for University Writing Instruction.* Logan: Utah State University Press.

Daniels, Em. 2022. *Building a Trauma-Responsive Educational Practice: Lessons from a Corrections Classroom.* New York: Routledge.

Edley, Christopher Jr. 2017. "At Cal State, Algebra is a Civil Rights Issue." *EdSource,* June 5. https://edsource.org/2017/at-cal-state-algebra-is-a-civil-rights-issue/582950.

Green, Draymond. 2022. "Reaction to J J Redick and Mad Dog Chris Russo 'Shut Up & Play' First Take Debate." YouTube video, 5:26. https://www.youtube.com/watch?v=Eiczolf6H6l.

Inoue, Asao B. 2015. *Antiracist Writing Assessment Ecologies: Teaching and Assessing Writing for a Socially Just Future.* Anderson, SC: Parlor.

Logue, Alexandra W. 2018. "The Extensive Evidence of Co-Requisite Remediation's Effectiveness." *Inside Higher Ed,* July 17, https://www.insidehighered.com/views/2018/07/17/data-already-tell-us-how-effective-co-requisite-education-opinion.

Meyer, Jan H. F., and Ray Land. 2006. *Overcoming Barriers to Student Understanding: Threshold Concepts and Troublesome Knowledge.* New York: Routledge.

Nicotra, Jodie. 2018. *Becoming Rhetorical: Analyzing and Composing in a Multimedia World.* Independence, KY: Cengage.

Perkins, D. N., and Gavriel Salomon. 1988. "Teaching for Transfer." *Educational Leadership* 46 (1): 22–32.

Schoenbach, Ruth, Cynthia Greenleaf, and Lynn Murphy. 2012. *Reading for Understanding.* 2nd ed. San Francisco: Jossey-Bass.

Smith, Kevin G., Kristi Girdharry, and Chris W. Gallagher. 2021. "Writing Transfer, Integration, and the Need for the Long View." *College Composition and Communication* 7 (1): 4–26.

Thonney, Teresa. 2011. "Teaching the Conventions of Academic Discourse." *Teaching English in the Two-Year College* 38 (4): 347–62.

Tinto, Vincent. 1997. "Classrooms as Communities: Exploring the Educational Character of Student Persistence." *Journal of Higher Education* 68 (6): 599–623.

Wardle, Elizabeth. 2007. "Understanding 'Transfer' from FYC: Preliminary Results of a Longitudinal Study." *WPA: Writing Program Administration* 3 (1/2): 65–85.

Wardle, Elizabeth. 2009. "'Mutt Genres' and the Goal of FYC: Can We Help Students Write the Genres of the University?" *College Composition and Communication* 60 (4): 765–89.

Kathleen Blake Yancey, Lianne Robertson, and Kara Taczak. 2014. *Writing across Contexts: Transfer, Composition, and Sites of Writing.* Logan: Utah State University Press.

PART II

Assessment

6
LABOR-BASED GRADING TO REDUCE ANXIETY, IMPROVE FLEXIBILITY, AND RECAST INSTRUCTOR-STUDENT RELATIONSHIPS

Mark Blaauw-Hara

The advent of a corequisite approach to developmental writing has spurred a sea change in the field of writing studies. Data gathered at a wide variety of institutions over the past decade strongly suggest that, for most students, corequisite models far surpass more traditional, standalone devclopmental courses in fostering student retention and writing improvement (Adams 2020; Complete College America 2021; Daugherty et al. 2021; Logue 2018). While there are a number of different models for how to schedule and teach corequisite writing courses, data suggest that as long as the models being used feature concurrent college-level and support courses (rather than simply offering a college-level course and then asking students to attend tutoring for extra help, or requiring students to take an entirely developmental course first and then a college-level course second in the same semester), most corequisite models outperform more traditional ones (Adams 2020). This means it is time to turn to more focused questions regarding how best to structure those corequisite courses and which methods work best for the students who take them.

It is helpful to remember that the populations we tend to see in developmental courses are different from those we see in college-level courses. Developmental sections tend to have a higher percentage of students of color, English-language learners (ELL), and working-class students (Anderst, Malow, and Shahar 2016; Avni and Finn 2021; Chen and Simone 2016), and some scholarship suggests students of color and women students experience significant negative effects from being placed into developmental courses (Jaggars and Stacey 2014).

These data underscore the urgent need for placement reform. As a recent collection by Jessica Nastal, Mya Poe, and Christie Toth (2022) illustrates, community colleges are well aware of this need and are responding in a variety of ways centering around informed or directed self-placement, multiple measures, and developing local assessments that address a given college's students. A concern for equity is driving most placement reform, and Jessica Nastal, Mya Poe, and Christie Toth's collection features several chapters that describe successful reform efforts that have increased equity for traditionally underserved groups, such as BIPOC students (Calhoon-Dillahunt and Margoni 2022; Del Principe, Broder, and Levesque 2022) and ELL students (Che 2022). While placement reform should certainly be top-of-mind for community-college WPAs and writing faculty, I think we can work at the same time to structure corequisite courses so they better support the students they currently contain.

In this chapter, I argue that labor-based grading contracts are an excellent fit for corequisite writing courses. As I detail through a blend of current scholarship and my own experiences teaching corequisite courses at a community college, labor-based grading contracts not only encourage writing habits (and habits of mind) that lead to improved fluency, they also help alleviate the anxiety and distress many students feel when they find themselves placed in developmental writing, and they recast the role of the faculty member as an ally rather than an arbiter. Because the nature of corequisite courses is that they are linked to college-level courses, I address college-level and corequisite courses as a pair, with examples drawn from each.

WHO ARE COREQUISITE STUDENTS, HOW DO THEY FEEL, AND WHAT DO THEY NEED

As alluded to above, I have grave concerns about the placement methods currently prevalent. Many schools have historically used placement systems chosen more for perceived efficiency than for their ability to place students in courses where they can benefit the most, and a number of scholars have raised concerns about racial, gender, and class bias implicit in standardized placement instruments (Elliot et al. 2012; Klausman et al. 2016; Nastal 2019; Toth et al. 2019). The student demographics in developmental writing classes—including corequisite classes—do not mirror the demographics of those in college-level writing classes. That fact alone should prompt us to question placement methods, but in the meantime, I think it can be productive to ask ourselves what we know about the students currently in those courses.

Many students who place into developmental courses find themselves disappointed and depressed (Matos 2017), frightened (Blackstock and Exton 2014), anxious (Inman and Powell 2018), and embarrassed (Daugherty et al. 2021). These negative emotions compound any real or perceived difficulties students may have with writing itself, making it important to implement curricula—including grading practices—that do not reinforce stress and anxiety. As I mentioned earlier, developmental writers are also disproportionately BIPOC, working class, or ELL, further complicating the situation, as these students are writing in the context of educational institutions predicated, for the most part, on white, middle-class language patterns and values (Inoue 2014b; Shafer 2018).

Because many developmental writers do, in fact, struggle to with what is widely termed Standard Edited American English (SEAE), and a better command of SAEA would likely help them navigate their writing tasks in the rest of the university, some instructors may be tempted to design much of the corequisite curriculum around instruction on SAEA. In addition to decades of research that strongly suggests traditional approaches to grammar instruction do not work (Blaauw-Hara 2006), many scholars have argued persuasively that college-level writing courses that focus uncritically on teaching and assessing SEAE serve to replicate sociocultural systems that elevate white, middle-class ways of being/communicating and subjugate other ways of being/communicating, particularly those practiced by students of color and users of other Englishes (Canagarajah 2006; Inoue 2019; Young and Martinez 2011).

Students in corequisite courses may say the main thing they want to learn is a command of "grammar," but even then, we should proceed cautiously. Gregory Shafer (2018) argues that the desire expressed by some developmental writers to elevate SEAE over their home dialects reminds him of Marx's concept of "false consciousness." As Shafer writes,

> False consciousness was used by Marx to describe how subjugated people could be manipulated to believe and practice the ideology of the oppressors above them. . . . It is also evident in the developmental writing class when teachers and pupils reproduce a pedagogy that treats developmental students—often populated by minority writers—as different and in need of special, often regressive policies. . . . False consciousness is conspicuous in writing practices that treat academic writing—the language of the upper class—as the exulted and final goal of the basic writer. (363)

Shafer argues that the resistance some students feel toward more liberatory pedagogies can be traced to this false consciousness: they "have long been laboring under the notion that their dialect is a point of disgrace" (366), and they have difficulty seeing that notions of linguistic virtue are constructs that serve to replicate unjust systems of power in US society (and by extension its educational systems).

Corequisite students can benefit from critical discussion of SEAE and individualized instruction that has as its goal an increased understanding and control of language. Bethany Davila (2016) presents some excellent methods for how to do this. But if we focus our curriculum and assessments in corequisite classes on grammar, we run the risk of signaling to students that adhering to SEAE is one of the most important parts of writing, we reinforce harmful social inequities, and we do all this in an environment that will likely lead to increased anxiety and stress because we are raising the stakes on something students already struggle with. Grammar has a place in corequisite courses, but it should be addressed in a supportive, low-stress environment in which we have critical discussions of language. Students in corequisite courses also need an introduction to the habits and practices valued in academia, as well as those practices decades of writing studies scholarship have shown result in better writing. Our grading practices should incentivize those habits and practices, emphasizing the specific things we want students to focus on.

Corequisite developmental writing courses are frequently not for credit and graded on a pass/fail basis, which was the case at the community college where I taught for twenty years. A traditional way to determine whether a student passed or failed would be to include a series of graded assignments and establish a cut-off score—say, 75 percent—above which a student would pass. This grade would be determined separately from the grade in the for-credit college-level course.

This traditional way of grading developmental courses is not the best way to address student needs in corequisite courses. Students in those courses have already had ample experience with what Asao Inoue (2014b) terms "quality-failure," or failure based on a teacher's determination that the student's work does not meet external standards of quality. In their pivotal article on grading contracts, Jane Danielewics and Peter Elbow (2009) outline the difficulties inherent in judging (and grading) the quality of student writing, difficulties our field has recognized since at least 1912 (Inman and Powell 2018). Students in our corequisite courses—anxious, disappointed, placed there in the first place by suspect testing mechanisms—do not need more of the same assessment practices with which they have already struggled and which have failed them. They need a supportive environment that still has rigor—but this rigor should be based on labor, not quality assessments. For those faculty reading this who worry a shift to labor-based contracts will mean everyone always passes, I can assure you it does not. Unfortunately, some students will still fail the course. However, they will fail because they did not meet objective standards that were clear from the start of the class—what Inoue (2014b) terms "labor-failure," which he argues is seen as fairer by students, including students of color.

My own introduction to labor-based grading was through Inoue's (2014a) chapter in Deborah Coxwell-Teague and Ronald Lunsford's outstanding book *First-Year Composition: From Theory to Practice*, and he has expanded on those ideas in many other places, most notably in his award-winning text *Antiracist Writing Assessment Ecologies: Teaching and Assessing Writing for a Socially Just Future* (2015). But I really like his rationale in "Theorizing Failure in US Writing Assessments" (2014b):

> It's arguable . . . that assessing writing only in terms of labor, effort, or quantity reorients students toward the work and behaviors most teachers hope students will learn, and thus toward performance-approach behaviors, noncognitive dimensions of academic success. It also avoids the damaging psychological effects, such as performance-avoidance and low self-efficacy, that grading by quality can cause many students, most notably students of color, working-class students, and multilingual students. Most importantly, when a piece of writing does not meet a teacher's sense of a local SEAAE [Standard Edited American Academic English], it does not require a failing grade, since writing quality does not denote labor-failure. Thus, labor-failure is produced only when students do not do enough work. This framework opens up room for translingual and other critical pedagogies that aim to question SEAAEs or broaden the academy. (345)

To me, at least, this seems exactly like what we should be focusing on in corequisite writing courses.

As Inoue (2014b) points out, labor-based grading also meshes well with the "Framework for Success in Post-Secondary Writing" (Council 2011), which lists eight habits of mind as "essential for success in college writing": curiosity, openness, engagement, creativity, persistence, responsibility, flexibility, and metacognition (1). The framework is focused primarily on credit-bearing college courses, but corequisite courses are explicitly designed to support student writers in their work for college-level writing courses—that is the fundamental way they differ from stand-alone developmental writing courses. Because of this linkage, corequisite courses should not just support the writing that happens in college-level courses, but also the thinking. Developmental writing students often do not just have difficulty with academic writing; they also tend to have felt a disconnect with academia in general.

While it is certainly true that, especially for BIPOC and working-class students, much of this disconnect likely stems from the white, middle-class ways academia is structured, it is also true that we want those students to succeed in college, and higher education is slow to change.

The corequisite course can serve as a place where we can discuss and interrogate not just writing but also the practices valued in academia. Additionally, several of the habits of mind—for example, engagement, persistence, responsibility, and flexibility—are also ones valued in the work world, and working-class students are likely familiar with them but have not yet considered how those practices might manifest in academia. (For more on the cognitive demands of working-class jobs, consider Mike Rose's [2005] *The Mind at Work*, Barbara Ehrenreich's [2011] *Nickel and Dimed*, or Matthew Crawford's [2010] *Shop Class as Soulcraft*.) A corequisite course can, by encouraging metacognition (another of the framework's habits of mind), support backward-reaching transfer wherein we ask students to explore how the practices connected to success in the work world might also set them up to succeed in college. (I have written elsewhere about transfer theory and writing studies in Blaauw-Hara 2014.)

In summary, corequisite writing courses should be structured in order to encourage students to interrogate and practice academic writing in ways that teach them to develop better linguistic control, and we should do so in a low-anxiety environment that encourages habits of thinking and working linked to college success. A labor-based grading system is a perfect fit for these goals.

MY OWN JOURNEY WITH LABOR-BASED GRADING

For about the first ten years of my career, I used a fairly standard non-contract system, with set weights for each essay, participation, the final portfolio, and so forth. I experimented with ways to encourage reflection and revision within this system, with the most effective being to weight the final portfolio more than any individual essay and have students include revised versions of two of their essays along with a reflective essay that discussed not only their revisions but also additional things they had learned in class. I also asked students to write short reflections after each essay and at other points during the semester. As I learned more about the value of metacognition in student learning and knowledge transfer, I put more emphasis on the reflective writing I asked students to do.

This system wasn't terrible by any means, and I used it in both my college-level and stand-alone developmental writing courses. My evaluations were generally very good, and students seemed to work hard and value the courses. They had no trouble understanding the grading system since it was quite similar to how they had been graded in the overwhelming majority of their prior academic experiences. Similarly, my own experiences as their professor were very standard—I spent a lot of time thinking about what grades they should get on their essays, and I used my feedback on their essays for two things: encouraging growth and justifying the grade. When I handed essays back, most students accepted their grades without comment, and I spent time answering questions (really, justifying grades) for the students who were unhappy. Occasionally, a student disagreed so strongly with their grade that they lodged a formal grade challenge; this was disheartening and took time away from what I'd rather have been doing, but I was a conscientious grader and my grades always stood up to scrutiny.

I started to get a sense that this system, although it was common and easily understandable to both students and administration, might be flawed when another writing professor gave me a copy of Elbow's (1993) "Ranking, Evaluating, and Liking: Sorting Out Three Forms of Judgment." In this relatively famous essay (that I had never heard of before), Elbow problematizes ranking—which includes assigning letter grades to essays—as unreliable and counterproductive to the goals most of us have as writing teachers. Elbow notes that even if grades are reliable, they still don't communicate in a very nuanced way to students what they should or shouldn't do to improve their writing. Elbow argues that grades also lead students to fixate on whether they do or do not achieve the mark they desire rather than thinking about their writing. Elbow also describes the emotional perils of grading: that poor grades can anger students or make them doubt their intelligence, and that even high grades can lead to feelings of fraud in students who have written to the grade, so to speak, and "sold out on their own judgment" (190).

I had to admit I had seen everything Elbow describes; however, I didn't know how to change my pedagogy. I already used portfolios, which Elbow recommends. For a few classes, I tried out a basic three-stage ranking system on individual essays—poor, adequate, and excellent, although I didn't use those terms—and saved the grading for the portfolio, but this approach seemed to inspire distress in students. They worried all semester about their grades, anxious their portfolios would be graded much lower than they hoped. I added midsemester and end-of-semester writing conferences, which worked very well, but they still didn't fully address the struggles I was having with grades. So even though I had come to think I was using a bad system, I went back to grading each essay, weighting the portfolio more, and I kept the midsemester and end-of-semester conferences. I continued to teach this way when our writing program shifted to the accelerated learning program (ALP) model, which two of my colleagues had brought to our college in 2012.

Then, in 2014, I read Inoue's "A Grade-Less Writing Course That Focuses on Labor and Assessing" (2014a) and was inspired. I sent him an email and asked him whether he thought labor-based grading would work well with working-class students at a community college. He was generous with his response and encouraged me to give it a try, so I did. My first semester, although I provided extensive feedback on essays and other work, I graded both my college-level and corequisite classes entirely based on labor contracts I had crafted. The contracts included things like completing rough drafts on essays, turning in final drafts, writing reflections, attending class, writing responses to readings, and the like. I put all these into a chart within the syllabus and discussed it on the first day of class. I scheduled midterm and final conferences in which I met with students, discussed their progress, and gave them a sense of where they fell on the chart and how that position would translate to a course grade.

Overall, these discussions went pretty well, although I did pick up on some discomfort with the process I think was similar to that outlined by Cathy Spidell and William Thelin (2006) in their article focusing on resistance to grading contracts. Like the students described by Spidell and Thelin, some of my students seemed suspicious of the system—they were waiting for the other shoe to drop, so to speak, for their grades to come out far lower than they hoped. Those who voiced these concerns tended to be higher-performing students who felt comfortable in the more traditional system of grading. In class discussions and privately, some of these students shared that they felt the labor grading system was a touch unfair—because it did not take "quality" into account, just labor, a student could conceivably write mediocre essays but do all the work, and they would get the same grade as a student who wrote excellent essays and also did all the work. When I pointed out (nonconfrontationally) that I, in turn, thought a more traditional system was unfair, I didn't make much headway. To my students who traditionally had struggled with writing, the labor contract felt wonderful—they said it reduced their stress and allowed them to focus on their writing without worrying about grades. But my students who already wrote well missed the grades, and they said they were less motivated to work hard on their essays because they knew I would not be grading on quality. These concerns resonate with those voiced by some of the students featured in Alan Blackstock and Virginia Exton's (2014) article on grading contracts for basic writers, in which a small number of "high-achieving students who rely on a steady stream of numerical grades to judge their own academic performance" experienced heightened anxiety in a contract-grading system (287–88).

These concerns put me in a quandary. I wanted my grading system to be equitable and transparent—goals I felt were served well by labor contracts—but I also wanted it to motivate students. My high-performing students said more traditional grading systems motivated them well, but they were also the students who, to be frank, needed the least motivation to produce good work. Still, I wanted a system that helped these more advanced students grow as writers, and I also wanted that system to motivate and support the students who struggled with writing.

I settled on a hybrid system for the college-level class, in which the majority of students' final grades (60%) were determined by a labor contract, but each of the four essays also received a grade. The essay grades were averaged together to constitute 40 percent of students' final grade. To increase the transparency of the essay-grading process and to help students (and me) feel as though the grades were determined in a way that honored student agency, we determined all essay grades in conference. These grading conferences, which were fifteen minutes long, let us dialogue about areas that were working and places to grow in each essay; they also gave us the opportunity to discuss sentence-level language issues in a way I hoped would build metacognitive awareness and rhetorical control. Many students found these conferences unnerving at first and shared they had never been asked to participate in their own grading before. Some asked me to assign a grade without their input. In those cases, I tried to respect their discomfort, but I also explained that I was genuinely interested in their own analysis of their writing and that practicing this sort of analysis would help them learn to recognize on their own which areas of their writing were strong and which needed work—a vital skill for their future writing endeavors. These writing conferences ended up being places of empowerment for students, once they worked through their discomfort.

In terms of the labor contracts, they were simple and flexible. Here is how I described them in my syllabus for the college-level course:

> The vast majority of your grade will be based on the "labor" you do in the course. Effective writing is a result of knowledge and skill: You will gain the knowledge through our readings, lectures, and discussions, but the skill comes from sustained hard work. You will receive credit for doing that hard work—if you do the work, you will get the credit, and that will greatly elevate your final grade. To help you out, I've created the following chart [table 6.1]:

To get a given letter grade for the "labor" portion, you need to meet ALL the requirements for that letter grade. If you don't meet all the requirements, you'll get less than that grade, even if you exceeded the

Table 6.1. Labor-based course grading rubric

	Total	A	B	C	D or lower
Attendance	24	≥ 21	20–19	18–17	< 17
Essays	4	4	4	4	3
Journals	17	≥ 15	12–14	10–11	< 10
Writing Reflections	3	3	3	2	< 2
Conferences	4	4	4	4	< 4
Field Interviews	1	1	0	0	0

requirements in another area. (For example, if you met the attendance, essay, and conference requirements for a B, but did not meet the journal and reflection requirements, you'd get a B- or C+.)

Elsewhere in the syllabus and the online learning-management system, I gave examples and descriptions of acceptable work in the areas in the chart—how to structure journals, for example, and how to prepare for conferences. As long as students met those measures of acceptable work, they received credit. To determine their final grades for the course, we held another grading conference in which we calculated their labor grades and essay averages and then figured out their final grades.

For the corequisite course, I stopped grading individual assignments altogether. Instead, here are my syllabus notes on grading to those students:

> This course is entirely designed to support your success in English 111. We will have a number of in-class discussions and assignments that roughly fall into four categories:
>
> 1. Previewing what we will work on in English 111.
> 2. Reviewing what we learned in English 111.
> 3. Providing extra practice on concepts and skills from English 111.
> 4. Exploring topics that impact college success.
>
> The class will feature many collaborative activities and free, open discussions. It is a safe space for you to ask questions and receive individualized help and feedback. I will touch base with each of you individually each class period.
>
> This is a pass/fail course. Your grade will be determined by whether you are present and prepared. Each class period, you will receive 0–2 points based on your attendance and preparation. At the end of the semester, if those totals equal greater than 75% of the possible points, you will pass the course.

This is, in essence, an extraordinarily simple labor contract. The four categories of coursework I outline are consistent with Peter Adams's

(2020) descriptions of the Community College of Baltimore County's corequisite ALP courses (20). To pass the class, students just have to do more than 75 percent of the work, all of which occurs during class time. (Here, I would like to note that in the entire time I taught ALP—around seven years—I had no instances in which students regularly attended the college-level course and then skipped the corequisite course, despite the corequisite course being pass/fail with the cutoff at 75 percent. Extremely infrequently, I had the opposite happen—students met passing requirements for the corequisite course but didn't pass the college-level course. In those cases, they were reenrolled in the college-level course the following semester but not required to take the corequisite course since they had already passed it. In the overwhelming number of cases, though, students either passed both courses together or failed both.)

Students in the corequisite class seemed to understand and appreciate this grading system. Students never requested more formal letter grades on assignments (as happened in the college-level courses very early in my experiences with labor grading, described above). Students seemed to understand immediately that since the purpose of the corequisite course was to support their learning and achievement in the college-level one, it would work best to keep the grading methods for the corequisite course simple and straightforward, based entirely on labor. A labor-based grading system also emphasized that the corequisite course was focused on hard work—a place for practice, not performance. As Blackstock and Exton (2014) note, "Basic writers perceive that they do not have control over their writing skills, but they can usually control their ability to attend class, engage in academic activities, and complete assignments. . . . Without a grade for each assignment, the learning outcomes shift from product to process" (284). I found this to be the case as well.

While I did not keep rigorous track of my course averages semester to semester, my sense is that overall grades went up as a result of labor grading. Since students could determine 60 percent of their final grade in the college-level class and 100 percent of their "grade" in the corequisite class by how much work they did, the overwhelming majority of them did at least as much work as they needed to earn a B in the college class and a passing grade in the corequisite class. Their essays, graded in conferences, earned around the same grades as they would have if I had graded them by myself, but students felt more invested in the process, and they left the conferences feeling as though they knew how their grades were determined. Since I settled on my eventual system of contract and conference grading, I have not experienced a student grade challenge—something that prior to contract grading had been infrequent but was nonetheless time consuming and distressing to both the students and to me.

The clarity of the labor contract and the collaboration of grading conferences helped me recast my role as more of a mentor and ally. If students started to fall behind on the labor contract, I was able to talk with them about why and help them troubleshoot ways to get back on track. The openness of the conferences let me ask questions about sections of their essays that were unclear and fine-tune wording together with the students; I could demonstrate structural changes, talk about places for development or revision, and more. This system of grading did much to reduce the air of mystery and subjectivity that surrounds much assessment in writing courses.

CONCLUSIONS

Admittedly, labor grading will not solve every difficulty in corequisite courses. As I note above, it does not address challenges with placement. While I have found anecdotally that labor grading helps reduce the anxiety of linguistically diverse students—including English-language learners—it does not automatically help such students write more fluently. While some scholarship suggests linguistically diverse students perform better in corequisite courses than in models that "isolat[e] them within an ESL track" (Anderst, Maloy, and Shahar 2016), others caution that corequisite instructors need more training in order to maximize the benefits for English-language learners (Avni and Finn 2021). Sheri Craig (2021) points out that contract grading, by itself, does little to address the racial inequities that run throughout higher education, and that all too frequently, white teachers turn to it as "low-hanging fruit" rather than striving for meaningful change in universities and the larger society (146). As Joyce Inman and Rebecca Powell (2018) write, contract grading "plung[es] students and instructors into the dissonance between our field's dismissal of grades and the institution's privileging of grades" (50). In sum, we must remember contract grading will not solve all the equity problems present in our writing programs, and we should be sure to view it as one intervention to make a biased educational system a little more equitable.

That said, it is an intervention well worth our time. As I outline in this piece, the grading systems in both the college-level and corequisite class should complement each other, and they should be chosen to decrease student anxiety and encourage activities writing scholarship tells us support student growth. Labor-based grading contracts serve these purposes well. In addition, they help recast the instructor's role as more ally than arbiter—a change that will not only feel welcome to most writing teachers but will do more to support student learning.

REFERENCES

Adams, Peter. 2020. "Giving Hope to the American Dream: Implementing a Corequisite Model of Developmental Writing." *Composition Studies* 48 (2): 19–34.

Anderst, Leah, Jennifer Maloy, and Jed Shahar. 2016. "Assessing the Accelerated Learning Program Model for Linguistically Diverse Developmental Writing Students." *Teaching English in the Two-Year College* 44 (1): 11–31.

Avni, Sharon, and Heather B. Finn. 2021. "Meeting the Needs of English Language Learners in Co-Requisite Courses at Community College." *Community College Journal of Research and Practice* 45 (8): 560–74.

Blaauw-Hara, Mark. 2006. "Why Our Students Need Instruction in Grammar, and How We Should Go about It." *Teaching English in the Two-Year College* 34 (2): 165–78.

Blaauw-Hara, Mark. 2014. "Transfer Theory, Threshold Concepts, and First-Year Composition: Connecting Writing Courses to the Rest of the College." *Teaching English in the Two-Year College* 41 (4): 354–65.

Blackstock, Alan, and Virginia Norris Exton. 2014. "'Space to Grow': Grading Contracts for Basic Writers." *Teaching English in the Two-Year College* 41 (3): 278–93.

Calhoon-Dillahunt, Carolyn, and Travis Margoni. 2022. "Narrowing the Divide in Placement at a Hispanic-Serving Institution: The Case of Yakima Valley College." In *Writing Placement in Two-Year Colleges: The Pursuit of Equity in Postsecondary Education*, edited by Jessica Nastal, Mya Poe, and Christie Toth, 131–49. Fort Collins, CO: WAC Clearinghouse.

Canagarajah, A. Suresh. 2006. "The Place of World Englishes in Composition: Pluralization Continued." *College Composition and Communication* 57 (4): 586–619.

Che, Charissa. 2022. "Mind the (Linguistic) Gap: On 'Flagging' ESL Students at Queensborough Community College." In *Writing Placement in Two-Year Colleges: The Pursuit of Equity in Postsecondary Education*, edited by Jessica Nastal, Mya Poe, and Christie Toth, 191–222. Fort Collins, CO: WAC Clearinghouse.

Chen, Xianglei, and Sean Simone. 2016. *Remedial Coursetaking at U.S. Public 2- and 4-Year Institutions: Scope, Experiences, and Outcomes. Statistical Analysis Report* NCES 2016–405. Washington, DC: National Center for Education Statistics, Institute of Education Sciences, US Department of Education.

Complete College America. n.d. "Corequisite Support." completecollege.org/strategy/corequisite-support.

Council of Writing Program Administrators. 2011. "Framework for Success in Postsecondary Writing." https://wpacouncil.org/aws/CWPA/pt/sd/news_article/242845/_PARENT/layout_details/false.

Craig, Sherri. 2021. "Your Contract Grading Ain't It." *WPA: Writing Program Administration* 44 (3): 145–46.

Crawford, Matthew B. 2010. *Shop Class as Soulcraft: An Inquiry into the Value of Work.* New York: Penguin.

Danielewicz, Jane, and Peter Elbow. 2009. "A Unilateral Grading Contract to Improve Learning and Teaching." *College Composition and Communication* 61 (2): 244–68.

Daugherty, Lindsay, Alexandra Mendoza-Graf, Diana Gehlhaus, Trey Miller, and Russell Gerber. 2021. *Student Experiences in English Corequisite Remediation versus a Standalone Developmental Education Course: Findings from an Experimental Study in Texas Community*

Colleges. RAND Corporation. https://www.rand.org/pubs/research_reports/RRA810-1.html.
Davila, Bethany. 2016. "The Inevitability of 'Standard' English: Discursive Constructions of Standard Language Ideologies." *Written Communication* 33 (2): 127–48.
Del Principe, Annie, Lesley Broder, and Lauren Levesque. 2022. "Tracking the Racial Consequences of Placement by Probability: A Case Study at Kingsborough Community College." In *Writing Placement in Two-Year Colleges: The Pursuit of Equity in Postsecondary Education*, edited by Jessica Nastal, Mya Poe, and Christie Toth, 173–90. Fort Collins, CO: WAC Clearinghouse.
Ehrenreich, Barbara. 2011. *Nickel and Dimed: On (Not) Getting By in America*. New York: Picador.
Elbow, Peter. 1993. "Ranking, Evaluating, Liking: Sorting Out Three Forms of Judgment." *College English* 55 (2): 187–206.
Elliot, Norbert, Perry Deess, Alex Rudniy, and Kamal Joshi. 2012. "Placement of Students into First-Year Writing Courses." *Research in the Teaching of English* 46 (3): 285–313.
Inman, Joyce Olewski, and Rebecca A. Powell. 2018. "In the Absence of Grades: Dissonance and Desire in Course-Contract Classrooms." *College Composition and Communication* 70 (1): 30–56.
Inoue, Asao B. 2014a. "A Grade-Less Writing Course That Focuses on Labor and Assessing." In *First-Year Composition: From Theory to Practice*, edited by Deborah Coxwell-Teague and Ronald F. Lunsford, 71–110. Anderson, SC: Parlor.
Inoue, Asao B. 2014b. "Theorizing Failure in US Writing Assessments." *Research in the Teaching of English* 48 (3): 330–52.
Inoue, Asao B. 2015. *Antiracist Writing Assessment Ecologies: Teaching and Assessing Writing for a Socially Just Future*. Fort Collins, CO: WAC Clearinghouse.
Inoue, Asao. B. 2019. *Labor Based Grading Contracts: Building Equity and Inclusion in the Compassionate Writing Classroom*. Fort Collins, CO: WAC Clearinghouse.
Jaggars, Shanna Smith, and Georgia West Stacey. 2014. *What We Know about Developmental Education Outcomes*. New York: Community College Research Center.
Klausman, Jeffrey, Christie Toth, Wendy Swyt, Brett Griffiths, Anthony Warnke, Amy L. Williams, Joanne Giordano, and Leslie Roberts. 2016. "TYCA White Paper on Placement Reform." *Teaching English in the Two-Year College* 44 (2): 135–51.
Logue, Alexandra W. 2018. "The Extensive Evidence of Co-Requisite Remediation's Effectiveness." *Inside Higher Ed*, July 16. www.insidehighered.com/views/2018/07/17/data-already-tell-us-how-effective-co-requisite-education-opinion.
Matos, Nicole. 2017. "What My Struggling Students Wanted Me to Understand." *Chronicle of Higher Education* 64 (9): 1.
Nastal, Jessica. 2019. "Beyond Tradition: Writing Placement, Fairness, and Success at a Two-Year College." *Journal of Writing Assessment* 12 (1): n.p. https://escholarship.org/uc/item/4wg8wong.
Nastal, Jessica, Mya Poe, and Christie Toth, eds. 2022. *Writing Placement in Two-Year Colleges: The Pursuit of Equity in Postsecondary Education*. Fort Collins, CO: WAC Clearinghouse.
Rose, Mike. 2005. *The Mind at Work: Valuing the Intelligence of the American Worker*. New York: Penguin.
Shafer, Gregory. 2018. "False Consciousness, Developmental Writing, and the Community College." *Community College Journal of Research and Practice* 42 (5): 362–72.
Spidell, Cathy, and William H. Thelin. 2006. "Not Ready to Let Go: A Study of Resistance to Grading Contracts." *Composition Studies* 34 (1): 35–57.
Toth, Christie, Jessica Nastal, Holly Hassel, and Joanne Baird Giordano. 2019. "Introduction: Writing Assessment, Placement, and the Two-Year College." *Journal of Writing Assessment* 12 (1): n.p. https://escholarship.org/uc/item/839356os.
Young, Vershawn Ashanti, and Aja Y. Martinez. 2011. *Code-Meshing as World English: Pedagogy, Policy, and Performance*. Urbana, IL: NCTE.

7
FINDING THE "RIGHT" AMOUNT OF RIGOR IN THE RESEARCH PAPER

Melissa Long

I began my most recent evaluation packet with the following statement: "I set the mark impossibly high and watch amazed as my students achieve it and prove its possibility. I've come to realize that the only limits to my students' capabilities are those I put on them." When I first began teaching accelerated courses in 2012, I was plagued by the need to prove my students could legitimately skip three levels of pre-transfer-level composition courses. My colleagues in the English department needed to give a stamp of approval to any student who wanted to make the leap, and I felt personally responsible for making sure the students' work not only reflected the quality of the average student entering our college composition course but transcended the quality of a student passing that course. My skeptical colleagues were amazed and allowed those students through the gates. They were comforted by the idea that this group was a handful of outliers who must have been tragically underplaced.

After the first few semesters of success, the other teachers in the department no longer wanted to read the portfolios of these students. They trusted the teachers of the accelerated courses to decide for themselves whether students were ready for transfer level. I should have been elated. Instead, I internalized the new responsibility for maintaining rigor and raised the bar even more. The English faculty continued to discuss our remedial students and the accelerated courses. I listened patiently as my colleagues complained without evidence that the courses were watered down, and I tried to quell the fears that we were simply passing students along. I felt the need to defend the acceleration movement and the crowds of teachers at other institutions who were "drinking the Kool-Aid." As far as I could see, the accelerated courses I was teaching were as rigorous, if not more so, than the transfer-level course the students took afterward. I had a long list of former students who attested that they'd worked harder, read higher-level texts, and turned in longer papers with me the semester before.

Five years later, accelerated classes were the norm for students placing below transfer-level composition, and I was one of two instructors piloting Porterville College's first corequisite courses, a new structure allowing students to take our college composition course at the same time as a support class aimed at helping students with the skills they lacked. The department raised the same concerns about the course—the material will be watered down, we'll just pass students along. What about the rigor? Compounding the doubts was the news that other English departments were paring down the research paper; a few were eliminating it altogether.

In part to address these concerns, my colleague and I structured the class in such a way that we demanded a great deal of our students, raising that bar a notch above what we thought our students were capable of achieving. They blew us away, and I continued with the same "successful" curriculum for the next two years, making sure to share the work they were submitting with those same colleagues who by this time had started to avoid me in the hallway, weary of another see-they-can-do-it story.

I was riding high at this point. I had battled the skeptics at never-ending department meetings, and our through-put rates were rising astronomically. I was presenting at conferences to promote the corequisite model, and I could see the difference I was making in students' lives. After finishing her twenty-five-page mini-graduate thesis, Shawna,[1] a middle-aged returning student who had struggled with the assignment, came to see me during office hours. Struggled is putting it lightly. She'd visited me the week before with angry tears asking how I could expect her to complete such a beast of an assignment and telling me how devastating this paper was for students who had worked hard all semester, so I was surprised to see her grinning ear to ear. I invited her to have a seat, and she could barely contain herself: "First, I want to apologize for last week. I was really upset, but I thought about what you said, and once I put everything together, the assignment wasn't that hard. I mean, we'd already done all the work, you know? And I wrote a book. Like a real book. With thirty pages."

I congratulated her, but I don't think she noticed or cared.

She went on, "I don't mean this disrespectfully, but I don't even care what grade you give me. I sent my book out to everyone in my family. I can't believe I wrote a book."

---

1. Name changed to protect her identity.

Shawna had been placed into the college's lowest level of composition. If she had followed her counselor's advice, the English course sequence would have taken her two years, and she passed my transfer-level class and corequisite with an A in a single semester.

NO NEED TO RAISE AN ALREADY HIGH BAR

I tell this story because it simultaneously illustrates one of my biggest success stories and perhaps my biggest failure as a teacher. I was setting the bar in my class based on what my colleagues might think (or, more appropriately, what I thought my colleagues thought). My hubris led me to demand more of my corequisite students than I ever did of those in my stand-alone college-level composition class; in fact, I was asking more of the students than most of the universities I was trying to prepare them to transfer to ask of their first-year composition students.

I understand now that my bar was too high, not because students couldn't reach it (the vast majority of them were doing so) but because I was placing unfair demands on my students' time and energy and requiring far more than the standards. At the same time, I have begun to worry that some English departments, especially early adopters of acceleration and corequisite models, are starting to drop the bar too low. Some of my colleagues at other institutions are getting rid of the research essay, a staple of first-year writing courses. In some ways, I see the early skeptics' fears realized in these conversations, and I have to admit, my immediate reaction is to recoil in horror. In many ways, the research essay is the embodiment of rigor in composition classes, and setting the bar for it is the equivalent of finding the "right" amount of rigor for transfer-level composition—a level that challenges students and holds community college English instructors accountable for teaching what students need as they move on to a four-year university but that does not reinforce inequities with unnecessary demands lingering from tradition and obsolete remembrances of university classes past. This elusive bar is the one I aim to set.

WHAT IS *RIGOR*, ANYWAY?

Let me begin by saying the horror with which I reacted when I first heard about eliminating research essays has not subsided. With thorough investigation and further contemplation, I am even more certain my initial reaction was correct. Rigor, and its maintenance in the form of the research essay, is as necessary for college composition courses as it ever was.

I realize *rigor* tends to be a bit of a dirty word in academia right now. Those who try to paint the term as obsolete use it to describe an instructor who is overly demanding and unbending, especially in ways unfeeling and unhelpful to students. Some who argue in defense of rigor use it as an excuse to refuse reflexively new andragogy that conflicts with tradition and would require significant disruptions to their classroom. The people clinging to the idea of rigor seem to be using their definition to continue to use outdated practices and ideas. I picture a grammar teacher with a ruler warning students about what lies ahead. I had one colleague in particular who fits this bill. He had a policy that docked points for every grammar error in a paper. He proudly told me as he sat in his office with a stack of papers ready to be butchered, the one in front of him bloodied by the red Vis-a-Vis marker poised in his hand, "After four different errors, I stop reading, and the paper gets a zero. No redos. They have to learn what to expect in the real world." I stared open mouthed and speechless. The overwhelming majority of my colleagues are not even close to this extreme, but to deny these outliers exist would be disingenuous.

Rigidity and rigor are not the same, and the former has no place in education. I sympathize with my colleague because he truly believed he was helping his students as they go on to face bosses with similar policies. Still, in my experience, real-world bosses are happy to get someone who can communicate clearly, and they will not fire someone who has a dangling modifier or a misplaced comma.

As an English teacher, I also know how easily I can fall into a similar trap. Grammar is the easiest part of the paper to grade and therefore (even for me) tends to be the fallback position. I can grade grammar, mechanics, and punctuation quickly and without a lot of effort. I must constantly monitor myself in my second-draft reviews so I don't focus on mechanics and instead concentrate on the often more difficult task of critiquing the organization in the argument or the logical progression of ideas. Those concepts require a great deal more thought and specificity, and sometimes I lose focus on the thirty-ninth paper.

Nor do I identify with colleagues who want to throw out any sense of rigor altogether. As we entered another semester of online learning in fall 2020, a colleague at another college relayed how she was showing her students grace in these unprecedented times: "I eliminated the final paper."

When she saw my look of disbelief, she quickly added, "They do an annotated bibliography, so they are mostly there. I can't expect anyone to work with the world the way it is."

I checked in with her last semester. She hasn't reinstated the assignment.

I can't help but think of all her former students who needed to demonstrate their research, critical thinking, reading, and writing skills in their final papers and how they would react to these current students meeting only a fraction of the standards.

EMBRACING THE (PRODUCTIVE) STRUGGLE

College should be challenging. If students are not challenged, they are not learning. When we remove all obstacles for our students, we don't do them any favors, but the hurdles should be in critical thinking and exposure to new ideas, not unnecessary barriers to their educational pathway (extra hoops in registration or confusing assignment instructions filled with jargon). Struggling with the material is necessary. We shouldn't treat it as part of an infestation we are trying to eliminate; instead, the productive struggle is what we must infuse into our classes, and it should be our goal. The obstacles should be placed intentionally and thoughtfully with the students' best interest as our motivation and a clear outcome as our guide. That is the rigor that must be maintained so our grades mean what we say they mean.

I am inclined to adopt the definition set forth in "The Anatomy of Academic Rigor: The Story of One Institutional Journey": "Academic rigor is illustrated when students are actively learning meaningful content with higher-order thinking at the appropriate level of expectation in a given context" (Draeger et al. 2013, 268). I fully admit that adherence to this definition might result from wishful thinking on my part. I want to describe my own teaching as reaching this level. After all, what teachers don't want to believe they are meeting these criteria? But, I also see this definition as best serving our students by holding our standards high but not jumping over the bar to unrealistic. Unfortunately, the line between rigor and impossible is hard to draw.

SETTING A REALISTIC BUT CHALLENGING MARK

Some argue when we get too close to impossible, we should erase the mark altogether. I don't believe we should discard goals because they are too difficult to meet. Elizabeth Wardle (2009), who writes extensively on the topic of first-year writing courses, claims "teaching students to write in the academy—or the slightly more manageable goal of teaching students about the genres of the academy" are lofty goals, and English professors should "lay such goals to rest" (783). My experience compels me to disagree with Wardle. Though we should always continue to question the central purpose of our courses, dismissing what we find as too challenging to teach seems defeatist and self-serving.

I understand the impossibility of teaching writing for all disciplines. As composition instructors, we can't prepare students for every audience, purpose, and style they will face. I wholeheartedly agree that writing should be taught in each discipline and that, more often than not, our colleagues in other disciplines shirk that responsibility, but I disagree we are best serving our students if we abandon teaching basic writing skills altogether. After all, we are an introductory course.

KEEPING THE BABY, THROWING OUT THE BATH WATER

Instead of throwing away the goal, I propose we focus our efforts on that which is most worthwhile and those skills that will transcend to serve our students in their future classes across the disciplines and their careers. We're going to have to open our eyes to some hard truths about composition classes. What are we really preparing students for? If we aren't preparing them for their other college classes or life after college, then what? Of course, this sober look in the mirror will force us to recognize that some of what we teach will need to be eliminated if that material is not driving our students to be better readers, writers, and critical thinkers.

I speak as someone who has spent too much time on MLA format, the bane of my existence as an English instructor. Yes, format is important, but if the only thing my students remember about writing in ten years is MLA format, I will have failed miserably. And yet, I used to spend an inordinate amount of time teaching the rules to them. I haven't eliminated MLA format from my lesson plans altogether; after all, the students must demonstrate the outcomes of the course, but teaching it takes a back seat to the skills I do want them to remember in ten years: writing to a specific audience with intent, thinking critically, and reading inquisitively.

I refuse to believe those skills do not transfer to other courses. I do think tracing those skills and the impact of their competency in students to other disciplines is incredibly tangled and problematic. That difficulty makes clarifying their focus all the more important. Rigor is maintained when we identify "meaningful content with higher-order thinking"; we can leave the "appropriate level of expectation in a given context" to the professors of other disciplines (Draeger et al. 2013, 268).

RECOGNIZING MEANINGFUL CONTENT

If we are to center our composition courses around meaningful content to maintain rigor, we need to come to a consensus about what that meaningful content is. A group of thinkers believes we should give up on teaching writing in general because the concept does not exist. Wardle (2017) asserts, "Writing is always in particular. . . . thus no single class or workshop or experience can teach people to write once and for all" (30). While I can't agree with Wardle completely because I do think writing is based on a universal set of skills that are teachable, I do think we should cut our curriculum to more manageable pursuits with a focus on research (whatever the new term for research may be), critical and creative thinking, and argumentative writing. Our courses may have to change fundamentally to allow for this transformation, but the recognition that we cannot teach all genres of writing and writing for every situation is necessary and valuable. When we pretend we are meeting the massive goal though we aren't, we fail not only our students who are not getting the education we are promising ("You will use this knowledge as you go forward in academia") but also future colleagues in English who will have to take up this burden, perhaps more as the demands continue to pile up for composition instructors.

When we clarify exactly what we attempt to teach our students, we can transfer the responsibility of more refined writing to the other disciplines. Wardle (2009) wishes to eliminate college composition as a required course in general education, proposing instead that the course focus on writing about writing and abandon any pretext of teaching writing across the disciplines. She believes her plan would allow composition instructors to "finally stop bowing to demands our research suggests can never be met by any one course or any one department." She goes further to conclude that the elimination of first-year composition would also force instructors in other disciplines to "assume more responsibility for the teaching of specialized academic writing themselves rather than relying on the false hope and promise of general skills writing courses" (785). Maybe Wardle's colleagues are entirely different than my own, but in my experience, faculty in other disciplines are not eager to pick up the slack and instead find it easier to eliminate writing from their classes altogether rather than teach writing skills along with content material in an already packed semester. We must take some responsibility in teaching our students to write with a clear conception of audience and purpose and be transparent and repetitious to our colleagues in other disciplines about the limitations of our instruction. Rather than throwing up our hands and bowing out altogether, let's work with our colleagues in anthropology, history, and biology. We can provide a base upon which our students can build, and we can communicate with our colleagues about what they should expect and that they will pick up where we left off. After all, if we can accomplish the task of teaching "basic skills in conducting research or structuring arguments," we are doing our job and shouldn't limit ourselves to "say[ing] that these skills are only specific to academic writing *in general*" (Branson 2017, 20). These are skills students will use that transcend academia.

FOCUSING ON TRANSFERABLE SKILLS

The transferable skills are writing to an audience with a clear purpose, conducting authentic research, and thinking critically in order to incorporate that research into one's own argument. The focus, then, must be on students executing these outcomes and demonstrating their mastery of those skills. These are threshold concepts and are integral to education (hence their inclusion in institution-level outcomes). Our mission then becomes teaching these threshold concepts and what should be the focus of our courses according to Doug Downs and Liane Robertson (2015): "Unlike narrow procedural (how-to) knowledge, which varies from task to task, threshold concepts apply broadly to almost every writing situation. A general education writing course is helped tremendously in its mission of teaching transferable knowledge about a situated activity when threshold concepts are the declarative content taught in the course" (105–6). Unfortunately, we veer from our mission when we become sidetracked and want all students to accomplish the goals at the same time and in the same way. We might even fall into the trap of pretending there is a formula for writing. This temptation is much greater in corequisite composition courses because those students want a formula, and we want to give it to them, a formula for writing that "works" in every situation. Regrettably, when we fall into this trap, we don't make our students better writers. Instead, we get abominations such as the five-paragraph essay.

The formula approach has permeated our culture to the degree that teachers in other disciplines want us to teach it. The five-paragraph essay is what they hold up as an example of good writing. However, as experts in our discipline, we must fight back against this pigeonhole, especially with our most at-risk students, and explain to our colleagues in other disciplines that "the concerns that shape texts are greater than replicating accepted language conventions, and thus composing writing requires more than attention to formal concerns. To write is to invent content, not just to arrange sentences" (Downs and Robertson 2015, 108). When we give in to formulaic thinking (in the way we are all apt to do because, as I enumerate earlier, doing so is easier and less time-consuming), we change our discipline into something it isn't. Putting words into grammatically correct sentences and fitting them into cookie-cutter paragraphs is not good writing, and we should not allow ourselves to be sucked into this illusion. Teaching good writing is a worthwhile endeavor, but doing so takes time and energy. When we allow ourselves to take shortcuts, we further feed this mathematical-equation deception of constructing an essay and further erode the base of knowledge our students take to other courses, undermining our argument that teachers of other disciplines must take students' writing skills and better shape them for the nuances of their area. We don't give them skills to further refine; instead, we offer a calculated recipe that not only does not serve students in their academic career but also fails them more tragically as they step into jobs and situations for which a five-paragraph essay and its ilk are laughable. When we are ensnared in this fantasy, we have exchanged the rigor of a true research essay for the ease of a paper that can be mass produced and replicated, and we continue to perpetuate its myth.

WRITING ABOUT WRITING IS BORING (FOR MOST PEOPLE)

Another argument faculty make is that college composition professors should only teach writing about writing. I disagree here as well. Writing about writing is boring (at least for most students and instructors). If I ask my students to write a paragraph about paragraphs, I get blank, disinterested stares, but if I ask them to write in response to a riveting article that produced lots of controversy in the classroom, I see students jumping right in.

If we are not writing about writing, we must give students something to write about, and if humans are making the choice of theme, we are bound to get flawed, biased, and controversial selections. But we cannot let fear drive us away from what we know to be right or good for our students. We must challenge our students to think critically and ourselves to teach critical thinking. At the same time, I see many colleagues who get off track in their classes in teaching the content they have chosen and forgetting the theme is a vehicle for our ultimate purpose: teaching writing. We can't just pick a topic and then assign readings (not teaching students to read, by the way) and writing (but not actually teaching students to write). Often, instructors think because they covered something or because they've assigned writing, they've taught it. As any experienced composition teacher will tell us, "Students need to be taught how to write rather than merely be tasked with writing" (Barger 2017, 47). I'm going to go ahead and make the ground-breaking assertion that if students haven't learned the skill (regardless of how many times I went over it), I haven't taught it to them.

TRANSFORMING KNOWLEDGE THROUGH THE RESEARCH ESSAY

Often, instructors are sidetracked in their assignments and give students a prompt that asks for knowledge-telling compositions. Even worse is when instructors ask for that knowledge to be the instructor's ideas and personal beliefs parroted back in an essay. In these instances, the papers students tend to write are knowledge-telling papers (in other words, research reports) and are often longer compositions that lend themselves to plagiarism. We must aim for what Julia A. Reynolds, Victor Cai, Julia Choi, Sarah Faller, Meghan Hu, Arthi Kozhumam, Jonathan Schwartzman, and Ananya Vohra (2020) call "knowledge-transforming assignments," or those that "require students to weigh evidence, construct an argument, or critique ideas" (12574).

A knowledge-transforming research essay should be used to assess the student's ability to demonstrate research, critical thinking, and competent writing. This assignment is the bar to set in order to maintain rigor in college composition courses.

The research essay is not simply a synthesis of sources (though that certainly might be some of the initial drafting) nor is it a wholly "original thought" (because, seriously, how unrealistic is that expectation and how much pressure are we unnecessarily burdening a student with when that is the requirement in an introductory course?). Instead, we must reimagine the assignment, not throw it out. We must ask how we can help students create arguments. One way to achieve that goal is to aid them in recognizing the valuable language framework with which they enter our classroom.

VALUING WHAT OUR STUDENTS BRING TO THE COURSE

I teach at a small, rural college in Central California. Porterville and the surrounding community are in a part of the state barren of higher education, with the closest four-year institution being over an hour away. Porterville College is designated by the state as a "Hispanic-serving institution," an understatement if there ever was one, with 81 percent of the student population self-identifying as Hispanic (Kern, n.d.). My students are overwhelmingly first-generation college students, and the vast majority come from generational poverty (Carley 2018). I mention these demographics because these attributes shape students' frameworks, and not only do we meet students where they are, we value where they are by beginning with the language and rhetorical structures they've built up to that point. Rather than jumping into lectures about proper grammar and paragraph construction, we make no assumptions about students' base knowledge; instead, we let students articulate what skills they already have. For example, they regularly research in their daily lives—deciding what phone to buy or what class to take—and that model is a starting point as we lead them to an understanding of what we mean by research in a college classroom. We go from there, wherever "there" is. In serving the students we have (rather than some idealized version of who they should be), and with them in mind as we consciously employ equitable teaching practices, we can concentrate on what the students bring rather than lamenting what they lack.

Some might argue the research essay should be removed because the concepts of research and clarity are raced and classed. I agree it *can be* raced and classed when the academic language required in the research essay is "a raciolinguistic ideology that frames the home language practices of racialized communities as inherently deficient" (Flores 2020, 24). But in my experience, when we approach the home-language practices with respect and inclusion, we are conveying a necessary message that the students are sufficient and are who college is for. We want students to hold onto those practices, as well as learn new ones, in order to have more choices, and therefore more agency, when making an argument,.

Nelson Flores (2020) believes educators should develop "new listening/reading subject positions that recognize the complex linguistic knowledge that their students have developed as part of their lived experience and make this central to the work that they are doing in classrooms" (24). Nelson's work is geared toward K–12 educators, but college instructors can make great gains in student success by recognizing students' knowledge and beginning with it in mind. However, the course must also proceed from there. I worry that when we eliminate academic discourse and spend the entire semester allowing students to only work with the base knowledge with which they entered the course, we are doing them a disservice. We want them to exit with pride and confidence in that base knowledge but also show proficiency in the rhetorical strategies involved in this new framework. We should aim to give students as many tools as we possibly can so they can write more powerfully, more persuasively, and more passionately and have a better chance of achieving their purpose.

I want to make it clear to my students that they belong in college, and I agree with Flores's (2020) three-pronged solution to the previous lack of an entry point in the college system:

> By framing the language practices that racialized communities engage in as legitimate in their own right, by rejecting the assumption that they are dichotomous with the language practices of schooling and by encouraging students from racialized backgrounds to appropriate language practices associated with school-based tasks that may be unfamiliar to them in ways that reflect their unique identities and voices, the language architecture framework offers an important point of entry for resisting the raciolinguistic ideologies that have historically framed and continue to frame their language practices as deficient and in need of remediation. (28)

This three-pronged approach is at the heart of the corequisite courses, and, I argue, what we aspire to do with the research paper.

Flores offers the metaphor of two architects, both hired to design a building. He says that "beyond some broad general parameters both must adhere to in order to successfully complete their tasks," the two architects participate in "a great deal of decision-making that . . . reflect[s] their own unique vision and voice" (25). I agree, but if one of the architects is educated in many different schools of thought and style and the other has been restricted to a single convention, the first architect will have more agency in those decisions. Our goal, then, is to help students discover as many tools as possible, teach them to wield the tools effectively, and allow them to make choices as to when to use the tools, and in what combinations, to have the greatest outcome. Our hope is that by the end of the semester, a student is making choices intentionally and thoughtfully in order to make a strong argument with audience and purpose as the propellers of those decisions.

Though we value the skills and experiences students bring to the course, we must keep our focus on the threshold concepts (reading, writing, and critical thinking) and be careful of letting other factors seep into our assessments. A student's grade usually depends on much more than demonstrating these three outcomes. Instead, students are graded on other elements, such as how the essay is produced. I do think the writing process is important, and I teach it in my composition courses and insist that my students learn it, but ultimately, if a student can produce an acceptable research essay without demonstrating the process to me, they should not be held back because of my own hubristic my-way-or-the-highway mentality. I suspect that, in the same way, if a math student can do a problem in their head and demonstrate they are able to do so without calculators or other aids (in other words, the student isn't cheating), we should not penalize that student for having a mind that works differently than our own. We need to value the product and release our "obsession over the writing process" that has kept us from "a healthy appreciation of finished drafts—of writing itself" (Butts 2017, 110). The writing process is a technique, a good technique, but still, it is one way of going about a complicated task. It is one option, not the only option, and we do our students a disservice when we treat it as such. The outcome is not learning the process. The outcome is the paper, and the process is a solid technique that works for the majority of students in reaching that outcome, but "it's not the only way to approach the writing process, and it doesn't work especially well for some tasks." Unfortunately, "this good option becomes the only option" (Dufour and Ahern-Dodson 2017, 121–22). We teach the process, but we should not be rigid or forget the end goal.

REALIZING THE PURPOSE OF THE COREQUISITE COURSE

Teaching the writing process can be the purpose of the corequisite course. The instructor focuses on the process in the support course (still recognizing the process is one way of writing, not the only way), and the product (the essay itself) can take center stage in the transfer-level composition course. In this way, rigor is maintained (the bar is set at producing a quality research paper), but the students who need support are getting what they need in the scaffolding of the corequisite course.

We return to my central belief about student capacity: students are capable of meeting the mark we set if we support them. My experience with the corequisite composition courses illustrates this. The students who fail my course do so for many external reasons: taking the time to care for a family member, job commitments, illness, or a death in the family. We can't lose sight of this important truth. At the same time, we can't internalize every failure. While we can do much to minimize the impact of these external factors, we certainly can't prevent them or, in most cases, even soften their blow. Life happens. Sometimes life happens, and a student needs to take the course next semester. Or next year. Or next decade. We can only control the educational opportunity, not the result for all students.

COREQUISITE AS THE ZONE OF PROXIMAL DEVELOPMENT

We do not pretend all students come in at the same level—doing so would be absurd! In all our courses, especially the corequisite courses, we must balance the "line between challenge and frustration." We know that introducing support in "elements such as scaffolding, alignment, learning context, and supportive environments can greatly modulate learner frustration" (Wyse and Soneral 2018, 2). That way, students make gains in their educational experience right from the beginning of the semester.

Our job, then, is to offer help to those who need it and wean them off that support as they are able by aiming for each student's zone of proximal development (ZPD). ZPD is the "zone of activity in which a student can achieve with support what they cannot achieve alone or can only achieve with difficulty" (Vygotsky quoted in Bukhari et al. 2021, 5). ZPD is the ultimate goal of scaffolding. We should offer this support in our corequisite courses, keeping the work challenging but not impossible so all students are meeting the same levels of rigor but are getting different degrees of assistance in order to meet the requirements. In K–12 education, this strategy is called *differentiated learning*. This model should be a reality in college composition courses and should be the aim, especially of the corequisite courses. All successful students should demonstrate skills at the same level regardless of whether they took the corequisite or not, but this bar must remain steady and cannot continue to be a moving target.

ENTER THE RESEARCH ESSAY

Suppose we want students to leave our college composition course having learned the skills of research, critical and creative thinking, building an argument, and communicating through writing. In that case, our desired outcome for the course is simple: make a clear, logical, and persuasive argument incorporating research in an essay generally free of errors. Most college composition courses already have a student learning outcome that conveys this general idea. Granted, this outcome is much easier to pinpoint than for a department to agree on what the terms actually mean (How many errors can a paper have and still be generally free of errors? What kinds of errors?), not to mention how difficult these skills are to teach (after all, good teachers work to master their craft their entire career and still never reach a surefire technique for all students), but at least we have a clear goal at the outset. Best of all, we have an assessment method that requires all the skills: the research essay. Now, I must throw in some huge caveats.

Caveat 1: Essay, Not Report
The assignment must call for a research essay, not simply a paper. When we require a research paper, we imply we want the knowledge-telling rote assignment I bemoaned earlier. Instead, we want the student to showcase their own thinking and not simply a regurgitate others' thoughts. Assignments should be knowledge transforming. We must ensure the essays adhere to the definition of academic argument Julie A. Reynolds et al. (2020) put forth requiring that the student "create and share new knowledge . . . the student's position as supported by the evidence that they have synthesized and evaluated." The students have an opportunity in this assignment to "synthesize and make meaning of their prior knowledge, biases, and opinions" (1575). Unfortunately, many English instructors continue to assign the research report out of habit because it is what they know as the traditional assignment in the composition class.

Caveat 2: Rigor Is Not Rigid
While I am adamant that we must maintain rigor, I wholeheartedly dispute the idea that we must stay the same. Rigor does not mean static. We must be open to these changes as long as they do not take away from the demonstration of skills necessary to assess whether students have met the demands of the research essay.

For instance, our outdated notions of page length and word count as measures of rigor might change. After all, in my life, I am more often faced with the difficulty of limiting my words and making a succinct, clear argument in the "real world" than I am expected to draw out my argument in detailed (and usually boring) lengthy prose.

English professors are depicted in pop culture and public opinion as training "students to churn out 20-page academic essays," and students' ability to produce those papers are touted as "examples of intellectual rigor in first-year writing," but we don't have to believe and live up to this stereotype ourselves (Branson 2017, 19). We shouldn't hold to tradition for tradition's sake or to fit the mold of what outside influences want us to be. We must consider our students and what they need, and we must eliminate, or severely limit, the amount of arbitrary instruction in our courses. And to be clear, I do think some instruction is a bit arbitrary—MLA citations are one example, but we can list many more—and I am as guilty as anyone of spending an inordinate amount of time on minutiae of grammar and proper mechanics. Barbara Fister (2011), a college librarian, asks why "composition instructors get to put first year students through the grueling paces of writing about sources they barely understand in a format that few will ever use again after college." But if we are concerned with what will serve our students in a year, five years, ten years, thirty years, then a research paper and the skills writing one entail are anything but arbitrary, though the format may be.

Caveat 3: Creativity and Rigor Are Not Mutually Exclusive

We also should seek out new, creative approaches to imagining the assignment. Like many professors, I have incorporated project-based learning in my composition courses. Students are still required to write the research essay, but they do so in conjunction with an art project that depicts their sources sitting around a table having a conversation, and a piece of creative writing describing the fictional exchange. I believe these opportunities help them envision how the sources speak to each other, and I must admit I am entertained by the fictional account of the Dalai Lama and Gretchen Rubin debating whether or not Epicurus should buy a car. Here, students can put these sources in the cultural context and framework that makes sense to them. If John Stuart Mill is reimagined as a drunk, belligerent uncle in a backyard barbecue in order to make his ideas relevant to a student, not only should we encourage the student to reframe him that way, we should congratulate that student for making connections elusive to those who only have the tool of academic discourse and lack the diversity of frameworks such a reimagining might take. I argue that this short story involves much more critical thinking than would a twelve-page paper on the pros and cons of the death penalty with a couple of disjointed quotations from sources the student didn't actually read thrown in.

The skills are important and need to be preserved no matter what we call the product in the future. The criticisms of the research essay are not unfounded. For instance, Julie Myatt Barger (2017) points out that the research paper assignment often "has no audience other than the teacher, no purpose beyond earning a grade, leaving students with little motivation to locate quality sources and use them thoughtfully" (46). We need not give every essay (or even the research essay) a real-life audience (writing an opinion piece for the local paper, publishing a blog), but we do need to explain to students why they are doing what they are doing and not assume "because I said so" is motivation or reason enough. Giving students an external audience is one way of making the assignment relevant and meaningful, but those feats can also be accomplished with a choice of topic, an infusion of creativity, and/or collaboration with the rest of the class.

Caveat 4: Reimagining Research

Another major change in the assignment must come in the way we teach and how students "do" research. Currently, many instructors construct the research-paper assignment in such a way that students are only confirming their own preresearch argument and are just finding sources to reinforce it. No learning is actually happening. Students aren't thinking and considering an argument from multiple points of view. Actually, doing so would punish the student and put them behind necessary deadlines because real thinking takes time. Instead, we boil down the research paper to pro/con dichotomies, and a plethora of sources and databases cater to this simple-minded rote assignment. Alison C. Witte (2017) correctly labels this method as "information locating and idea confirmation" (229).

We must get away from research as a method of cherry picking quotations from sources students aren't reading to authentic intellectual curiosity filled with twists and turns, wrong ways, and dead ends. The assignment must necessarily shift to one that is "information generating and problem-solving" (Witte 2017, 229). I call this *rabbit-hole research* in my class because I don't want my students to have any idea where they will come out on the other end. They begin with one text, and if they find it interesting, useful, and relevant to their inquiry, they look into the sources used in that text. The process continues until they meet a text that does not fulfill those criteria. Mostly, I want to break students of the false illusion that research is a straight line.

They are not responsible for this illusion; we are. Instead of giving students assignments that lend themselves to this form (I mean, come on, how many of us give our students a prompt that asks them to choose a topic and make an argument before they've done any research at all?), let's help all of our students get to a point where they are mimicking Wernher von Braun, an inventor in the US space program, who says, "[Research is] [w]hat I'm doing when I don't know what I'm doing" (quoted in Wierszewski 2017, 232). Though the concept is paradoxical (to me as well as my students), when they get to the point of being entirely lost and throwing up their hands, I know they are on the right path. We must reiterate to students that "research isn't just for backing up our hunches"; it should "be used as a method of investigating areas of uncertainty, curiosity, conflict, and multiple perspectives" (232). In this manner, we get to authentic research students can use throughout their lifetimes.

We may want research to be less messy because it would be easier to teach, but in the same way we recognize the five-paragraph essay isn't a myth we should perpetuate, we shouldn't present research as if it were a clean, direct process that always takes the same amount of time and as if sources can always be found in simple prepackaged formats: "The messiness of research requires us to be flexible, often modifying our approaches along the way. When we enter the research process with a narrow and rigid focus on our thesis, we can become discouraged and inclined to abandon our ideas when the research process does not unfold neatly" (Wierszewski 2017, 232). In short, we as instructors must admit we don't know how to research everything, and we'll have to get our hands dirty with our students grinding out these new answers in pursuit of authentic research driven by intellectual curiosity.

Our definition of research might (and probably should) change substantially. Some instructors still require certain kinds of sources—books, for example. Do we really expect a student to read an entire book along with the assigned readings? Aren't we setting them up to cherry pick quotations from sources we deem appropriate rather than teaching them to think for themselves about what sources are appropriate for their argument and audience? Many of us roll our eyes at Wikipedia and make a blanket rule that it shouldn't be used in the research essay, but our reasons not to use Wikipedia tend to stop at it's being unreliable or not academic. More important, though, at the end of the day, Wikipedia is still an encyclopedia and, as such, it focuses on factual overviews. But as a college professor, I want my students to do more than read the well-established facts, regardless of where they come from. I want them to read multifaceted perspectives, and, more important, to grapple with the issues.

The problem, then, isn't Wikipedia or the easy access to a firehose of resources; the problem is that we are assigning research papers that allow students to use sources like Wikipedia to complete routine assignments that ask them to do no more than regurgitate information. Instead of putting labels like *legitimate* or *valid* (or even *academically appropriate*, one I use often) on sources before students find them, let's really teach students to make those choices and understand what baggage their sources carry. Teaching students to use tools like the CRAAP test[2] lets them determine how they will support their arguments. If they use Wikipedia and complete the assignment fully, maybe the problem isn't the student. The problem is the assignment. I want my students to have some sources with crazy opinions that are published in the larger world because those

---

2. The CRAAP test is an information evaluation technique developed in the Meriam Library at California State University, Chico. CRAAP is an acronym for the assessment criteria: currency, relevance, authority, accuracy, purpose.

are the kinds of sources my students need to discern in the future. Yes, I want them to question peer-reviewed scholarly articles, but honestly, what kinds of exposure are they likely to have with those sources outside academia? Granted, I want them to be skeptical of anything they read or hear regardless of where they find it, but when we limit their pool to this set of "good" and "acceptable" choices, we are not really giving them the freedom to do authentic research and the kind of critical thinking we hope they'll carry with them beyond the course. Shouldn't we instead let them use nonscholarly sources so they can analyze why the sources aren't scholarly and locate any flaws in logic?

Along the same lines, I don't understand the idea that students must step foot into the school library to get their sources. We have everything our library has (and more) at our fingertips on our phones. So much has changed in ten years, and yet composition instructors are holding onto outdated and arbitrary rules of conducting research: "Long gone are the days when one major function of the research paper was to bring students into contact with libraries" (Lockett 2017, 236). Why are we holding on to vestiges of the past? Instead of clinging to the *how* (research means combing through stacks of books at the library or searching the library databases), shouldn't we focus on the *why* (we want students to learn the skill of research,—discerning which sources are relevant, trustworthy, and useful in forming an argument)?

We must develop new research approaches for the digital age that allow us to embrace the abundance of information and help students create their own "process that blends technological comfort and savvy with academic standards and rigor" (McClure 2011, 239). I confess I am at the nascent stages of building such an approach and am constantly searching for strategies for the future. I can't claim to have the answers, but I don't want to pretend the world isn't changing and that researching the old-fashioned way is better than not researching at all because I'm not sure that is true. Wasting time teaching students outdated research methods is detrimental because we lose our focus on those skills that are important, and what we teach will not serve the students moving forward.

Caveat 5: Grading Thoughtfully and Giving Feedback Intentionally
In the same way we must reconsider the meaning of and the way we teach research, we must think in advance about how we grade research essays. What are the important components? In my mind, the argument, support, and integration of research are the highest priorities. Next, I put

style and organization. Finally, I put conventions and word choice. If I am putting these skills in such a hierarchy, I must practice what I preach. If the majority of the points are for argument, support, and research, a proportional amount of class time should be directed at those endeavors. I also must tailor my comments to what I deem important. When the feedback on a paper is obsessed with grammar or style, but the rubric emphasizes argument, we have a disconnect, and students become frustrated as they concentrate on fixing the mistakes detailed in the feedback but do not see an improvement in their grades. Using a rubric at all stages of writing can help me keep my focus and can aid students in "making dependable judgments on their task-specific strengths and the aspects which they need to revise and improve, resulting in deep learning, better self-regulation, and grade improvement" (Bukhari et al. 2021, 4).

Departments need a shared rubric in order to maintain a sense of norming in what can be a subjective discipline. Such a rubric, if developed and maintained through collaboration, does not infringe on academic freedoms but instead is an instrument of equity providing students with some assurance they will be held to the same level of rigor no matter which instructor they get (and we know the instructor they get is often based on circumstances beyond their own choosing). An English department working together to create a rubric "promotes shared expectations and grading practices" (Bukhari et al. 2021, 4). Though a rubric is not a fix-all for maintaining consistency across all sections of college composition, it is an invaluable tool.

The collaboration on and use of a rubric can also help the department to grade the outcome, not the process. Because the focus in norming is on the product itself (the research essay), instructors are forced to abandon considerations of how the student created the paper, the struggles the student faced in the process, or whether the student took advantage of scaffolding but instead evaluate the writing itself, and thus rigor is maintained.

Caveat 6: Metacognition to Make the Skills Stick

Though metacognition would not factor into the faculty assessment of the research essay, I would be remiss if I did not mention self-assessment as a powerful tool we should include in our composition courses. Metacognitive practices are the strongest tools we have in helping students learn the skills we are teaching and in transferring that knowledge to future courses and situations. Suppose we want to teach so that creative and critical thinking, writing arguments, and researching transcend the one semester we have with students. In that case, we must follow the "one consistent recommendation for doing so," which is "incorporating metacognitive exercises into writing courses." Self-assessment and self-reflection are essential to a "better understanding about how we and others learn in our everyday lives and what types of learning experiences facilitate transfer not just in academic contexts but across all the contexts we inhabit, including—but certainly not limited to—school, home, and work" (Carillo 2017, 36).

If we truly want to provide a foundation for our students, we must include metacognition in our instruction. The foundation doesn't help our students if they don't know it is there. Howard Tinberg (2015) relays why we need this type of reflection in the composition classroom:

> The need for metacognition assumes special importance when writers find themselves required to work in unfamiliar contexts or with forms with which they are unfamiliar. In those cases, metacognition allows writers to assess which skill and knowledge sets apply in these novel situations and which do not. In the end, while cognition remains critical to effective writing, it is metacognition that endows writers with a certain control over their work, regardless of the situation in which they operate. (76)

The skills must be transferable, and students will only be able to apply them if they recognize how they can adapt them in their college classes and beyond.

CONCLUSION

As we model metacognitive practices in our own teaching, we can better adapt to what our students need to attain the necessary skills we teach in the composition classroom. We can be open to future innovations. After all, maintaining rigor does not mean keeping the status quo. I am not the naïve professor I was ten years ago when I began work in acceleration, nor am I still the faculty member who pushes students to the limits of their capacity in order to show the world they are capable. I can't claim to have all the answers as to how we help our students meet these lofty goals, nor can I say with confidence I won't look back on my teaching practices now and shake my head at the seemingly obvious changes I needed to make. As people much smarter than I have recognized, the only constant in the world is change. My hope is that as writing instructors, we can innovate in andragogy, assessment, and procedure and, at the same time, hold steady to the foundations of college composition in maintaining rigor. I realize we've set a high mark, but I am confident we can rise to meet it.

REFERENCES

Barger, Julie Myatt. 2017. "Reading Is Not Essential to Writing Instruction." In *Bad Ideas about Writing*, edited by Cheryl E. Ball and Drew M. Loewe, 44–50. Morgantown: West Virginia University Libraries.

Branson, Tyler. 2017. "First-Year Composition Prepares Students for Academic Writing." In *Bad Ideas about Writing*, edited by Cheryl E. Ball and Drew M. Loewe, 18–23. Morgantown: West Virginia University Libraries.

Bukhari, Nurliyana, Jamilah Jamal, Adibah Ismail, and Jauriyah Shamsuddin. 2021. "Assessment Rubric for Research Report Writing: A Tool for Supervision." *Malaysian Journal of Learning and Instruction* 18 (2): 1–43.

Butts, Jimmy, 2017. "The More Writing Process, the Better." In *Bad Ideas about Writing*, edited by Cheryl E. Ball and Drew M. Loewe, 109–14. Morgantown: West Virginia University Libraries.

Carillo, Ellen C. 2017. "Writing Knowledge Transfers Easily." In *Bad Ideas about Writing*, edited by Cheryl E. Ball and Drew M. Loewe, 34–37. Morgantown: West Virginia University Libraries.

Carley, Michael. 2018. "Poverty in Porterville." Slides presented at Porterville College's "Poverty and Its Effect on Learning," Porterville, CA.

Downs, Doug, and Liane Robertson. 2015. "Threshold Concepts in First-Year Composition." In *Naming What We Know: Threshold Concepts of Writing Studies*, edited by Linda Adler-Kassner and Elizabeth Wardle, 105–21. Logan: Utah State University Press.

Draeger, John, Pixita del Prado Hill, Lisa R. Hunter, and Ronnie Mahler. 2013. "The Anatomy of Academic Rigor: The Story of One Institutional Journey." *Innovations in Higher Education* 38: 267–279.

Dufour, Monique, and Jennifer Ahern-Dodson, 2017. "Good Writers Always Follow My Rules." In *Bad Ideas about Writing*, edited by Cheryl E. Ball and Drew M. Loewe, 121–25. Morgantown,: West Virginia University Libraries.

Fister, Barbara. 2011. "Why the 'Research Paper' Isn't Working." *Inside Higher Ed*, July 5. www.insidehighered.com/blogs/library-babel-fish/why-research-paper-isnt-working.

Flores, Nelson, 2020. "From Academic Language to Language Architecture: Challenging Raciolinguistic Ideologies in Research and Practice." *Theory Into Practice* 59 (1): 22–31.

Kern Community College District. n.d. "KCCD Enrollment Dashboard." *KCCD Institutional Research and Reporting*. Updated August 8, 2022. ir.kccd.edu/data-directory/enrollment/kccd-enrollment-dashboard/index.html.

Lockett, Alexandria. 2017. "The Traditional Research Paper Is Best." In *Bad Ideas about Writing*, edited by Cheryl E. Ball and Drew M. Loewe, 236–41. Morgantown: West Virginia University Libraries.

McClure, Randall, 2011. "Googlepedia: Turning Information Behaviors into Research Skills." In *Writing Spaces: Readings on Writing*, edited by Charles Lowe and Pavel Zemliansky, 221–41. Anderson, SC: Parlor.

Reynolds, Julie A., Victor Cai, Julia Choi, Sarah Faller, Meghan Hu, Arthi Kozhumam, Jonathan Schwartzman, and Ananya Vohra. 2020. "Teaching During a Pandemic: Using High-Impact Writing Assignments to Balance Rigor, Engagement, Flexibility, and Workload." *Academic Practice in Ecology and Evolution* 10 (22): 1573–1580.

Tinberg, Howard. 2015. "Metacognition Is Not Cognition." In *Naming What We Know: Threshold Concepts of Writing Studies*, edited by Linda Adler-Kassner and Elizabeth Wardle, 75–76. Logan: Utah State University Press.

Wardle, Elizabeth. 2009. "'Mutt Genres' and the Goal of FYC: Can We Help Students Write the Genres of the University?" *College Composition and Communication* 60 (4): 765–89.

Wardle, Elizabeth. 2017. "You Can Learn to Write in General." In *Bad Ideas about Writing*, edited by Cheryl E. Ball and Drew M. Loewe, 30–33. Morgantown: West Virginia University Libraries.

Wierszewski, Emily A. 2017. "Research Starts with a Thesis Statement." In *Bad Ideas about Writing*, edited by Cheryl E. Ball and Drew M. Loewe, 231–35. Morgantown: West Virginia University Libraries.

Witte, Alison C. 2017. "Research Starts with Answers." In *Bad Ideas about Writing*, edited by Cheryl E. Ball and Drew M. Loewe, 226–230. Morgantown: West Virginia University Libraries.

Wyse, Sara A., and Paula A. G. Soneral. 2018. " 'Is This Class Hard?' Defining and Analyzing Academic Rigor from a Learner's Perspective." *CBE—Life Sciences Education* 17 (4): 1–14.

PART III

Reading

8
INTEGRATING READING AND WRITING
A Four-Step Process

Peter Adams

The corequisite model of developmental education has been adopted widely and has resulted in significant improvement in student success. Complete College America (2021) reports that "corequisite support works—and it's gaining momentum at institutions across the country." Lexa Logue (2019) writes in the *Chronicle of Higher Education* that "decisions about whether to deliver traditional or corequisite remediation should be based on evidence. The evidence clearly favors corequisite remediation." I have personally worked with more than two hundred schools as they implement such a model. Most corequisite models also include the integration of reading and writing (IRW). Curiously IRW has received much less attention than other innovations like corequisite courses, multiple-measures assessment, and math pathways. This lack of recognition is unfortunate, as integrating reading and writing is both very beneficial for students and very challenging to implement.

In this article I provide a brief history of integrated reading and writing, explain the sources of its difficulty of implementation, and suggest solutions to those difficulties.

The English profession has struggled for several centuries with the question of where reading belongs in our courses and in our scholarship, and the issue is not resolved today. As Nancy Nelson and Robert Calfee (1998) point out, even though most educators know that "literacy includes both reading and writing, that a measure of one is often used as an index of proficiency in the other, that writing is produced to be read . . . historically the two components of literacy have been largely *dis*connected in education in the United States" (1).

The following brief overview of the history of reading in higher education owes much to Ellen Carillo's (2015) important study of this history, *Securing a Place for Reading in Composition*.

In his study of English textbooks, Robert Connors (1996) summarizes the state of writing instruction in the early twentieth century: "Almost every text covered obligatory elements like the levels of composition—word, sentence, paragraph, whole composition—and modes of discourse—narration, description, exposition, argument—as well as minor fields that shifted with the book's emphasis—grammar, punctuation, figures of speech, outlining, proofreading, letter-writing etc." (189). As much as we might disagree today with this pedagogy, it is clear this was a writing course; little or no reading was involved.

Simultaneously, however, a different approach to writing instruction—an approach that placed reading at the center of instruction—was developed by Thomas Lounsbury at Yale University and imitated at many institutions across the country. Lounsbury explained his approach to writing instruction in *Harper's Monthly* in 1911: "To become thoroughly conversant with the work of a great writer, to be influenced by his method of giving utterance to his ideas, to feel profoundly the power and beauty of his style, is worth more than the mastery of all the rhetorical rules that were ever invented" (quoted in Carillo 2015, 51). Here the reading of literature was at the heart of the course.

In the first half of the twentieth century, the combined literature and composition courses gradually drifted apart so that, as James Murphy (1982) explains, "in virtually every department there is a deeply rooted division between those who teach 'reading,' commonly called 'literature,' and those who teach 'writing,' commonly called 'composition' " (4). Carillo argues that "the overwhelming popularity" of New Criticism from 1930 to 1950 "seems to have cemented the idea that attending to reading fell within the domain of literary studies, not composition" (53–54).

While students continued to be asked to read in composition courses throughout the sixties, *instruction* in reading receded into the background, perhaps as a result of two events: the publication of Rudolf Flesch's *Why Johnny Can't Read—And What to Do about It* (1955) and the Dartmouth Seminar of 1966. The Flesch book set off a national discussion of how to improve reading instruction, at first in elementary and high school, but eventually also in college, resulting, in 1967, in the publication of Jeanne Chall's major study of reading instruction, *Learning to Read: The Great Debate*, and the establishment, within the School of Education at Harvard, of a graduate program on instruction in reading led by Chall. As Carillo puts it, "[The school of] education was emerging as the public face of research in reading" (64).

Earlier, in the summer of 1966, at Dartmouth, fifty prominent English instructors from the United States and England met for three weeks to discuss the proper content of English. The Englishman James Britton introduced the idea of teaching the *process* of writing, an idea, still operant today, that came to dominate writing instruction for years, leaving little room for reading.

Despite this emphasis on a process approach to writing instruction and coolness toward the New Critical theories about literature, participants at Dartmouth were more supportive of one particular theory: reader response. With its emphasis on the act of reading, the response of a reader to a text, this theory provided a way to include instruction in reading without turning composition into an introduction to literature course. As Mariolina Salvatori and Patricia Donahue (2012) point out, "What had been so innovative about theories of reading in the 1980s and early 1990s, and their potential for change, was that they shifted the conversation away from *what* to read to *how* to read" (206). Carillo (2015) summarizes more than a decade of evolution in theory about reading: "In the 1980s and early 1990s, textbooks, collections of essays, conferences on the subject of reading (on its own) and on connections between reading and writing were plentiful" (74). Among these were Charles Bazerman's (1980) "A Relationship between Reading and Writing: The Conversation Model," David Bartholomae and Anthony Petrosky's (1986) *Facts, Artifacts, and Counterfacts* and their exceedingly popular textbook, *Ways of Reading* (2002), and Thomas Newkirk's (1986) edited collection of essays *Only Connect: Uniting Reading and Writing*.

It seemed compositionists had finally found an appropriate place in their discipline for instruction and theorizing about reading. But barely a decade later, reading had dropped off the composition radar. Starting in the early nineties, the number of journal articles, the number of conference papers, and even the amount of classroom time devoted to the teaching of reading dropped dramatically. Salvatori and Donahue (2012), after examining CCCC proposals from 1991 to 2007, observe that "it remains puzzling that for seventeen years the word *reading* was completely invisible" (210). Explaining this absence requires considerable speculation. Daniel Keller (2014) suggests that the struggles of writing faculty for legitimacy in English departments and the desire to distance themselves from literary scholarship contributed (29). Carillo (2015) points out that in the discussions of reading, often the verb slides into a noun as scholars argue about what *readings* are useful in first-year composition (81–84). I add to Keller's and Carillo's speculations the frequent tendency of college faculty to view reading as either a remedial topic or one that belongs in high school, certainly inappropriate for a college-level writing course.

So, after more than a decade of flourishing, the teaching of reading simply disappeared from the scholarship and conduct of writing instruction ... from 1991 to the early 2000s. It's difficult to pinpoint when the inclusion of reading in writing courses and scholarship reemerged.

Perhaps it was with the publication in 2002 of Marguerite Helmer's *Intertexts: Reading Pedagogy in Writing*, an edited collection representing a range of theoretical approaches to the teaching of reading.

Or perhaps the rebirth began when Salvatori and Donahue (2004) published *The Elements (and Pleasures) of Difficulty*, which provides important advice for writing teachers trying to teach reading. Salvatori and Donahue suggest focusing on the various difficulties students experience as they tackle challenging readings.

Or perhaps, the impetus for integrating reading and writing came from outside the composition community altogether. In 2008 and for several years thereafter, Thomas Bailey and others at the Community College Research Center (CCRC) at Teachers College, Columbia University, conducted important studies of how effective developmental education, including developmental writing, was at helping students succeed. The news was not good. Based on data from more than 250,000 students in Achieving the Dream schools, Bailey concluded that

> many students who are referred to developmental education never enroll in it. Many who complete one remediation course fail to show up for the next course in the sequence. Overall, fewer than one half of students who are referred to developmental education complete the recommended sequence. What is more, many students who do complete their developmental courses do not go on to enroll in the associated college-level courses. (17)

Based on this study, Bailey suggested a reform and research agenda based on three recommendations, only two of which are germane to this discussion:

> Abandon the dichotomy between developmental and college-ready students for a wide range of students above and below current developmental cutoff scores by opening college-level courses to more students and by incorporating academic support assistance for all students who need it into college-level courses.... [F]or those students whose skills are so weak that they could not be successful even in augmented college-level courses, explicitly work to minimize the time necessary to prepare students for entry into those courses. (18)

The first recommendation has led to corequisite developmental models like ALP. The second—that we minimize the time students spend in developmental courses—has led many schools to integrate their developmental reading and writing courses so students spend less time in developmental reading and writing. These courses typically involve three or four credits, meaning students placed in the lower levels of each could need to take as many as fourteen credits before they are eligible for first-year composition. Integrating the courses cuts the number of developmental credits these students need in half and, as a result, ideally, reduces the student attrition rate.

Much of the impetus for integrating reading and writing came from the desire to reduce the number of developmental credits students had to take before taking credit English, but other factors contributed to the trend. On reflection, many faculty realized separation of reading and writing was illogical. How can a writer revise a piece of writing without reading it? How can a reader annotate a text without writing? Is writing a summary reading or a writing? Is doing research writing or reading?

Whatever the catalyst was, integrating reading and writing has been accomplished widely across the country—sometimes as a result of state mandates but more often as a result of local faculty efforts . . . and that is a welcome first step. In the rest of this article, I want to address the three steps remaining.

Developmental reading and writing at most community colleges and open-admissions universities has, for decades, been taught in two completely separate courses, taught by two separate faculties, often located in two separate departments. The faculty teaching developmental reading, for the most part, have received their preparation in schools of education. The faculty teaching writing have often done their graduate work in literature, not composition. So, the two faculties have very different attitudes and pedagogies.

In addition, at most schools, the English faculty considerably outnumber the reading faculty, which means most of the IRW courses are taught by writing faculty, with very little preparation or experience at teaching reading. Steps must be taken to ensure reading instruction isn't neglected, not because writing faculty don't believe it is needed but because they simply don't know how to do it. So, the second step we must take is to ramp up faculty development in reading instruction.

Faculty development is not strongly supported at most colleges and universities. The assumption seems to be that faculty should have learned how to perform their jobs during their graduate education. The problem is that teaching reading was not expected of composition faculty until recently and so was not part of most faculty's preparation. One obvious way to address this problem is for graduate programs in English to start including the teaching of reading, but that change will take years. In the meantime, it is imperative that English departments who have or who are contemplating the integration of reading and writing develop extensive faculty-development programs for their composition faculty.

This change will require significant effort on the part of faculty, but this effort should also be supported with resources. Our argument is that we are being asked to do something we were not prepared to do in our graduate programs, teaching reading (and also teaching in a corequisite model), so support is more essential than it usually is.

The state organizations—legislatures or boards of higher education—that have mandated these changes should be pressured to provide the support for sorely-needed faculty development. Ironically, according to "Getting There: A Statewide Progress Report on Implementation of AB 705," "A key source of funding for this work—[California's] Basic Skills and Student Outcomes Transformation Program—ended, just as colleges were gearing up for AB 705, and no additional state funding has been earmarked to help colleges make the dramatic shifts the law requires" (Campaign 2019, 24). Texas enacted HB 2223, mandating the gradual adoption of corequisite models, in 2017. When HB 2223 passed, funding was provided for faculty development; unfortunately, the workshops offered primarily addressed the arcane regulations included in the bill, topics like how to calculate the percentage of students enrolled in corequisite courses, descriptions of exemptions, what counts as a corequisite course, how to use Non-Course Competency-Based Options, and rules for English-language learners. Seldom were pedagogical issues included. These examples from California and Texas show state support is possible but that it doesn't come easily.

Grant support is also possible. At the Community College of Baltimore County, our faculty development was supported initially with a grant from the Hewlett Foundation and later a grant from the Kresge Foundation. With that support, we were able to offer what I think of as the "Cadillac" model, a five-day workshop, six hours per day, offered in January and August to twenty faculty each time for a total of five times. Major portions of each workshop were devoted to IRW. Faculty who attended received a stipend of $700.

Even with little or no outside support, departments adopting integrated reading and writing have come up with a creative array of approaches to faculty development. In many cases, the small cohort of reading faculty has conducted much of this training, which includes

- breaking CCBC's thirty-hour model into fifteen two-hour sessions and spreading them out over several semesters;
- holding full-day workshops before classes start in September or January;
- assigning experienced faculty as mentors to new faculty;
- posting collections of materials on a website—sample syllabi, assignments, activities, readings, videos;
- supporting travel to national, regional, and state conferences;
- prioritizing IRW preparation or experience in hiring decisions.

To contribute to the profession's taking this second step, in this next section I have compiled a number of strategies for the teaching of reading, strategies that could be addressed in faculty development. As I have stumbled toward becoming an effective teacher of reading, I have learned much from my reading colleagues at CCBC, from presenters at conferences, and from published scholarship.

In working with composition faculty across the country, I have often encountered the comments of writing faculty about reading teachers: "They just teach phonics or word-attack skills"; "They give their students short paragraphs and ask them merely to underline the main idea. They're not really teaching reading." On the other hand, the reading faculty I've talked with tell me English faculty "think they're 'teaching reading' when they assign a reading and then ask students to write about it or to discuss it in class." Much work is needed to reconcile these misunderstandings of each other's pedagogy. I argue that what is needed for effective integration of reading and writing is to harvest the strengths of the two pedagogies, which will not be as difficult as it might seem because there is more overlap between the two than one might expect.

For example, *reading* scholar Frank Smith (2004) observes that

> reading is the most natural activity in the world. I am not taking liberties with language here. The word "reading" is properly employed for all manner of activities when we endeavor to make sense of circumstances; its original meaning was "interpretation." We read the weather, the state of the tides, people's feelings and intentions, stock market trends, animal tracks, maps, signals, signs, symbols, hands, tea leaves, the law, music, mathematics, minds, body language, between the lines, and above all—a point I must come back to—we read faces. "Reading," when employed to refer to interpretation of a piece of writing, is just a special use of the term. We have been reading—interpreting experience—constantly since birth and we all continue to do so. (2)

Elsewhere, in a definition I love, Smith asserts that "reading might be defined as thought stimulated by a written text" (27).

Students should know about Smith's observations because they lead to a deeper understanding of just what *reading* means. Take Smith's first example—reading the weather. This kind of reading doesn't mean looking up in the sky and recording what you see—a few puffy white clouds overhead but some dark heavy clouds on the western horizon. Reading the weather means looking at the sky and assembling the signs in order to figure out what they mean, what kind of weather to expect. So *reading* a text doesn't mean just deciphering the words; it means assembling those words to actually create meaning.

Ursula LeGuin's analogy (1979) captures Smith's observation beautifully: "As you read a book word by word and page by page, you participate in its creation, just as a cellist playing a Bach suite participates, note by note, in the creation, the coming-to-be, the existence of the music" (127).

David Bartholomae and Anthony Petrosky, describing the reading-writing course at the University of Pittsburgh (Bartholomae and Petrosky 1986), argue, much like Smith, that "a text in our class becomes an occasion for meaning, not a meaning in itself, and the possibilities for meaning in any given text remain open until, as a class, we see what we have done and begin to imagine what else might be done." Bartholomae and Petrosky encapsulate their view of readers concisely: "We choose to represent our student readers as composers rather than decoders" (15). They also identify one of the primary sources of anxiety in student readers: "Our students . . . equate comprehension with sheer memory, and they are haunted by the fact that they cannot remember all that they have read, whether it be a passage or a chapter or a book of 300 pages. And what they do remember, they suspect, is the very stuff they should have forgotten" (17).

Oddly, this same problem—a fear of not being able to remember what you've read—is at the heart of high-school reading teacher Cris Tovani's (2000) book *I Read It, but I Don't Get It: Comprehension Strategies for Adolescent Readers*, in which she tells a story about her own experience with reading. Having spent her entire Christmas vacation reading *Heart of Darkness*, she asks her teacher, "What do you do if you read every page but still have no idea what the book is about?" Tovani's teacher's responded, "Obviously, you weren't concentrating. Reread the book and this time pay attention" (5).

Bartholomae points out that inexperienced readers "have not developed a procedure to make a book available to them once they've read through all the pages. They need to learn, in other words, to create [a] kind of index. They leave their books blank and so a rereading stands only as the act of going back to an empty text" (Bartholomae and Petrosky 1986, 18). One effective procedure for making the text available for a second reading is annotation, which as Bartholomae suggests, can serve as an index when students return to the text.

Often inexperienced readers must resolve two problems in order to annotate effectively. First, they need to find a way around their reluctance to write in their books, a reluctance often left over from high school, where they were warned not to write in their books because they would be recycled to a new class the next year. A little discussion should be able to alleviate this reluctance.

A more significant obstacle occurs when students don't want to write in their books because they need to sell them back at the end of the semester. While a little more cumbersome, writing their marginal comments on "sticky notes" circumvents this problem. You might suggest they use different colors of sticky notes for different types of comments—red for important information, blue for text they don't understand, green when they want to add their own thought to what the author says, yellow to mark where they disagree with the author, and so forth. Increasingly, digital platforms allow annotation in a sidebar and/or highlighting in various colors, which can be used like the colored sticky notes.

This kind of annotating provides a way back into a text when students are rereading to gain a better understanding, or to study for a test, or to find support for an assertion in an essay they are writing. But it has other benefits as well: it encourages active, thoughtful, and engaged reading. It eases the reader into viewing reading as having a conversation with the text, as Bazerman (1980) recommends.

Ann Berthoff (1987) popularized a second method by which students can create a conversation with a text: a double-entry journal. On a sheet of paper or in a word-processing document, the students create two columns. In a digital document, I recommend using the "table" function to create two columns, making it easier to keep the passage and the response to it aligned. In the left column, the students note any passages that catch their attention (with a page number)—passages that are interesting, important, surprising, puzzling, or that engage them for some other reason. In the right-hand column, they write an entry that responds to the passage. They might disagree, provide additional evidence, relate the idea to something else they've read or experienced, or explain the idea in their own language. This double-entry journaling encourages the kind of active reading we want our students to engage in, creates a written conversation with the text, and serves as another kind of index to the text.

Most instructors have had the experience of assigning a text we find quite interesting and coming into class looking forward to a vigorous discussion only to run headlong into silence, into "it was boring," "I couldn't get into it," or "I was confused." In other words, the students had difficulty with the text. Facing such a response, it is all too easy for an instructor to fall back on an all-too-familiar strategy: launching into a lecture to explain how interesting the text is and why. I want to suggest a couple of alternative strategies.

Mariolina Salvatori and Patricia Donahue (2004), in their important text, *The Elements (and Pleasures) of Difficulty*, suggest that, instead of retreating to a lecture,

> it is at [this] point that the teacher needs to perform a new kind of move, by posing a different kind of question: What is confusing? Show us. Where did this text surprise you? What did you expect it to do? Where did it fail to meet your expectations? Where did you stop reading? What might be necessary for you to do to resume your reading? What students say in response to these questions is then used to guide classroom inquiry, as they engage in the work of naming what they know and do not know. (xvii–xviii)

For example, you could ask the students—perhaps individually or perhaps in groups—to make a list of the difficulties they experienced with the text. I sometimes ask them to identify the place in the text where they *first* encountered difficulty. Sharing a selection of these lists in class can lead to interesting outcomes. Students realize they are not alone in having difficulties. They can reflect on what it is about a text they find difficult. Students can look for patterns in the class's lists, as well as outliers that can also be interesting.

As an instructor, I like to look for difficulties that lead to greater insight, clearer understanding of the text. I like to ask students why they think the author included whatever it was that caused them difficulty. Was it a mistake? Was it intentional? Where did the difficulty reside—in the text or in the reader of the text or both?

Finally, by the end of the class, I want to leave my students with an awareness that encountering difficulty in reading is not a sign of their inadequacies as a reader. Difficulty is often a sign of careful, engaged reading.

Salvatori and Donahue (2004) suggest an additional strategy to encourage students to view their difficulties with readings as opportunities to read more effectively and to understand more about their reading processes, a strategy they call "The Difficulty Paper." Students are asked, in conjunction with many of the reading assignments, to write a short paper, half a page to a page, in which they identify a difficulty they had with the reading and analyze the causes of their difficulty. A few of these papers are used to stimulate class discussion as the class as a whole attempts to sharpen the identification of the difficulty and the analysis of its causes.

One last source of difficulty for students often involves encountering words and phrases they are not familiar with. I have, over the years, often asked my students what they do when they encounter such a word or phrase. Several students invariably respond, "I look it up in the dictionary." Not always, but in most cases, it is what they think I want them to do; but ironically it's not. I want them to have a collection of strategies for dealing with difficult language, and looking it up in the dictionary is the strategy of last resort. If a reader must look up a large number of words as they read, they have a much more difficult time with their primary task: constructing a meaning from the text.

Here are five strategies I recommend students try *before* resorting to the dictionary:

1. **Derive the meaning from the context.** In other words, look at the rest of the sentence, and maybe the sentence before and after, and ask yourself if that clarifies the meaning of the term. For example, in the sentence, "She threw some clothes into her portmanteau and ran to the train station," it seems fairly clear, from the context, that a portmanteau is something like a suitcase.

2. **Decide the word is not important.** This strategy is a bit of a gamble. You may be wrong, but if you are and not knowing what the word means causes you difficulty, then you can look it up.

3. **Analyze the parts of the word.** You bump into the word *polysyllabic* while reading one of your textbooks. Dredging up a memory from high-school geometry, you might remember that a polygon has many sides. And the second half sounds a lot like *syllable*, so *polysyllabic* would seem to mean a word with many syllables.

4. **Back up and reread the passage.** Writers often provide clues to technical or other unusual terms before they use them.

5. **Keep reading.** Writers often explain challenging words in the next sentence.

Cognitive scientists have proposed that the only way we can make sense of the world is through our repertoire of schemata (the plural of *schema*). A schema is a representation of patterns or regularities in the world we inhabit. We have schemata for places like restaurants, classrooms, and bathrooms. We know in general how they are laid out and what we will find in them. We also have schemas for events—baseball games, marriage ceremonies, and buying groceries. And we have schemas for texts—how they are organized into paragraphs, pages, and chapters. We expect newspapers to be laid out in sections and columns, novels into chapters, poems into stanzas. Smith (2004) argues that "many experiments have demonstrated that our ability to recognize scenes and to remember them depends on the extent to which they conform to our expectations of what such scenes should be like, to the [schemata] that we already possess" (21).

Kathleen McCormick (1994) provides a dramatic example of how schemata work:

> In other experiments on how schemata affect comprehension and memory, subjects are presented with passages that could "activate" more than one schema. For example, Anderson, Reynolds, Shallert, and Goetz gave students in a music education class and a weightlifting class a passage that began this way:
>
> Tony slowly got up from the mat, planning his escape. He hesitated a moment and thought. Things were not going well. What bothered him most was being held, especially since the charge against him had been weak. He considered his present situation. The lock that held him was strong but he thought he could break it.... He was being ridden unmercifully.... He felt that he was ready to make his move.
>
> The students in the music class assumed that Tony was in jail, whereas the students in the weight-lifting class assumed he was in a wrestling match. The students' different backgrounds led them to "access" different schemata. (20–21).

To make it more likely they will activate the appropriate schemata, students should take a little time to preview a text before diving into it—to take a look at the title, the opening sentences, any headings, the concluding paragraph—so they are aware generally of what the text is about and so the appropriate schemata will be activated.

This process of previewing serves another purpose, as well. It allows readers to prepare themselves to read the text, to predict what it will be like. They can judge how difficult the text seems to be, how long it is, whether it takes a position they agree or disagree with, and whether it was written for an audience something like them.

Two additional strategies faculty teaching reading will find useful are Peter Elbow's "believing and doubting" and John Bean's "What does it say? What does it do?"

Elbow (1973) proposes students be asked to read texts in two ways, believing and doubting. When reading as a believer, students are to adopt the attitude that they agree with the author, they see the world through the author's eyes. As a doubter, they read as an opponent; they question the author's assertions, look for weaknesses in the argument, and think of counter evidence. This strategy can be used for writing assignments, for small-group work, and even as the basis of classroom debate.

Bean (1996) suggests asking students after reading a short portion of a text, perhaps just a paragraph, to answer the question, "What does it say?" After responding to that question, they are next asked a different question, "What does it do?" Both questions invite students to read actively. The second question leads them into an analysis of structure. How does this paragraph fit into the overall structure of the reading? Does it set the context? Does it provide a transition from one topic to the next? Does it explain a complicated term? Does it explain what opponents might say? What is the paragraph "doing" in the essay? (170).

I have found Bean's two questions also to be useful when I'm conferencing with students about their own writing. When I notice a problematic passage, I ask the student to explain to me what the passage says and then what it does. Usually, in the process of answering these questions, the student sees the problem and even thinks of a way to solve it.

Robust faculty development is the greatest need as we move forward with IRW, but there are others. The reading-writing courses we have ended up with are quite different from those described by scholars in the 80s: in most cases, integrated reading and writing takes place only in developmental courses. The integration of reading and writing today, unfortunately, seldom affects first-year composition. There is no reason to assume students in first-year composition classes don't need help to become more sophisticated readers. The third step we must take is to integrate reading and writing in these college-level courses.

Finally, we need more scholarship. You may have noticed that a preponderance of the scholarship I have referred to in this article is more than twenty years old. There is a pressing need for more of today's scholars to address the many questions and challenges presented by integrated reading and writing.

It is remarkable that we have taken the first step toward integrating reading and writing. Now we must ramp up faculty development, extend IRW into first-year composition, and generate an avalanche of new scholarship to make the integration of reading and writing successful.

REFERENCES

Bailey, Thomas. 2008. "Challenge and Opportunity: Rethinking the Role and Function of Developmental Education in Community College." *CCRC Working Paper* 14, Community College Research Center, Teachers College, Columbia University. https://ccrc.tc.columbia.edu/media/k2/attachments/challenge-and-opportunity.pdf.

Bartholomae, David, and Anthony Petrosky. 1986. *Facts, Artifacts, and Counterfacts: Theory and Method for a Reading and Writing Course.* Portsmouth, NH: Boynton Cook.
Bartholomae, David, and Anthony Petrosky. 2002. *Ways of Reading: An Anthology for Writers.* Boston: Bedford/St. Martin's.
Bazerman, Charles. 1980. "A Relationship between Reading and Writing: The Conversational Model." *College English* 41 (6): 656–61.
Bean, John. 1996. *Engaging Ideas: The Professor's Guide to Integrating Writing, Critical Thinking, and Active Learning in the Classroom.* San Francisco: Jossey-Bass.
Berthoff, Ann E. 1987. *The Making of Meaning: Metaphors, Models, and Maxims for Writing Teachers.* Portsmouth, NH: Heineman.
Campaign for College Opportunity and the California Acceleration Project. 2019. "Getting There II: A Statewide Progress Report on Implementation of AB 705." https://collegecampaign.org/publication/getting-there-ii-a-statewide-progress-report-on-implementation-of-ab-705.
Carillo, Ellen C. 2015. *Securing a Place for Reading in Composition.* Logan: Utah State University Press.
Chall, Jeanne. 1967. *Learning to Read: The Great Debate.* New York: McGraw-Hill.
Complete College America. 2021. *No Room for Doubt: Moving Corequisite Support from Idea to Imperative.* https://completecollege.org/wp-content/uploads/2021/04/CCA_NoRoomForDoubt_CorequisiteSupport.pdf.
Connors, Robert J. 1996. "Textbooks and the Evolution of the Discipline." *College Composition and Communication* 37 (2): 178–94.
Elbow, Peter. 1973. *Writing without Teachers.* Oxford: Oxford University Press.
Flesch, Rudolf. 1955. *Why Johnny Can't Read—And What You Can Do about It.* New York: Harper.
Helmer, Marguerite. 2002. *Intertexts: Reading Pedagogy in Writing.* New York: Routledge.
Keller, Daniel. 2014. *Chasing Literacy: Reading and Writing in an Age of Acceleration.* Logan: Utah State University Press.
LeGuin, Ursula. 1979. *The Language of the Night.* New York: Putnam.
Logue, Lexa. 2019. "Evidence Clearly Favors Corequisite Remediation." *Chronicle of Higher Education*, December 19. https://www.chronicle.com/blogs/letters/evidence-clearly-favors-corequisite-remediation/.
McCormick, Kathleen. 1994. *The Culture of Reading and the Teaching of English.* Manchester: Manchester University Press.
Murphy, James. 1982. "Rhetorical History as a Guide to the Salvation of American Reading and Writing: A Plea for Curricular Courage." In *The Rhetorical Tradition and Modern Writing*, edited by James Murphy, 3–12. New York: MLA.
Nelson, Nancy. 1998. "The Reading-Writing Connection Viewed Historically." In *The Reading-Writing Connection*, edited by Nancy Nelson and Robert C. Calfee, 1–52. Chicago: University of Chicago Press.
Newkirk, Thomas. 1986. *Only Connect: Uniting Reading and Writing.* Portsmouth, NH: Boynton/Cook.
Salvatori, Mariolina Rizzi, and Patricia Donahue. 2004. *The Elements (and Pleasures) of Difficulty.* New York: Longman.
Salvatori, Mariolina Rizzi, and Patricia Donahue. 2012. "Stories about Reading: Appearance, Disappearance, Morphing, and Revival." *College English* 75 (2): 199–217. www.jstor.org/stable/24238139.
Smith, Frank. 2004. *Understanding Reading.* Mahwah, NJ: Lawrence Erlbaum.
Tovani, Cris. 2000. *I Read It but I Don't Get It.* Portland, ME: Stenhouse.

9
TEA WITH A FRIEND
Teaching Challenging Reading in the Corequisite Classroom

Jami Blaauw-Hara

Writing teachers know good writers are often good readers. In her survey of scholarship on reading and writing, Cheryl Hogue Smith (2012) notes that the academic consensus is that "college students' ability to write is limited by their ability to read" (60). Though the fix would seem to be assigning more reading, it is not that simple. Faculty report teaching "around" texts, with lectures and slide presentations, to protect students from difficult readings or avoid awkward classroom discussions when no one has read the assignment. This workaround generally comes from a place of empathy rather than poor teaching skills. As W. Norton Grubb and Robert Gabriner (2013) note, "Out of concern for students and the busy conditions of their lives, many basic skills instructors place very few demands on [students]" (51). Corequisite writing courses can seem challenging enough to developmental students.

Much scholarship in reading and writing focuses on how teaching writing or reading in isolation is less authentic and less relevant for students than teaching them together (Bickerstaff and Rauffman 2017). However, reading and writing instruction are often separated in the college curriculum. The practice of teaching reading and writing in isolation in part grew from siloed developmental programs disconnected from the rest of the college curriculum. This system felt as if it would attend to the many needs of developmental students with care, but in the early 2000s, research found the extra courses were slowing students down and creating barriers to success in college (Bailey, Jeong, and Cho 2010). Corequisite models have allowed us to keep students on track to achieve college-level success with the extra support they need. This revision of developmental education improved college success rates (Community College 2021), but we must recognize the continued and important role of reading instruction in our corequisite writing classrooms.

Teachers of corequisite courses who care about reading can find it challenging to choose the right texts—manageable for students yet engaging. Dense, academic texts can seem too difficult to comprehend for students in the developmental section while perhaps being just right for college-level writers. These choices are more complicated without a clear set of strategies for mentoring students in college-level reading skills. As Linda Adler-Kassner and Heidi Estrem (2007) note, the attention devoted to writing processes should also be afforded to reading. *Deep Reading*, edited by Patrick Sullivan, Howard Tinberg, and Sheridan Blau (2017), is part of a recent return to teaching reading in composition classrooms, and this resurgence in thinking about reading was recently encouraged by the Conference on College Composition and Communication in its statement on the importance of teaching reading in the writing classroom issued in 2021. The statement provides recommendations that focus on reading as a skill requiring purposeful, reflective instruction. After some background on reading in composition classes, I discuss four levels of reading depth that invite students to grow in confidence and capability. The levels are inspired by the metaphor of the Burkean parlor (Burke 1973). While the original metaphor focuses on rhetors engaging in a debate, I am enacting a feminist reimagining in which the engagement is less confrontational and more supportive and participatory. As readers come into the parlor, they need to feel comfortable before they can enter into the conversation. As established academics, we enter the Burkean parlor knowing the rules and as friends. Our students need support to understand the rules of academic reading and writing before they participate.

First, we enter the room through basic comprehension skills, which can be difficult when the reading is challenging. Second, we take a seat in the room, signaling we are comfortable with the reading and ready to go beyond basic comprehension into some of the subtler points. Third, we have a cup of tea and reflect on our experience in the reading through metacognition, engaging with what we still do not understand. And, finally, we take note of the conversation and prepare for participation by examining the superstructures of the reading experience. Through a scaffolded model like this, students can access deeper levels of reading comprehension and begin to participate in academic conversations as they progress through a corequisite writing course.

SOME CONTEXT

Developmental education was in crisis at the beginning of this century. Students placed into developmental courses, especially those at two-year colleges, were failing at astounding rates, and this failure led to them dropping out and not realizing the promise of higher education (Community College 2021). As a developmental instructor who deeply cared about the lives of my students, I felt wary of a developmental model that separated the complicated tasks of academic writing into simple sentences and paragraphs. In the early 2000s, I attended a conference session on integrated reading and writing in accelerated writing courses, and I saw how developmental education could be as rich and complex as the students in my classes (Stahl 2017). This model reinvigorated my developmental classes, and I was reminded of the messages of empowerment and hopefulness from scholars I had read from the late 1970s and early 1980s like Mike Rose (1980), Sondra Perl (1979), and Janet Emig (1977). Those early scholars reminded us writing is a skill that takes time and is aided, through thoughtful intervention, by instructors who have insight into its complexity. Integrated reading and writing models were a helpful reminder of the nature of reading and writing, the fact that we read as we write and rewrite as we read.

Later, at a conference in Baltimore in 2012, a colleague and I discovered the corequisite model, which we brought back to our small, rural community college as a pilot. With departmental and administrative support, the corequisite model became our standard developmental sequence. As we experienced success with the corequisite model, we integrated threshold concepts and a writing-about-writing (WAW) curriculum, specifically using Elizabeth Wardle and Doug Downs's (2020) text *Writing about Writing*. One unexpected challenge with integrating this curriculum was instructor pushback about the difficult readings. While many researchers argue we should treat developmental writers academically like transfer-level students and provide challenging reading (Barhoum 2017; McCracken and Ortiz 2013; Stahl 2017), others worry that developmental students will feel overwhelmed by the difficulty of WAW readings and that such readings are inappropriate for students who are not studying rhetoric and composition (Miles et al. 2008). I have found over and over that students rise to the challenge as long as I can tolerate their initial discomfort and provide support for their growing reading skills. One of the founding ideas of a WAW curriculum is the importance of fostering high-road transfer by supporting the development of a general theory of writing instead of teaching specific genre strategies. As Ellen Carillo (2014) argues, the broader context of WAW can apply to reading as well. When students understand how to read "mindfully," they may be better prepared "to read in a range of contexts" (119) and thus be better prepared for future literacy activities in their chosen field.

Still, we struggled for buy-in with WAW strategies and readings from some faculty at our college. Spurred on by the controversy about WAW and its challenges, some colleagues and I studied the efficacy of a WAW approach. We found that developmental writers do really well with the WAW curriculum in a corequisite model and that, specifically, the skills and strategies they use to understand the readings give them confidence as both students and writers (Blaauw-Hara et al. 2020). We found that their reading comprehension grew and they developed self-efficacy. Self-efficacy theory, which was pioneered by Albert Bandura (1977), deals with a person's expectation of success and how it affects actual success. Developmental students in corequisite courses tend to have poor confidence because of past challenges. When we interviewed our students about their feelings concerning challenging reading after a WAW approach (Blaauw-Hara et al. 2020), they told us how confident they were about college in general. One of the students we interviewed noted that his approach to future courses would be to "go in and tackle the class" (64). Another student said, "Before, I just didn't care and I would give plain basic answers and now I go into depth and explain things" (64). It's clear that learning to read difficult texts improves students' confidence. Our students expected to do well in the future instead of fearing challenges.

In addition to using integrated reading and writing strategies, a WAW approach, and a corequisite model, my reading pedagogy has been influenced by Reading Apprenticeship, a model for teaching reading through WestEd, which follows Lev Vygotsky's work on social mediation in learning: apprentice readers (students) learn from skilled readers (instructors and other students) through metacognitive conversations about the reading. Vygotsky's work also connects to the corequisite model and its zones of proximal development. In Reading Apprenticeship, just as in corequisite courses, learners of varying skill are placed together, and some teach others as they learn together. The assumption is that reading is a complex process for which proficiency varies based on the situation and the experiences of the reader (Schoenbach, Greenleaf, and Murphy 2012) This model is useful because it helps correct any assumptions that reading instruction is a K–12 project that involves learning to decode text. In fact, reading is complex and varied; proficient readers share key characteristics like persistence and strategic monitoring of the reading process (Schoenbach et al. 2012). Although Reading Apprenticeship (2023) offers little new in terms of scholarship on reading, it does bring together many proven strategies that can assist reading instruction in the writing classroom.

So far in this chapter, I have been treating reading as a stable idea, an activity with a known function and purpose, but such stability is only true for the act of decoding text. How we process decoded text and how we use it is incredibly variable and weighted with expectations for the role of reading in different disciplines (Ihara and Del Principe 2018). Many disciplines and instructors at our institutions promote reading as just another way to acquire class content. In corequisite classrooms, our focus on reading is analytical, often asking readers to challenge texts and learn from them, both in terms of structure and the exchange of ideas within texts. If the goal was only to acquire knowledge, simple comprehension would suffice, but understanding structures and maintaining self-awareness of comprehension as we read is vital to learning to construct our own texts. We need models to help us guide students beyond simple comprehension.

The metaphor of the Burkean parlor is one students find compelling, and it aligns with the ways reading skills allow access to academic conversations. The new rhetor is quiet upon entering the parlor not just to understand what has been said but also to read the timbre of the conversation and the moves and mores of its members. New readers in academic conversations benefit from someone whispering some context to them, giving them a cup of tea, and helping them feel comfortable and welcome before diving into the conversation. This is the role of the instructor of corequisite courses. We are in the parlor and welcome our students warmly, provide them with a little context, get them a cup of tea, and help them feel comfortable before they feel ready to join in. The metaphor reminds me of the warmth with which I must approach challenges for students because I truly want them to enter academic conversations with skill.

ENTERING THE ROOM

When we talk about comprehension, we're not talking about decoding texts or learning new words. As noted by Ruth Schoenbach, Cynthia Greenleaf, and Lynn Murphy (2012), few students in college need assistance with decoding texts. Most developmental and college-level students, however, require help with comprehension, unfamiliar vocabulary, and engagement with the ideas in the text. Upon entering the "room" of a text, students need to understand what is going on and be able to orient themselves within that space. Academic texts, while comfortable to many instructors, are initially inscrutable to novice academic readers. Additionally, faculty in jobs that do not require them to stay current with scholarship, as is the case for many two-year college instructors, can be reluctant to assist students with understanding academic texts they long ago stopped reading. There is reluctance on the part of both the student and the marginalized faculty. Academic texts require some orientation to begin the process of comprehension.

Think-aloud protocols were staples of early composition research and are a standard model for improving basic comprehension in the reading-apprenticeship model. As the name suggests, readers say aloud what they are thinking as they read. This protocol is modeled by the instructor and then practiced by students in small groups or pairs. Ideally, this modeling should be the authentic problem-solving responses of the reader approaching a text. When using a WAW approach, this protocol isn't difficult to model in an authentic way, as the texts are fairly challenging. However, if the instructor is comfortable with the text, modeling is more of an approximation of the kinds of reasoning one might use to understand a particular text. For instance, when I model think-aloud protocols with a common and popular first-year composition (FYC) text like "Shitty First Drafts" by Anne Lamott (1994), which addresses the importance of writing bad first drafts, I am remembering my thoughts in my first reading and positing questions and observations I might have had. When I model with a reading like James Paul Gee's (1989) "Literacy, Discourse, and Linguistics," which introduces the idea of discourse as an identity kit, I am authentic in my reaction to the challenges of unpacking the article's dense sentences and embedded concepts. Think-aloud protocols help students understand that texts are challenging for good reason. Such texts have complicated ideas that relate to other complicated ideas. All readers, even skilled ones, must slow down when the writing is most dense and then speed up in other sections.

In practice, think-aloud protocols involve sharing metacognitive thoughts for short passages of a text, focusing especially on the challenging parts. Instructors can project sections on a white board and use a pen to highlight, question, and mark up a text just as if it were in front of them on a desk. Then, instructors ask students what strategies they noticed the instructor using to understand the text, including slowing down, rereading, making connections to other texts, predicting, and so forth. Afterwards, students can practice the same strategies with each other in pairs or small groups. I do this extensively at the beginning of a course, and I continue to model my thinking as I read, especially when we read texts that are different from our normal reading or with sections that are particularly challenging or important to our work. Allowing students to preread before doing think-aloud protocols in pairs can be helpful to alleviate self-consciousness.

In addition to think-aloud protocols, basic comprehension is aided by composing reading journals, another practice from Reading Apprenticeship. The format of these journals can change for different readings and situations. At the simplest, reading journals serve to keep readers aware of their cognitions about the text, in terms of both exciting or interesting elements and places where the text drags or where readers lose interest or become confused. The standard format is basically a double-entry notebook in which the left column is a summary or quote from the section of the text the readers finds themselves in, and the right side is used for reflection, questions, struggles, and so forth. In this way, the reader is tracking key moments in the reading experience, from questions to breakthroughs. I ask students to submit these logs before class and use excerpts to begin conversation about the reading. I also have students use them to start conversations with one another. Sometimes I ask students to focus their entries on confusing sections or to make connections to the current writing project. At the beginning of a course, reading logs focus on noticing elements of the reading and then shift in specificity as students become more confident with the academic readings. Later in the course, they concentrate on struggles in the text, and then students begin to start solving their reading problems themselves, which leads to deeper understanding.

Reading journals and think-aloud protocols communicate to students that every reader has strategies to aid comprehension, no matter how skilled the reader. When journals are graded, they convey that the texts must be finished before the class period, and they put reading conversations at the center of the classroom experience.

SITTING DOWN

Once students have entered the parlor, instructors can create experiences to help them delve into textual complexities. Patrick Sullivan (2017) writes at length about "deep reading," and this orientation similarly encourages students to contemplate the troublesome implications of a text (Meyer and Land 2006). As Sullivan writes, "Deep reading pedagogy . . . is most essentially designed to provide opportunities for students to engage in metacognitive thinking about the process of learning, and to help students assess and reassess their own mental models for understanding the world" (147). When texts have sufficient depth, there is room for far-reaching learning and reflection on resonant questions about writing and language. The key is to frame the reading expansively so students have the freedom to examine how the text might connect to experiences beyond what is happening in the classroom and the specific paper or project currently underway.

Though the reading journals of the previous section help readers home in on locations in the text and connect to the conversation in their minds at that time, a strategy to move beyond basic comprehension is what Mariolina Salvatori and Patricia Donahue (2005) call a "difficulty paper." Students write a half to a full page on what made a reading particularly challenging, foregrounding the struggles of reading and yet working to understand in spite of the challenge. Often, these papers open a window into liminal concepts or new vocabulary students benefit from. These papers encourage students to move beyond the surface-level strategies for avoiding reading that Sullivan (2017) notes, like reading tactically just to complete whatever assignment is due. Salvatori and Donahue (2005) further suggest that instructors choose a couple of insightful difficulty papers to make available to the class so the class can discuss not only student readers' struggles but the elements of the text that make it particularly demanding. Students find it challenging to articulate what it is about a reading that makes it difficult, but this assignment helps readers turn challenges into insights, especially when done in a warmly established community of practice. I use difficulty papers with readings students historically struggle with, like James Porter's (1986) "Intertextuality and the Discourse Community."

Another strategy to encourage reading that goes beyond the surface is the triple-entry notebook, a strategy borrowed in one form from Ann E. Berthoff and modified by Salvatori and Donahue. Students may be familiar with double-entry notebooks, in which the left side is used to record what the reader notices and the right side records the reader's reflections at that point in the text. The reading journals Reading Apprenticeship uses, and which I detail in the previous section, are an example of that kind of process. Triple-entry notebooks add a third column in which readers extend their learning to other contexts, raising the level of abstraction. These journals are helpful when the reading I have assigned is specifically chosen to help students with a paper they are working on. The third column can be used to find connections from the reading to the drafts they are currently working on or to help them focus on textual features I want them to notice. This process connects readers to their current writing project and then allows deeper connection to the text they are reading.

Deeper reading helps writing because students begin to understand how texts make meaning known by understanding how it can be concealed from some readers. They see strategies for making writing both more transparent and more obscure, even if this understanding is still liminal for students. They also begin to create deeper meaning through rhetorical reading strategies a superficial reading might avoid. This is the deep listening required in the Burkean parlor to truly understand before participation.

HAVING A CUP OF TEA

I've written this chapter with countless cups of tea in my hand, and I often pick up a cup and sip when I'm stuck in my writing. Stopping to think, reflecting on where I am and where I want to go, prepares me to move forward with purpose. The same is true for metacognition in reading. It's a moment to stop, reflect on what's been gained, and consider what still needs integration. Many strategies I suggest already use metacognitive elements, as they are vital for high-road transfer (Perkins and Salomon 1988). This section explores metacognition in greater depth.

While reading journals can address basic comprehension, they are also useful for understanding deeper structures within the text, notably increasing metalinguistic awareness. Miriam Moore (2021) studied metacognitive journals in two sections of FYC that followed a WAW syllabus. When students were asked to respond to focus-on-language questions, she found they were able to show the beginning of skilled awareness of language structures, with an emphasis on lexical structures. However, Moore notes that even students who spend most of their time on content comments in journals are also using syntactical cues to scan, skim, and preview texts before and during reading. What they may lack is an awareness that they are using those structures. The focus-on-language prompts specifically ask students to zoom in on particular paragraphs and identify power sentences or structures that convey a lot of meaning. While more than 80 percent of these journals initially focus on content, they eventually open up to syntactical structure, lexis, and genre. Journal prompts help students focus on the writer's stance and engagement with the audience and on significant paragraphs and sentences. Such prompts encourage readers to see beyond their superficial reading experience and increase their metalinguistic awareness. I ask students to use their journals to identify power sentences and paragraphs, especially when their writing assignment asks them to perform more challenging activities like rhetorical analysis or primary research. It's important to understand key sections of text that do significant work like setting up the research question or identifying exigency.

In her chapter on mindful reading, Ellen Carillo (2014) argues that we also should help students use metalinguistic awareness to identify when a particular reading strategy has ceased to work and when a new one is required. An awareness of the ways texts shift from simpler, organizational transitions to dense explanations of concepts is important for flexible reading, something most experienced academic readers already know. Reading naturally speeds up and slows down, even within the same text. According to Carillo, "Reading knowledge is less likely to transfer from one context to the next unless students are constructing this knowledge within a metacognitive framework that fosters generalization" (124). Strategic metacognition is generalizable and prepares students for reading in other contexts because they are accustomed to monitoring their comprehension and developing multiple strategies to respond to reading. Carillo also recommends a passage-based paper, which asks students to choose a short passage of three to five sentences and then "unpack" the passage, considering its "language, tone, and construction" (133). In addition to asking students to complete a short paper, Carillo asks them to reflect on how they fulfilled the requirements of the assignment, as well as comment on the difficulties of the assignment. Metacognition tied to deeper analysis of texts helps readers understand which strategies work for them and to what effect. It moves them past a simple comprehension of the content for a summary or a quiz. I use passage-based papers when we have shifted to a new essay assignment and the reading provides an example of what I want students to do. I have them focus on key transitions or rhetorical moves specific to the genre we are working on.

LISTENING IN AND FINDING WAYS TO ENGAGE

Awareness, through metacognition, leads to interest. When we understand how to adapt and move within a text to make meaning, we are able to examine some elements more closely, focusing in, growing curious. When we have had our tea, we are comfortable and can look around and make connections, noticing small details not apparent at first glance. We can make plans to join the conversation. Metacognition reflects on the reader's understanding of the text, but a deeper awareness of structure and patterns in a text can be encouraged by asking students to focus on specific sections or elements of a text. In a parts-to-whole approach to developmental education, readers start with the identification of parts of speech or simply read a paragraph. One of the problems with this approach is that focusing on parts limits how deeply a student may comprehend a text. Students never surprise themselves because they are never given access to the entire piece of writing or are led to believe it's bad to move ahead (Grubb and Gabriner 2013). Examining the structures and patterns of texts encourages us to open up to broader academic conversations.

The CCCC statement on reading focuses its final recommendations on textual structures, but I argue it is also important, given complex comprehension and metacognition, to consider textual superstructures. In other words, what do we bring to readings through the contexts in which we read and our beliefs about text and ourselves? As Adler-Kassner and Estrem (2007) argue, "Good reading involves at least an awareness that iterating with and interpreting text is not neutral in that it is always 'sponsored'" (38). The idea of sponsorship comes from Deborah Brandt's (1998) argument that literacy is sponsored by agents who wish to take advantage of the skill. Once we understand the basic concepts of a text, we become aware that our reading is bounded by, sponsored by, and invested in certain systems, values, and beliefs.

According to Paulo Freire and Loretta Slover (1983), "Reading is not exhausted merely by decoding the written word or written language, but rather anticipated by and extending into knowledge of the world" (5). Reading is an application of our worldview onto a text. We bring our world to the reading, and we take our reading out into the world. It's important for students to see that, even if we never speak or write in the parlor, we are changed by what has occurred in it. As Freire and Slover further note, "Reading the world always precedes reading the word, and reading the word implies continually reading the world" (10). A shift from viewing reading as transactional for information to viewing it as transformational for the world is emancipatory for our students, especially if they have felt like outsiders in academic conversations.

Asao Inoue (2020) offers an antiracist approach to reading because "to read is to make judgments about language" (135), and racism is essentially a judgment. Inoue argues that in order to engage in antiracist reading, we must understand where our judgments about language come from. He argues that understanding comes from "a practice of reading words and pausing to pose questions about the reader's relation to their material situation, their reality, and conceiving of those conditions as structures and systems, which are both outside and inside them" (140). This view is consistent with the metaphor we've been developing in this chapter. One enters a text, sits down, thinks reflectively, and notices details before joining the conversation. This last noticing includes understanding the structures and systems that drive our reading of texts and how structural bias complicates this process.

Two clear practices suggested by Inoue (2020) bear mention. The first is based on contemplative traditions: the reader notices an emotional reaction to a reading, pauses for at least ten seconds, takes three breaths, locates sensation in the body, and then asks, "What habits of judgment and language am I using to make that meaning? How would I describe them and their affordances and limitations? . . . Where did I get those habits in my life? What other habits might reasonably be applied here?" (145). This reflection is then brought to small groups and the larger classroom to understand our habits of language and judgment as we read. I use this strategy with readings like Vershawn Young's "Should Writers Use They Own English?" (2010) because students often have strong reactions to it that reveal a lot about their expectations of language and experiences with standardization.

The second practice Inoue advocates for comes from Bob Broad (2003): dynamic criteria mapping (DCM). Though this practice is used for mapping the values of a particular writing program, it can also be used to focus on what we value in reading. In DCM, faculty map the textual qualities and features they consider in judging a text. The map is a community-based conversation about textual assumptions and readings, an analysis of all the features that drive a community's overall assessment of a text. Students begin with their reflections on readings and then instructors help them map the resulting judgments. This map can be as simple as creating a word cloud of key terms students used to describe the reading. If it is deemed too dense but also full of good ideas, the community can be aware of this judgment and its implications. This approach helps develop a picture of "the diverse values a community of readers really has when they read and judge texts together" (Inoue 2020, 138). This process is helpful after a few readings have been completed and students are getting better at comprehension but may be trapped in a groupthink about the difficulty of the readings. I often see that difficult texts also yield some of the most interesting ideas. When criteria mapping is used periodically throughout the semester, we can examine how our community of readers is changing and growing over time.

Awareness of the community's reading practices is crucial to make clear that reading is performance (Adler-Kassner and Estrem 2007). Readers take on roles, engage in socially bounded situations, and articulate perspectives that seem consonant with the needs of the instructor and the performance of critical, academic reading as they see it. While performing these roles, we also learn about new ideas, participate in engaging conversations, and challenge previously held ideas. Academic texts require a knowledge of the social system in which the text resides before readers can reach the ideas embedded within. The writing classroom is an ideal place to help students enact the disciplinarity of reading difficult texts.

CONCLUSION

The expectations for teachers of developmental courses are tremendous; we are burdened with the constraints of our institutions and buoyed by our hopes for the students' futures. Faculty teach developmental students because they have an investment in the most marginalized students and perhaps even know the power of developmental education for themselves. It's challenging to place another expectation on corequisite courses, yet the benefits of mindfully incorporating challenging reading with supportive classroom strategies is exciting. The conversations in my classrooms are richer and more purposeful. My students have grown more confident; their self-efficacy has improved. In addition, I am able to understand these rich, theoretical texts better through teaching them in conversation with my students. A return to reading is a return to engagement in big ideas and theoretical conundrums rather than teaching bits and pieces in order to get the students through the course. I choose to walk with them into the Burkean parlor, serve them some tea, and help them join the ongoing conversation that will continue into the night.

REFERENCES

Adler-Kassner, Linda, and Heidi Estrem. 2007. "Reading Practices in the Writing Classroom." *WPA: Writing Program Administration* 31 (1/2): 35–47.

Bailey, Thomas, Dong Wook Jeong, and Sung-Woo Cho. 2010. "Referral, Enrollment, and Completion in Developmental Education Sequences in Community College." Community College Research Center, Teachers College. Columbia University, NY. https://ccrc.tc.columbia.edu/publications/referral-enrollment-completion-developmental-education.html.

Bandura, Albert. 1977. "Self-Efficacy: Toward a Unifying Theory of Behavioral Change." *Psychological Review* 84 (2): 191–215.

Barhoum, Sim. 2017. "Community College Developmental Writing Programs Most Promising Practices: What the Research Tells Educators." *Community College Journal of Research and Practice* 41 (12): 791–808.

Bickerstaff, Susan, and Julia Raufman. 2017. "From 'Additive' to 'Integrative': Experiences of Faculty Teaching Developmental Integrated Reading and Writing Courses." Community College Research Center, Teachers College, Columbia University, NY. https:

//ccrc.tc.columbia.edu/publications/faculty-experiences-teaching-developmental-reading-writing.html.
Blaauw-Hara, Mark, Carrie Strand Tebeau, Dominic Borowiak, and Jami Blaauw-Hara. 2020. "Is a Writing-about-Writing Approach Appropriate for Community College Developmental Writers in a Corequisite Class?" *Composition Studies* 48 (2): 54–73.
Brandt, Deborah. 1998. "Sponsors of Literacy." *College Composition and Communication* 49 (2): 165–85.
Broad, Bob. 2003. *What We Really Value: Beyond Rubrics in Teaching and Assessing Writing*. Logan: Utah State University Press.
Burke, Kenneth. 1973. *The Philosophy of Literary Form: Studies in Symbolic Action*. 3rd ed. Oakland: University of California Press.
Carillo, Ellen. 2014. *Securing a Place for Reading in Composition: The Importance of Teaching for Transfer*. Logan: Utah State University Press.
Community College Research Center. 2021. *Developmental Education Policy Fact Sheet*. https://ccrc.tc.columbia.edu/media/k2/attachments/developmental-education-fact-sheet.pdf.
Conference on College Composition and Communication. 2021. "CCCC Position Station on the Role of Reading in College Writing Classrooms." March. https://cccc.ncte.org/cccc/the-role-of-reading.
Emig, Janet. 1977. Writing as a Mode of Learning. *College Composition and Communication* 28 (2): 122–28. https://doi.org/10.2307/356095.
Freire, Paulo, and Loretta Slover. 1983. "The Importance of the Act of Reading." *Journal of Education* 165 (1): 5–11.
Gee, James. 1989. "Literacy, Discourse, and Linguistics: Introduction." *Journal of Education* 171 (1): 5–17.
Grubb, W. Norton, and Robert Gabriner. 2013. *Basic Skills Education in Community Colleges: Inside and Outside of Classrooms*. Oxfordshire: Routledge. https://doi.org/10.4324/9780203094297.
Hogue Smith, Cheryl. 2012. "Interrogating Texts: From Deferent to Efferent and Aesthetic Reading Practices." *Journal of Basic Writing* 31 (1): 59–79.
Ihara, Rachel, and Ann Del Principe. 2018. "What We Mean When We Talk about Reading: Rethinking the Purposes and Contexts of College Reading." *Across the Disciplines* 15 (2): 1–15. https://doi.org/10.37514/ATD-J.2018.15.2.06.
Inoue, Asao B. 2020. "Teaching Antiracist Reading." *Journal of College Reading and Learning* 50 (3): 134–56.
Lamott, Anne. 1994. *Bird by Bird: Some Instructions on Writing and Life*. New York: Anchor Books.
McCracken, I. Moriah, and Valerie Ortiz. 2013. "Latino/a Student (Efficacy) Expectations: Reacting and Adjusting to a Writing-about-Writing Curriculum Change at a Hispanic Serving Institution." *Composition Forum* 27. http://composition-forum.com/issue/27/.
Meyer, Erik, and Ray Land. 2006. *Overcoming Barriers to Student Understanding: Threshold Concepts and Troublesome Knowledge*. New York: Routledge.
Miles, Libby, Michael Pennell, Kim Hensley Owens, Jeremiah Dyehouse, Helen O'Grady, Nedra Reynolds, Robert Schwegler, and Linda Shamoon. 2008. "Commenting on Douglas Downs and Elizabeth Wardle's 'Teaching about Writing, Righting Misconceptions.'" *College Composition and Communication* 59 (3): 503–11.
Moore, Miriam. 2021. "Grammatical Concepts and Metalinguistic Awareness in First-year College Writers: A Study of Reading Journals." *Journal of College Reading and Learning* 51 (3): 178–202.
Perkins, David, and Gavriel Salomon. 1988. "Teaching for Transfer." *Educational Leadership* 46 (1): 22–32.
Perl, Sondra. 1979. "The Composing Processes of Unskilled College Writers." *Research in the Teaching of English* 13 (4): 317–36.

Porter, James. 1986. "Intertextuality and the Discourse Community." *Rhetoric Review* 5 (1): 34–37.

Reading Apprenticeship. 2023. https://readingapprenticeship.org/.

Rose, Mike. 1980. "Rigid Rules, Inflexible Plans, and the Stifling of Language: A Cognitivist Analysis of Writer's Block." *College Composition and Communication* 31 (4): 389–401.

Salvatori, Mariolina, and Patricia Donahue. 2005. *The Elements (and Pleasures) of Difficulty.* New York: Pearson.

Schoenbach, Ruth, Cynthia Greenleaf, and Lynn Murphy. 2012. *Reading for Understanding: How Reading Apprenticeship Improves Disciplinary Learning in Secondary and College Classrooms.* San Francisco: Jossey-Bass.

Stahl, Norman. 2017. "Integrating Reading and Writing Instruction in an Accelerated Curriculum: An interview with Katie Hern." *Journal of Developmental Education* 40 (3): 24–38.

Sullivan, Patrick. 2017. "'Deep Reading' as a Threshold Concept in Composition Studies." In *Deep Reading: Teaching Reading in the Writing Classroom*, edited by Patrick Sullivan, Howard Tinberg, and Sheridan Blau, 143–71. Urbana, IL: NCTE.

Sullivan, Patrick, Howard Tinberg, and Sheridan Blau. 2017. *Deep Reading: Teaching Reading in the Writing Classroom.* Urbana, IL: NCTE.

Wardle, Elizabeth, and Doug Downs. 2020. *Writing about Writing.* 4th ed. Boston: Bedford St. Martin's.

Young, Vershawn. 2010. "Should Writers Use They Own English?" *Iowa Journal of Cultural Studies* 12 (1): 110–18.

10
MORE THAN BUSYWORK
Journals as a Method of Success in First-Year Composition and Corequisite Courses

Gregory Ramírez

INTRODUCTION

The separation of reading and writing courses at the remedial level baffled me for many years. Such a split did not occur when I was teaching English A—a course one level below first-year composition (FYC)—as a graduate student at California State University, Fresno (CSUF). Even before majoring in English, my beginning nonfiction professor proclaimed to the class, "If you want to write, you have to read." As a result, requiring students to pass separate reading and writing courses made as much sense as requiring them to pass separate addition and subtraction courses for remedial mathematics.

My attendance at California Acceleration Project (CAP) events in 2015 affirmed my skepticism, as I learned how traditional remediation hindered throughput and student success, especially for students of color. This information was personally noteworthy. According to the Strategic Plan for Madera Community College (MCC)—where I have taught English full time since 2008—66 percent of the student population in the fall 2020 semester identified as Hispanic/Latinx (Madera Community College, n.d., 11). I also discovered how CAP leaders espoused reading apprenticeship to refine student reading skills in lieu of additional courses. The passage of California Assembly Bill 705 two years later "would require a community college district or college to maximize the probability that the student will enter and complete transfer-level coursework in English . . . within a one-year timeframe" (Seymour-Campbell 2017, 1). When coupled with the advocacy of corequisites over courses below FYC, it is fair to say AB 705 eradicated developmental reading.

Nevertheless, it is imperative that we FYC instructors do not abandon efforts to improve students' reading skills, especially when teaching

https://doi.org/10.7330/9781646424788.c010

corequisites. As Michael Bunn (2013) writes, "Teaching reading in terms of its connections to writing can motivate students to read and increase the likelihood that they find success in both activities" (512). If puzzlement persists on how to structure corequisite courses, focusing on students' reading skills provides the answers.

The most productive method is to include journal entries as low-stakes assignments and to provide comments of affirmation, as opposed to assessing them for accuracy of reading comprehension. To ensure the journals are more than busywork, it is essential to alter the format among the journals. This flexibility allows the instructor to address various features of writing as the course progresses. Limited scholarship exists on the application of journal assignments in corequisite courses specifically; however, this article explores how reading journals refines both reading and writing skills, especially among students of color.

THE READING-WRITING CONNECTION

MCC began offering sections of ENGL 205—the two-unit corequisite to ENGL 1A—in the fall 2018 semester. This change followed the discontinuation of Accuplacer—which determined the levels of English and mathematics for incoming students—in favor of multiple-measures placement, in which counselors referred to high-school transcripts. Wayne Au (2009) writes that "the weight of the high-stakes testing environment falls heaviest on the shoulders of low income students and students of color who are disproportionately affected by high-stakes, standardized testing" (3). Combined, the corequisite offerings and multiple measures were paramount in MCC's work towards equity.

With course titles such as Reading and Composition for ENGL 1A and Strategic Skills for Success in English for ENGL 205, the connection of reading and writing in FYC courses at MCC, along with the supportive nature of the two-unit corequisite, became evident. But their respective Course Outlines of Record (CORs) elaborate on what the course titles establish. For example, towards the end of the course objectives on the ENGL 1A COR are the words, "Read and understand college-level prose," whereas the ENGL 205 COR states, "Further utilize appropriate pre and post reading strategies to analyze patterns of organization within a variety of texts."

Among the student learning outcomes (SLOs) found on the ENGL 1A COR, the following is listed: "Summarize and comprehend college-level prose (will include a full reading)." This language not only reiterates the foundational nature of FYC but also corroborates Edward

Behrman's (2006) assertion that "reading and writing are not merely communicative acts but part of the habits, customs, and behaviors that shape social relations" (497). It is therefore critical for instructors to use the corequisite course to supplement the efforts of improving students' reading skills.

The exact number of journals each instructor assigns, along with the number of points each journal is worth, is up to that instructor. Two other aspects of instructional agency are how often to assign journals and whether students complete a journal for each reading assignment. During an eighteen-week semester, I have assigned as many as seventeen journals and seldom assign more than two per week. It is also recommended that the total amount of points for the journals does not exceed the combined total for rough drafts and student responses to rough drafts. This way, the drafting process, the reflection on drafts, and the reflection on reading assignments are prioritized in the corequisite course.

Regardless, marking each journal as Complete or Incomplete is important to maintain its low-stakes nature. Some instructors categorize journals as homework, and as Joe Feldman (2019) asserts,

> homework is the space for students to make mistakes, and if mistakes are necessary for learning, then to grade homework based on whether the answers are correct sends contradictory messages. When we award homework points based on how correct students' answers are, we simultaneously tell them that mistakes during practice are to be avoided and that mistakes during practice are to be desired. We can't deduct points for incorrect answers on homework—which penalizes students for mistakes—and at the same time tell students that homework is just practice and that mistakes are a necessary part of learning! When we do, it's no wonder that we confuse students about what learning is and make it much easier for them to measure success simply by point totals. (129)

But more is needed than simply marking a journal as Complete or Incomplete in order for it to be considered low stakes. Instructors should not overwhelm students with journals as complex as out-of-class essays nor should instructors structure all journals the same so students consider them rote. Creating journals that are only one or two pages each conveys to students that brevity and importance can coexist. When an instructor teaches the corequisite face to face—which I have not been able to do since the COVID-19 pandemic began—hard copies of the journals can be distributed to students.

An online instructor, however, is by no means at a disadvantage, as students may either submit Word documents or scanned copies of handwritten journals. (Accepting smartphone pictures of handwritten journals is an easy way to solve any problems with submissions in the event that students lack access to a scanner.) Despite the technical details of handout length and file types, instructors and students alike will appreciate the commitment towards simplifying assignments.

FORMATTING

To ensure journals do not become repetitive, varying the format is a necessity. This is not to say no two journals can be alike; however, the instructor should provide a feature (e.g., an example, a passage, a list of characters or individuals) so each journal is *at least* distinct. Providing two constants—which I address later—will promote inquiry. The various formats on which I elaborate include *dialectical (or double-entry) journals; character map; summary, paraphrase, citation; metacognitive bookmark;* and *features of essays.*

Dialectical (or Double-Entry) Journals

Arguably the format with which I am most familiar both as a student and as an instructor, dialectical journals only require two side-by-side columns: the left one for a passage from the text, the right one for the reader's response. If the instructor wants, students can simply write down the page and/or paragraph number for the passage instead of writing the passage verbatim. Because the right column is for the reader's responses, there is no right or wrong answer so long as the response is on topic and related to the text. Students can share how much they enjoy the stylistic delivery of the passage, how they agree or disagree with the claim and/or support given, how the passage confuses them (i.e., any questions they have), or how the passage reminds them of a personal experience or of another reading assignment. Robert Eaglestone (2009) articulates it best when he writes, "Reading a text, interpreting a text, is not an activity that has a right or wrong answer. It is not like making a bet" (84).

At the very least, the dialectical journal conveys a writer-reader dynamic FYC instructors hope to demonstrate to students. Louise Rosenblatt (1982) points out how "reading is a transaction, a two-way process, involving a reader and a text at a particular time under particular circumstances. . . . The words in their particular pattern stir up elements of memory, activate areas of consciousness. The reader, bringing past experience of language and of the world to the task, sets up tentative notions of a subject, of some framework into which to fit the ideas as the words unfurl" (268). By juxtaposing significant passages and student responses, both instructors and students can reflect on the power of the written word.

In the two sample dialectical journals below, we see *variation within variations* in which the former assists students with filling in the blank columns on their own, whereas the latter gives the option to select one of three passages from the text, with students writing their own responses.

Example 1 of Dialectical Journal

Name:_____ Due: Sunday, August 22

Journal for Pico Iyer's "The Nowhere Man"
In the boxes provided on both sides of this handout, use the left column to write word-for-word a passage (*at least* one full sentence but **no longer than** one paragraph) from the text that catches your attention. (For this reading assignment, you may write down either the page number on the PDF or the paragraph number.)

In the right column, specify why that passage catches your attention. (This can range from—but is not limited to—how you like the wording, something you agree or disagree with, possible confusion. However, avoid simply rewording what the passage says.)

An example has been provided below.

Passage	*Response*
"While I was growing up, I was never within 6,000 miles of the nearest relative—and came, therefore, to learn how to define relations in non-familial ways" (¶ 1).	This sounds like it would have been difficult. Then again, he probably didn't know any different. It also sounds as though Iyer adapted to something that differed from a traditional living arrangement.
Passage	*Response*
Passage	*Response*

Example 2 of Dialectical Journal

Name:_____ Due: Sunday, August 22

Journal for Scott Russell Sanders's "Staying Put"
Circle one passage from the list below and write your response to that passage in the box provided.

    A. "In our national mythology, the worst fate is to be trapped on a farm, in a village, in some dead-end job or unglamorous marriage or played-out game. Stand still, we are warned, and you die" (¶ 1).

    B. "But who would pretend that a history of migration has immunized the United States against bigotry? And even if, by uprooting ourselves, we shed our chauvinism, is that all we lose?" (¶ 2).

C. "People who root themselves in places are likelier to know and care for those places than people who root themselves in ideas" (¶ 4).

Response

Such formats are applied early on so students may grow accustomed to the dialectical format and to journals overall. Either way, the main goal is for students to engage as readers with the text. As Carol Olson (2011) states, "The dialectical journal can be an excellent way for students to access all of the cognitive strategies in their tool kit—tapping prior knowledge, asking questions, making predictions, making connections, revising meaning, evaluating, and so forth" (131).

Character Map

The next type of journal assignment can entail differing formats, depending on what the instructor wishes the students to accomplish. Essentially, the use of a character map is best applied when students need to keep track of numerous characters or individuals. Initially designed for works of fiction, character maps can also work for nonfiction. Like the dialectical journal, there is an open-ended aspect to what the students may write for each character or individual, as it is up to the student to decide what distinguishes each one from the others.

An additional technique worth noting is having students jot down significant page numbers. These can relate to when a character or an individual first appears in a text, a key detail about that character or individual, or the relationship to someone else on the character map.

A character map, along with noting page numbers, can assist students with future texts, particularly book-length ones. I encourage students to use the extra pages found at the beginning and the end of a book to make notes and to write down the characters' names. This gives students a reference, whether it be while reading the text itself or in composing an out-of-class essay, regardless of the course. Students may be aware of highlighting, but it can be daunting to skim through hundreds of pages to find a passage they have highlighted or circled. Having specific page numbers on the front and back sheets of the book aids the task, particularly if they are locating passages for the purpose of summary, paraphrase, or citation.

Summary, Paraphrase, Citation

One skill we FYC instructors want our students to refine is the use of parenthetical documentation for supportive purposes within out-of-class essays. What better way to give students practice with this skill than to offer them a journal that has them summarize, paraphrase, and cite a reading assignment? Providing either a box or a space for all three truly takes advantage of the low-stakes nature of the journal assignment. The refinement eventually translates to the out-of-class essays.

One word of caution: students have confused citation for an entry that appears on a Works Cited or bibliography page. Therefore, instructors should provide examples or detailed instructions. Additionally, instructors must be explicit if they want students to work with signal phrases such as "Morrison writes," "Márquez argues," or "Soyinka points out." Examples should ensure that most (if not all) students will do more than simply write a passage word for word encased in quotations.

Metacognitive Bookmark

I was first introduced to the Reading Apprenticeship's metacognitive bookmark (Schoenbach, Greenleaf, and Murphy 2012, 106) while attending the California Acceleration Project's Community of Practice in 2015. In recent years, I have made copies of it on cardstock and distributed them to my face-to-face students. I have also provided a PDF file so they may make copies on their own.

In the case of journal assignments, I have created spaces for the seven headings along with the two to three phrases that accompany each. In the instructions, students are told to circle one of the phrases in each section and to complete the sentence as they are reading through the text. Students therefore are doing more than simply using a bookmark for the purpose of a bookmark; they are engaging with the text in a manner that encourages engagement through think-aloud protocols such as predicting, picturing, questioning, summarizing, and identifying a problem (Schoenbach, Greenleaf, and Murphy 2012, 106).

Features of Essays

The final format worth focusing on applies to FYC instructors who use rubrics. Those elements of the essay that will be graded are listed in one column of the handout. (Whether there are multiple boxes similar to what we have for dialectical journals is entirely up to the instructor's discretion.) Then, the student selects a passage from the text that demonstrates that particular feature.

For example, one box may be titled "Organization" and have among its features the word *transitions*. In order for students to apply their knowledge of effective transitions in an essay, they locate an example from the reading assignment. Not only are they able to locate examples from the reading assignment, but they will also be able to interpret the scoring and comments on a rubric for an out-of-class essay. The connection between their reading and writing assignments thus becomes clearer.

Two Constants

Although not a format per se, two suggested constants for every journal are boxes or spaces dedicated to Vocabulary and Additional Comments/Questions. Including these terms helps students to be mindful of words or phrases with which they are unfamiliar and to keep track of certain aspects of the reading assignments. These boxes can help students see what they are learning as the course advances throughout the semester.

Nothing is inserted in the boxes or spaces by the instructor, showing that there are no prescribed words or phrases the students are expected to learn. The lack of judgment from the instructor comforts the students in their intellectual growth. These boxes also allow for two possibilities. The first is a dialogue among the students; in a face-to-face setting, students can compare their words and questions while engaging in group dialogue prior to whole-class discussion. The second is a dialogue between the student and the instructor; when the assignment is being graded, the instructor can use the opportunity to answer any questions the student may have.

Whichever format they use, instructors ought to resist the idea of grammatical correction. As stated earlier, the journal assignment is low stakes; practice and mistakes should be allowed. Doing so works towards countering what Asao Inoue (2015) calls "judgments of student writing that use a local Standardized Edited American English (SEAE) with populations of people who do not use that discourse on a daily basis" (6). Randy Bomer (2011) adds, "When teachers say that a student lacks language, what they really reveal is that they have not yet found a way to engage this other human being in communication, that the differences between teacher and student have not yet been bridged in the teacher's imagination, and that the teacher is predisposed to thinking all of this distance and misunderstanding is the fault of the kid. That is deficit thinking" (23).

At its core, a journal is intended for students to strengthen their comprehension of a specific reading assignment. Grammatical errors or even misinterpretation should have no bearing on the journal's grade whatsoever. This approach can also serve as practice for instructors when assessing of out-of-class essays. As Lucy Spence (2010) explains, "Generous reading offers a structure to think about students as people in the process of developing their own views of the world. Classroom teachers can benefit from this as an alternative to traditional assessment and gain a new perspective on how their students appropriate the words of others as they construct their personal identities" (640). When the assignment is marked as Complete or Incomplete, grading the journal traditionally is unnecessary and does not add to an instructor's work load.

BENEFITS

When journals are assigned in the corequisite courses, FYC students see advantages they are traditionally unaware of in the absence of journals. Before teaching corequisite courses myself, I discontinued journals because I concluded they were no more than busywork. However, journal assignments are most appropriate for the corequisite, which serves the purpose of furthering the students' skills. The low-stakes nature of journal assignments gives them several advantages.

At the very least, the journal assignments—when delivered in one of the formats aforementioned—promote active reading. Journals ensure that students see reading as something more dialogic than simply watching a movie or a video on social media. Instead of passively consuming information, they are writing down words and phrases and details somewhere so they can remember what they read after they finish reading.

Another benefit students experience with journals is that they encourage metacognition. Given the purpose of the two-unit corequisite in relation to the four-unit FYC course, the role of metacognition could not be more suitable, particularly when the format mirrors the metacognitive bookmark. If we can get our students to focus more on their processes with reading, they can apply those processes to their own writing. As Sandra Stotsky (1983) affirms, "Correlational studies show almost consistently that better writers tend to be better readers (of their own writing as well as of other reading material), that better writers tend to read more than poorer writers, and that better readers tend to produce more syntactically mature writing than poorer readers" (636).

The third benefit students experience is that journals provide practice for essential composition skills. As they do when completing the summary-paraphrase-citation and the features-of-essays assignments, students can strengthen their skills for using outside sources and better interpret the feedback they receive on rubrics. Being able to identify with the writer of the reading assignment can bring about empathy, as well as appreciation for the writing process. According to Maryanne Wolf (2018), "Reading at the deepest levels may provide one part of the antidote to the noted trend away from empathy. But make no mistake: empathy is not solely about being compassionate toward others; its importance goes further. For it is also about a more in-depth understanding of the Other, an essential skill in a world of increasing connectedness among divergent cultures."

Sugi Goen and Helen Gillotte-Tropp (2003) point out the parallel between the writing and reading processes: "Journals help students understand that we 'draft' a first reading and revise or elaborate on it in subsequent readings, just as we do in writing. We want our students to learn that readers construct the meaning of texts they read by degrees in the same way writers gradually construct meaning in the texts they write" (99–100). This construction of meaning "by degrees" aligns with applying a growth mindset in the FYC classroom and suggests how even professional writers must revise their work. Students can have a firsthand experience and realize effective writing is not a state of nirvana but rather a discipline requiring effort.

But the benefits of journals are not confined to the solitary spaces produced by reading and writing. When students bring completed journals to a face-to-face class meeting, the journals can serve as springboards for class discussion. Students arrive prepared with their insights and questions for the group and whole-class discussions, where comprehension of a text is often refined. Oftentimes, the formatting of the journals translates into activities for face-to-face courses. There are several occasions on which I have asked students to write dialectical journals on either the whiteboard or on flip boards. This approach can also work for character maps and for summary-paraphrase-citation exercises. FYC instructors can use whichever of these formats they want for the whiteboard, a flip board, or even a smart panel to foster class discussion and student engagement. Granted, the discussions themselves would most likely occur in the FYC course to avoid time constraints. But having students work with any one of the formats serves as a segue from small-group to whole-class discussions and extends the possibility of the whole-class discussion beyond the traditional lecture format.

An online instructor is by no means out of luck compared to a face-to-face instructor. If the instructor holds Zoom meetings, the use of Google Docs in breakout rooms easily accommodates journal work. Instructors who teach asynchronous online courses can also provide a Google Docs link for students in either a small-group or a whole-class discussion forum. Video recordings of the instructor, including anonymous responses from submitted journals, are yet another way for asynchronous online courses to mirror the engagement of face-to-face courses.

During a unit and even throughout the semester, journal assignments can also nurture student appreciation for the selected texts. As mentioned with dialectical journals, students may identify a connection between (or among) reading assignments. This kind of connection aligns with Angela Goddard and Neil Carey's (2017) claim that "texts do not exist in isolation, but form networks or relationships with other texts" (22). Such a skill will serve the students in FYC and throughout their college career, as they will recognize concepts and ideas various writers—who may be contemporaries or from different eras—affirm and debate.

One key benefit to journal assignments is that they eventually serve as a reference for students while they are composing out-of-class essays. Instead of scrambling through notes (assuming students take them), the students can refer to the handout they were given, they printed out, or they saved on their devices. Students can direct more attention towards composing itself, managing their time more effectively. By having the journal assignments on hand, the students are further empowered in the writing process.

STUDENT PERSPECTIVES

Toward the end of the semester, as either a one- to two-page reflection or as part of the final exam, students in the ENGL 205 share their thoughts about the corequisite courses. They either give advice to future students or reflect on how taking the corequisite is better than traditional remediation. Students often comment positively on the journal assignments as part of the course.

Chris—whose name, like the other students', has been changed—was among the first students at MCC to enroll in ENGL 1A and ENGL 205. He wrote, "The journals in this class really developed on what to look out for in the book and to keen in on specific things so that we knew what we would talk about in the next class meeting, rather than just have the book assigned and being left in the dark as what to look for and truly look into." Journals allowed Chris to be prepared as he anticipated class discussion in the ENGL 1A section.

His classmate Amanda took the class along with her mother. At the time they took the course, students were able to earn one extra credit point if they turned in their journals at the beginning of the ENGL 1A class meeting. They could earn a total of fifteen of the twenty-five possible extra credit points if they were to do this for every journal assignment. As a result, Amanda made the following comments: "The journals will become helpful tools that you will use in order to complete timed writings. Keep this in mind when you fill them out it is best to put some actual thought into them. Manage your time wisely and submit those journals early if possible, because an extra point might not seem like much in the beginning, but it definitely adds up. Trust me, every point will count."

Veronica was my student during fall 2020, the first full semester during the lockdown: "I agreed to take English 205 along with English 1A because I need additional help on this class. It was helpful to do the journal's that came along with the reading assignment given by the professor. I liked that it collaborated with the topic of the essay which usually followed. It gave us a better understand on the assignment and the vocabulary section gave me time to find out the definitions to the words that I did not know. I am a student that needs to re-read a chapter to have a better understanding but with the additional assignments in this class it helped me to remember what the chapter was about." In this response, we see a student whose comprehension improved, whose vocabulary expanded, and whose recall increased. Veronica is undoubtedly a clear example of who the journals were designed for.

Tara, a student from the fall 2021 semester, gave her thoughts as part of the final reflection for the course (prior to the final assignments). An immigrant from El Salvador, Tara opens her reflection by saying that she moved to the United States when she was twenty-one years old and that English is her second language. Although she does not mention journals explicitly, Tara writes in her final paragraph, "In my opinion, I think it is good to take these two classes together because one class helps the other to understand it better. They are two classes that complement each other very well and give more information and help to students. It also avoids us taking another semester, which can help us take other classes, and move faster in our process of reaching our goals." As one can see, Tara articulates the purpose of corequisite courses: to improve the chances for student success and to streamline the time it takes for students to attain their academic goals.

CONCLUSION

Like the fast pass we have grown accustomed to seeing at amusement parks in recent years, corequisites allow all students to have the same educational experience as traditionally defined "college-level" first-semester students, but without the hurdles community colleges have traditionally placed in front of them in the form of below-transfer courses. Peter Elbow (2011) addresses the futility of traditional remediation—especially for English as a second language (ESL) students—with these words:

> "We could . . . restrict our *regular* one semester first year writing class to those students who don't need instruction in conventions of usage or copy-editing, and put the others in remedial or basic classes devoted to those matters. But if we take that path, we tend to focus the basic course on 'error' and send just the wrong message to students who are least skilled at [Standard Written English]: 'If you want to learn to write, you must first concentrate most of your attention on grammar and correctness. Only after you master surface features do you get to concentrate your attention wholeheartedly on the substance of your thinking.' Also, segregation on the basis of surface features of language can result in segregation on the basis of race and class. I am not arguing against all basic writing courses, but I am troubled by how they often function" (648–49).

When these concerns are addressed with corequisites, there is no extra money to be paid by the students, simply extra professional development and a reassessment of traditional methods on the part of instructors. If the goal of FYC instructors is in fact to improve equity and success among our student population, then corequisites are the route toward achieving what we have wanted for our students for many years.

Journals may seem like a simple solution for improving the efficacy of corequisites, but they are perfect for the job. Reading journals serve to partially mitigate the discontinuation of developmental reading courses. As an English instructor at a community college with a predominantly Hispanic/Latinx student population, I can affirm that obstacles to direct enrollment in FYC, successful completion of FYC, and persistence beyond FYC must be removed. But by no means should academic rigor be sacrificed. An FYC instructor can still assign complex texts as reading assignments as long as the proper supports are in place, which includes well-structured journal assignments.

It would be difficult (if not, impossible) for anyone who has attained a college degree and even sought one at the graduate level to argue against the importance of reading and writing. Likewise, the roles of reading and writing in any career requiring a college degree cannot be ignored. Reading and writing are inseparable, and journals are a simple yet effective method to ensure students refine their skills.

REFERENCES

Au, Wayne. 2009. *Unequal by Design: High-Stakes Testing and the Standardization of Inequality.* New York: Routledge.

Behrman, Edward H. 2006. "Teaching About Language, Power, and Text: A Review of Classroom Practices That Support Critical Literacy." *Journal of Adolescent and Adult Literacy* 49 (6): 490–98.

Bomer, Randy. 2011. *Building Adolescent Literacy in Today's English Classrooms.* Portsmouth, NH: Heinemann.

Bunn, Michael. 2013. "Motivation and Connection: Teaching Reading (and Writing) in the Composition Classroom." *College Composition and Communication* 64 (3): 496–516.

Seymour-Campbell Student Success Act of 2012: Matriculation: Assessment. AB 705. California State Legislature. 2017.

Eaglestone, Robert. 2009. *Doing English: A Guide for Literature Students.* 3rd ed. London: Routledge.

Elbow, Peter. 2011. "Inviting the Mother Tongue: Beyond 'Mistakes,' 'Bad English,' and 'Wrong Language.'" In *Cross-Talk in Comp Theory: A Reader*, 3rd ed., edited by Victor Villanueva and Kristin L. Arola, 641–72. Urbana, IL: NCTE.

Feldman, Joe. 2019. *Grading for Equity: What It Is, Why It Matters, and How It Can Transform Schools and Classrooms.* Thousand Oaks, CA: Corwin.

Goddard, Angela, and Neil Carey. 2017. *Discourse: The Basics.* London: Routledge.

Goen, Sugie, and Helen Gillotte-Tropp. 2003. "Integrating Reading and Writing: A Response to the Basic Writing 'Crisis.'" *Journal of Basic Writing* 22 (2): 90–113.

Inoue, Asao B. 2015. *Antiracist Writing Assessment Ecologies: Teaching and Assessing Writing for a Socially Just Future.* Anderson, SC: Parlor.

Madera Community College. n.d. "2021–2026 Strategic Plan." https://www.maderacollege.edu/faculty-and-staff/madera_communitycollege_strategicplan2021.pdf.

Olson, Carol Booth. 2011. *The Reading/Writing Connection: Strategies for Teaching and Learning in the Secondary Classroom.* 3rd ed. Boston: Pearson.

Rosenblatt, Louise M. 1982. "The Literary Transaction: Evocation and Response." *Theory Into Practice* 21 (4): 268–77.

Schoenbach, Ruth, Cynthia Greenleaf, and Lynn Murphy. 2012. *Reading for Understanding: How Reading Apprenticeship Improves Disciplinary Learning in Secondary and College Classrooms.* 2nd ed. San Francisco: Jossey-Bass.

Spence, Lucy K. 2010. "Generous Reading: Seeing Students Through Their Writing." *Reading Teacher* 63 (8): 634–42.

Stotsky, Sandra. 1983. "Research on Reading/Writing Relationships: A Synthesis and Suggested Directions." *Language Arts* 60 (5): 627–42.

Wolf, Maryanne. 2018. "What Does Immersing Yourself in a Book Do to Your Brain?: On Neurochemistry, Lucia Berlin, and the Dangers of Empathy Loss." Literary Hub, August 8. https://lithub.com/what-does-immersing-yourself-in-a-book-do-to-your-brain/.

PART IV

Noncognitive Learning

11
ACCELERATING SUCCESS
Noncognitive Learning in Composition Courses

Margaret Nelson Rodriguez

INTRODUCTION

Accelerated composition weaves into the curriculum noncognitive learning that leads to successful student behaviors. This approach differentiates accelerated composition from traditional English composition and benefits students and faculty in many expected and unexpected ways. The accelerated composition pioneers of the California Acceleration Project (CAP) and the Community College of Baltimore County's Accelerated Learning Program (ALP) encouraged a holistic approach to students and their success. These early accelerated composition experiments and subsequent programs established across the country were being implemented with the backdrop of financial, political, and institutional pressures to transform noncredit/remedial course work from discrete, multilevel class sequences to accelerated and contextualized corequisites. The acceleration movement aimed to improve student outcomes, especially for the historically underserved student population, and to shift the paradigm of viewing students as underprepared to making our institutions better prepared for these students.

Through our accelerated composition work that prioritizes teaching student-success habits along with the reading and writing curriculum, we have learned that since our students are multidimensional human beings, when we focus only on the cognitive aspects, the academic, we have success with students who will succeed no matter what, the students who typically have social capital and college knowledge; however, we do not have as much as success with a broad spectrum of students, especially with first-generation and historically underrepresented student populations. Noncognitive learning incorporated with antiracism pedagogy, practices, and assessment educates and empowers students as learners, thinkers, and advocates. Promoting noncognitive learning in accelerated composition, therefore, advances equitable outcomes for historically underserved students and updates pedagogical approaches for our nation's incredibly diverse student population. Through exploring El Paso Community College's journey, I assert the importance of noncognitive learning in accelerated composition. Also, I investigate current efforts to incorporate antiracist practices in accelerated composition professional development, pedagogy, and assessment.

INSTITUTIONAL CONTEXT

El Paso County, located in the far west corner of Texas, is closer geographically to Phoenix and San Diego than Austin or Houston, respectively, and closer culturally to New México and California than the rest of Texas. Our unique geography on the international US-México border and at the convergence of three states (Texas, New México, and Chihuahua, México) makes the El Paso Borderlands area vibrant and diverse. El Paso County is also home to a large military installation, Fort Bliss, and is driving distance, about 78 miles, from Holloman Air Force Base.

Established in 1969, El Paso Community College (EPCC) is the only community college serving residents of El Paso and Hudspeth counties. El Paso County is largely urban, with rural outlying areas and a population of approximately 867,000 residents over 1,012 square miles; Hudspeth County is mostly rural and sparsely populated with, approximately 3,000 residents over 4,566 square miles (United States Census Bureau 2020a, 2020b). These geographic details convey the vastness of far west Texas, its remoteness and isolation, which lends itself to strong collaborations between educational institutions and strategic leveraging of scarce resources. Since its inception, EPCC has awarded more than 85,000 degrees and certificates. Eighty-five percent of EPCC's students are Hispanic, and, according to the magazine *Hispanic Outlook on Education*, EPCC has led the nation in granting associate degrees to Hispanic students for over thirteen years. EPCC and its major four-year-university partner, the University of Texas at El Paso (UTEP), share students and resources; more than 70 percent of UTEP students have EPCC course credit on their academic transcripts (UTEP 2021), and students swirl between both institutions.

Our shared students must be creative and strategic in determining class schedules, managing their scarce time and financial resources, and working toward degree completion. As an example of students swirling between the two institutions, an EPCC math course is one third the cost and has a smaller class size than the equivalent course at UTEP, yet the course still transfers and applies to the student's UTEP degree plan.

The student may take this math class at EPCC, along with four courses at UTEP, to save money and to receive the benefit of more individualized instruction from the EPCC math faculty. EPCC and UTEP have agreements and share data that allow students to swirl without institutional barriers.

EPCC's student population is majority first generation, economically disadvantaged, and working class. Like most community colleges, over 70 percent of EPCC students are pursuing their degrees part time, which makes completing their degrees more subject to delay and disruption. The data on the EPCC graduation chart (table 11.1) is from the 2021 *Texas Higher Education Coordinating Board Almanac*, which is published online annually and publicly accessible (Texas Higher Education 2021c).

Table 11.1. EPCC graduation rates

	Full time	Part time
3-year	24.1%	10.3%
4-year	29.8%	15.5%
6-year	37.8%	21.3%

Although EPCC's graduation rates have increased and semester credit hours to completion have decreased over the last ten years, work still must be done to improve student outcomes such as retention, persistence, and completion. One promising area of improving student outcomes has been developmental education reforms and students' successful completion of college-level composition and reading-intensive courses such as history, government, and biology.

ACCELERATED COMPOSITION BACKGROUND

In 2012, an El Paso Community College (EPCC) team attended the 4th Annual Conference on Acceleration in Baltimore, Maryland. Peter Adams and his colleagues were successfully piloting the accelerated learning program (ALP) English corequisite models at the Community College of Baltimore County, and our team was ready to absorb as much knowledge and resources as possible. My colleagues and I left the conference excited, motivated, and primed to conduct our own ALP pilot. During that same time period, the state of Texas mandated integrating reading and writing developmental/remedial instruction, so developmental education was undergoing many changes simultaneously.

In developing and implementing an ALP English corequisite and integrated reading and writing (INRW) models, we quickly learned the importance of noncognitive learning for student success. At EPCC, INRW courses are noncredit and are designed to support student learning in the college composition or reading-intensive courses. At EPCC, the majority of INRW courses are corequisites to a college course with the exception of one basic-skills INRW course that precedes the corequisite. This INRW course is for students who need adult basic education or English-language learner support. The majority of EPCC students who need additional support, however, take the INRW corequisite course discussed in this chapter. Although the curriculum was, of course, imperative, our department began to prioritize and emphasize noncognitive learning in these accelerated models. This priority was a sea change from the previous mentality that only academic learning objectives mattered to a more holistic, nuanced view that academic and noncognitive objectives both mattered. We emphasized students' development of the following metacognitive and noncognitive factors:

- mindfulness of how they learn;
- awareness of behaviors and attitudes that affect learning;
- ability to improve their learning practices and approaches;
- empowering themselves to learn (recognizing and addressing learned hopelessness and other disempowering mindsets); and
- attentiveness to all the noncognitive factors that affect students' learning, especially in the community college setting.

In order to implement accelerated writing models with fidelity, a culture change was needed. Changing the syllabus and curriculum was only the first step. Meaningfully incorporating noncognitive learning, metacognition, and a completely different approach to teaching developmental writing courses required engagement with faculty, collaboration with other disciplines and student services, and ongoing, high-quality professional development for faculty. Our theoretical and research foundation for a noncognitive learning approach was mostly derived from Daniel Goleman's (2006) research on emotional intelligence and Svetlana Holt's (2007) research on emotional intelligence in higher education. Asao Inoue's scholarship on antiracist writing assessment, and his other and other scholars' work on labor-based grading contracts, have also helped inform our continuous improvement and professional development.

Although INRW corequisite models were state mandated, our initial offerings of ALP corequisite models were truly a labor of love, a passionate grassroots attempt to help our most vulnerable students. Once Texas mandated corequisites in 2018, with 75 percent of all exit-level developmental courses required to be corequisites by 2020–2021, we finally received full institutional support to scale our corequisites to *all* students, not just those students fortunate enough to be placed in a pilot program. We knew ALP corequisites were the most effective approach because of internal student outcomes data and external qualitative student data (from research primarily conducted by researchers at the RAND Corporation). Students were able to articulate best that the classes were not only effective in *what* students learned but also *how* they learned.

The metacognition we frequently discussed in developmental education was finally evidenced in students' learning, and students were empowered for the next step of their educational journeys. However, shifting from deeply ingrained attitudes, assumptions, and misconceptions about students placed into remedial classes in the English department and throughout the institution was challenging. This paradigm shift necessitated a clear, coherent, cohesive approach that made students' development and success the foci and goals for the endeavor, even if the endeavor was not as revenue producing as traditional developmental models or as easy to implement when it came to scheduling, faculty compensation, curriculum alignment, and interdisciplinary collaboration, just to name a few of the necessary considerations.

Presenting relevant data about the lack of student success and upward trajectory in traditional developmental sequences, without alienating or offending colleagues who cared deeply about students but had been stuck in an ineffective model, took finesse and savvy. Showing data about the grim chances students typically face in actually finishing a degree when placed into traditional developmental sequences and the significantly more promising corequisite data also helped. For example, in fall 2019, 52 percent of students in Texas in reading and writing corequisites completed their first college-level course versus only 24 percent of students enrolled in traditional developmental education courses (Texas Higher Education 2018). Our institution's scaling of accelerated models has positively impacted thousands of additional students who now complete their first college-level course within their first year of college, gaining invaluable momentum towards degree completion. Showing faculty and other stakeholders this type of data is influential and empowering—we all want more students to succeed. Corequisites help more students succeed and gain momentum towards degree completion. How can we argue against that? In fact, because corequisites have been so successful, El Paso Community College has scaled its corequisites to 100 percent of eligible students in reading and writing. This scaling has provided faculty opportunities to experiment with different noncognitive learning strategies to see what works well and what does not. Transitioning from traditional developmental education and traditional thinking about teaching underprepared students has helped inspire and embolden faculty to prioritize noncognitive learning and holistic supports for student success.

IMPLEMENTING ACCELERATED COMPOSITION AT SCALE

Although we had broad faculty and administrative support for our accelerated learning program (ALP) English corequisites in the pilot phase, there were many structural challenges to implement corequisites at scale, and we were only able to accomplish this feat once the state mandated it, thereby increasing institutional buy-in and support. Through our corequisite scaling efforts, we gained valuable knowledge and experience, particularly incorporating noncognitive learning to promote student success. Our corequisite journey became interwoven with our integrated reading and writing (INRW) journey, as now our corequisite courses are INRW and not stand-alone writing or reading courses as in the early days of our corequisite experimentation.

At El Paso Community College (EPCC), the English discipline had previously led the stand-alone writing developmental courses, and the reading discipline had previously led the stand-alone reading developmental courses. With the advent of integrating reading and writing skills into one course, the two disciplines collaborated on the curriculum and course design, which was useful with the corequisite movement. Both disciplines used an integrated reading and writing course for their corequisites; however, each discipline tailored the course to meet the needs of the paired corequisite course. The English discipline's corequisite course is more writing intensive and is paired with students' first college-level composition course. The reading discipline's corequisite course is more reading intensive and is paired with students' first reading-intensive course, such as biology, history, government, and speech. At EPCC, students enrolled in writing corequisites are mainstreamed with peers who placed directly into the college composition course without additional corequisite support. In this chapter, I explore the writing-intensive corequisite courses.

NECESSARY CURRICULAR CHANGES

Transitioning from corequisite pilots to full-scale acceleration was accomplished in four phases. Our goal was to have 25 percent of eligible students enrolled in corequisites by fall 2018, 50 percent by fall 2019, and 75 percent by fall 2020. During implementation, the institution and disciplines decided to try to scale closer to 100 percent. We exceeded

75 percent implementation by fall 2020, and we were 100 percent accelerated writing by fall 2021, even with the challenges brought on with the pandemic.

It all starts with the syllabus, right? Beyond making the textual changes on the syllabus, there was extensive work to engage faculty and provide the right support and professional development to make sure the syllabus changes led to real changes in the classroom and student outcomes. I am going to touch on curricular changes in our INRW and ALP journeys; many of the changes connected and cascaded, as both interventions were designed to accelerate developmental education. One of the first curricular changes was transitioning from the exit exam, a high-stakes essay included in the English's discipline's standalone developmental writing courses, to a more aligned and equitable capstone assignment. No matter the student's final grade at the end of their developmental writing course, the English discipline required all students to write an essay, called the *exit exam*, with the same prompt and instructions. Even the assignment name was ominous and intimidating to students, and the results were very often disheartening for these beginning college writers.

The exit exam prompt was developed by a discipline committee, and although we tried to generate topics that would interest students (Elbow 2002, 5–13), often students did not have the base knowledge to reasonably write about the topic, let only address the prompt effectively, and students were not allowed to conduct research to learn more about the topic. Students' lack of topic knowledge often impeded their essay success since it is very difficult for college writers at any level to generate ideas on a writing topic for which they have no previous knowledge or experience. The essay mode was persuasive, further compounding the negative effects of unfamiliar topics for students. The discipline tried to create topics familiar to many people, but it is impossible to know what will be familiar for hundreds of students with different classes, faculty, and experiences. Students only had fifty minutes to write the essay (the shortest class time to be fair to all class meeting times), so a large number of students ended up failing the exit exam simply because they ran out of time. The department did offer an appeal exam (with a different topic and prompt) during the college's final-exam week that provided students two hours to complete the essay; however, students were often so demoralized after failing the exit exam that their appeal-exam performance suffered and the same issues with the exam and its assessment persisted.

The department graded these essays without any identifying information to help make the process as fair, objective, and accurate as possible;

however, the grading process often did not seem fair, objective, or accurate, especially when instructors witnessed students who were passing their courses fail the semester because of one seemingly arbitrary essay graded by instructors who knew nothing about the student, their development and progress, and their overall readiness demonstrated by their semester's worth of work.

Despite good intentions, the exit exam was repeating our students' mostly negative standardized-testing experiences from high school and from the college placement exam. Students' learning and readiness were not really being assessed or measured. Students were being told that, despite all their hard work and positive writing assessments from their writing professor that semester, one single essay test would determine whether they could move on to their college writing course. The exit exam attempted to measure students' writing abilities in one high-stakes assignment instead of viewing "writing and other forms of literacy . . . as purposeful, meaningful activities" (Moss 1994, 110), like the semester's writing activities and assignments, of equal importance and assessed accordingly. We were unknowingly reinforcing hegemonic hierarchies and racist writing assessments in our exit exam assessment process by only using one, noncontextualized writing assignment to serve as a barrier to credit-bearing courses and degree completion. We had constructed an unnecessary, destructive barrier that would negatively affect our most underresourced students who could least afford to take these developmental courses multiple times. Additionally, students' grit, mindset, and motivation were all ignored, as was their writing accomplished with time and process. We were just starting to incorporate noncognitive learning into our accelerated and integrated reading and writing models, and the exit exam was completely contrary to these ideals. Of course, students are not solely graded on their grit, mindset, and motivation in any writing course, but these noncognitive factors help propel students to improve academically throughout a semester, especially in writing, which is so much about process, not just a final product.

Overall, the exit exam had a detrimental effect on students and faculty and represented a punitive approach and pedagogy not holistic or aligned with the ALP philosophy and approach. Since our discipline was piloting accelerated models and designing an integrated reading and writing (INRW) course, we had a golden opportunity to change this practice into a more equitable and effective assignment. In addition to the exit exam's problematic nature, it really did not fit into the accelerated or INRW courses. We were finding some students in the accelerated model passing the college-level writing course but failing the developmental course because of the exit exam. Since one of the major grading parameters of the exit exam was "The student demonstrates readiness to succeed in English 1301 [the college-level writing course]," the fact that we had students already succeeding in English 1301 but still failing the developmental writing exit exam showed a concerning mismatch of assessments and expectations. Further, the exit exam was based on a writing prompt with no connected reading assignment, making it completely unaligned with the expectations of INRW. We knew we needed to change this assignment and its associated culture in order to fully implement accelerated models and improve student success.

The teams working on accelerated and INRW models brainstormed and researched capstone assignments to replace the exit exam that were more fitting to our holistic view of student development and success. We settled on a common essay and portfolio to replace the exit exam in our developmental writing courses. These stand-alone developmental writing courses would soon fully transition to INRW courses, and eventually all stand-alone reading and writing developmental courses would transition to INRW corequisite courses. These transitions made EPCC's accelerated composition journey more centered on teaching reading *and* writing than other states' accelerated composition models. EPCC curricular development and faculty professional development also emphasized scaffolding and contextualizing to help students connect their reading and writing processes for maximal impact and success.

The common essay was based on an article and prompt that required students to read and understand the article before engaging with the writing process. The common-essay article, prompt, instructions, rubric, and any other resources were provided to students at least a week in advance, and instructors were allowed to discuss and conduct activities about the article, topic, and prompt and help students brainstorm and outline their essay. Students were encouraged to read the article several times and to practice the critical-reading strategies we were stressing in accelerated models, such as annotating, summarizing, and reflecting. Students were given double the original writing time, and, most important, the common essay was not high stakes. Instead, the common essay was worth 20 percent of students' final course grade. The department developed a more holistic rubric to go along with the new common essay and its approach. The department still convened to assess the essays with a common rubric. This action was important to help persuade colleagues who appreciated the productive discussions that often accompanied the exit exam group grading sessions to support the transition to a common essay. The grading percentage was also an important compromise for colleagues who may have not been completely convinced acceleration was here to stay. After all, faculty are often bombarded with educational fads that usually fade. Fortunately, acceleration, with its emphasis on noncognitive learning, has had staying power based on its outcomes and efficiency, especially in the state of Texas, but we did not know this for certain back in 2012. The common essay's weight as 20 percent of the final course grade was consequential enough for students and faculty to take the common essay seriously, but it was not high stakes enough to bring its own array of issues and potentially derail motivated students ready to continue on their academic journeys.

In 2013, the common essay replaced the exit exam and was a more accurate, aligned assignment for accelerated reading and writing courses; however, our curriculum-design teams wanted a more holistic and comprehensive way to evaluate students' growth in reading, writing, and noncognitive learning. Thus, a portfolio that worked for our students, faculty, and accelerated learning models was born.

First, we had to make the portfolio work for our unique situation: two separate academic departments (English and reading) embarking on radically new educational models for students. In many contexts, portfolios are a means to holistically assess a student's final grade primarily based on their entire body of work and not necessarily on individual assignment grades. Logistically and practically, this type of portfolio assessment was not going to work for our accelerated courses. Instead, we developed a framework for faculty to develop their own portfolio design, parameters, and specific criteria. Our only departmental portfolio requirements were that the assignment counted for at least 10 percent of students' final grade and students wrote a reflection to demonstrate metacognition. We developed sample portfolio instructions, rubrics, and reflection assignments and then conducted a pilot in a select number of ALP and INRW courses. We asked students for permission to use portfolios as examples. We included these student sample portfolios; sample portfolio instructions, rubrics, and reflection assignments; and lessons learned in our INRW pilot sections and faculty-training sessions. These INRW courses were not corequisites yet, as they are now, but they still gave the curriculum-design teams viable opportunities to learn what worked well for both the common essay and portfolio and what modifications were needed.

The common essay and portfolio had successes and challenges, and both assignments have evolved as our accelerated journey has continued. Successes included increased completion in developmental courses, increased student and faculty engagement, and improved alignment with accelerated course objectives. Challenges included sustaining engagement with the common essay, transitioning to e-portfolios, and additional curricular changes needed after accelerated models were mandated for all eligible students. In the first few years, the common essay and portfolio worked well in our integrated reading and writing and corequisite courses. Once our INRW courses became corequisites and all corequisite courses needed to be fully contextualized to a college-level course, the common essay became less necessary, ultimately leading to its termination in 2018. The portfolio was still determined to be useful pedagogically in the fully contextualized accelerated reading and writing courses. The portfolio now includes the body of work from the college-level writing and corequisite course. Students' reflections are arguably deeper and richer now. Students reflect not only on their learning and progression throughout the semester but also on their strengths and challenges with noncognitive learning and on noncognitive factors that affected their success in the college course. An example of guiding reflection questions on noncognitive learning include the following:

- What noncognitive skills (time management, grit, mindset, motivation, goal setting, personal responsibility, social responsibility, using college resources like the writing center, visiting office hours, asking for help, forming study groups, studying, taking care of your physical/social/emotional/mental health) have you developed in this course? What noncognitive skills did you already possess but strengthened during this course?
- How do you think your noncognitive skills have helped you succeed in this course, your college writing course, any other courses this semester, or in your life outside of school?
- What noncognitive skills have you struggled to develop? Why do you think that is? How will you try to develop those skills in the future?

With these questions, we are trying to get students to probe and investigate their own noncognitive learning. We also ask questions to reflect on their writing processes, products, and progression, prompting students to become more aware of their cognitive-learning processes, as well.

The corequisite course provides the time and space for faculty to help their students realize and become more aware of their learning, behaviors, and attitudes in high-quality reflections and discussions. These reflections also provide informal feedback for instructors on what writing and noncognitive skills their students were most aware of and if there are any noncognitive skills that can be incorporated differently or more deeply into the corequisite curriculum. For example, if none of my students mentioned that they developed the noncognitive skill of using college resources, like the writing center, I would reflect on how I could emphasize that important noncognitive skill and resulting positive action in my class activities and assignments, such as requiring all students to visit the writing center at least once a semester for one of their college compositions, scheduling a virtual or face-to-face writing center orientation, or scheduling a corequisite class at the writing center. These activities aim to help students understand the importance of using college resources to improve success. Often, students just need a little push to realize the benefits of using a college resource like the writing center. Once students see and experience the benefits, they usually adopt the practice of using the writing center not just for the corequisite class but for other classes too, and they begin to understand the value in using other college resources, as well. Like most community colleges, a sizable portion of our institution's students are first generation, so they may not fully understand resources available or feel comfortable accessing resources. Additionally, community college students are more likely to have full-time jobs and family obligations, causing time scarcity and a reluctance to spend time on something unless it is clearly and obviously beneficial and purposeful. Empowering and encouraging students to use campus resources may help students feel they belong at your institution, which can also improve student retention and success.

Another portfolio challenge was more logistical in nature; however, it provided a valuable opportunity to further define and refine our portfolio expectations and outcomes. Even before the pandemic (please see the "Virtual Acceleration" section of this chapter for additional curricular and logistical transitions necessitated by the pandemic), we had begun including e-portfolio training during our accelerated learning program (ALP) professional development. Some faculty adopted e-portfolios, but the majority of our faculty did not and continued to use the traditional, hard-copy portfolio. Many faculty who attended the training thought e-portfolios were intriguing but did not necessarily want to change their practices and learn a new virtual platform well enough to introduce it to students. Nevertheless, the pandemic forced us all to use virtual platforms, so e-portfolios were quicky adopted by faculty. The existing e-portfolio training was adapted to include more virtual platforms, lessons learned, and support for faculty and students. Our discipline's adoption of e-portfolios is particularly exciting for students. Students now leave our accelerated courses with a digital showcase of their work that can never be misplaced, and they learn valuable skills and knowledge about effectively communicating in the digital world and developing a professional digital footprint.

CONTEXTUALIZATION: FUNDAMENTAL TO ACCELERATED LEARNING

Contextualization is not a new concept in education or in developmental education reforms; however, the accelerated learning movement has brought this concept to the forefront of teaching and learning. Effective accelerated learning requires contextualization of the material in the corequisite, or developmental, course and the college writing course. Effective accelerating teaching also requires contextualization between the corequisite course and the noncognitive learning we want our students to develop and strengthen along with their academic skills. These noncognitive skills can cover a wide array of topics, but in our accelerated learning journey, we have prioritized the following noncognitive skills in our corequisite courses:

- using campus resources, like the writing center, tutoring, and advising;
- visiting professors' office hours;
- setting and achieving goals;
- cultivating a growth mindset;
- developing grit and resilience;
- managing time effectively; and
- recognizing and addressing main causes of procrastination.

Methods of incorporating noncognitive learning vary by professor, but generally these domains are emphasized in the syllabus and online-course shell, included in course readings and activities, and incorporated in low-stakes writing assignments like journals and reflections, particularly in the end-of-the-semester portfolio reflection. Contextualization has different meanings and applications depending on the circumstances, so it is worth explaining its significance to accelerated teaching and noncognitive learning.

Contextualization is key to accelerated teaching, including noncognitive learning, because it provides the framework for the developmental course to be purposeful and meaningful to students. Contextualization also bridges content learned in a semester to future courses and to life. Through metacognitive activities and focus, students are more likely to transfer and apply their knowledge and skills to future classes and situations. Dolores Perin and Rachel Hare (2010), researchers at the

Community College Research Center, define contextualization and its benefits:

> Instead of teaching reading and writing skills in the abstract, contextualized literacy instruction focuses on "authentic content." The guided assumption is that skills learned through contextualized instruction are more likely to transfer beyond the course in which they are taught. According to this theory, such transfer would result from the similarity between the contexts of learning and eventual application as well as from increased student motivation. (2)

Perin and Hare conducted a quasi-experimental study on contextualization at three community colleges and six cohorts of students with a specific contextualization tool called the Content Comprehension Strategy Intervention (CCSI). Both student groups received the CCSI intervention. The first student group received the CCSI intervention along with contextualized reading and writing instruction from a biology course, "authentic content in that many community college students must pass a science course to earn a degree" (2). The other student group received the CCSI intervention with "a variety of unrelated themes drawn from developmental education textbooks" (2). These unrelated themes were current, controversial social topics commonly used in developmental reading and writing courses. The researchers found that contextualized instruction produced promising results in students' literacy learning, particularly in the identification and inclusion of main ideas and accurate information from a text into a written summary.

Another study conducted by Paulette Golden (2018) shows promising results from contextualized reading and writing instruction. Golden aimed to find any quantifiable differences in student learning outcomes when students were taught with contextualized, purposeful instruction that helps them realize the content is meaningful and relevant to their lives. Golden conducted a study of first-year writing students receiving contextualized writing instruction with scenario-based learning (SBL), defined as "a subset of problem-based and case-based learning" (2). Golden found "promising results in critical thinking, analytic reasoning, and problem solving" (7) but less conclusive results with students' transferability of writing skills. Low-stakes SBL activities alone did not appear to improve students' transferability of writing skills; however, low-stakes SBL activities coupled with more challenging SBL assignments did appear to improve students' transferability of writing skills.

Through this sampling of contextualized reading and writing instruction research studies, we can see why, collectively, so many community college faculty are moving towards accelerated learning models. Contextualization is foundational to accelerated learning, and contextualization has been demonstrating positive and promising results in student learning outcomes for many years. Contextualization is a primary reason accelerated writing instruction has been delivering improved student success and completion measures in comparison to traditional developmental courses. Because the corequisite course is contextualized by using authentic content, it is more meaningful and purposeful for students. The corequisite course's just-in-time instruction enables students to focus their time and attention, improving their chances of succeeding in the college writing course. The corequisite course's noncognitive learning emphasis equips students with the self-efficacy, self-awareness, and self-confidence to succeed in and beyond the classroom. Just when we were finally feeling as if we had a good handle on our accelerated composition courses, every facet of life was disrupted by the global pandemic, and we had to quickly adapt to online and hybrid modalities.

REFLECTING ON NONCOGNITIVE LEARNING IN ACCELERATED COMPOSITION

Accelerated learning models have upended traditional ways of thinking and teaching college students. In order to teach accelerated models effectively, we must understand and accept that students' success in college has many influencing factors beyond academics. In addition to a large body of theoretical research and practical experience to support this claim, accelerated learning models rely heavily on noncognitive learning and thinking for their success.

Accelerated learning is based on the philosophy that academically underprepared students can learn and succeed with additional academic and social supports and that noncognitive learning and support are just as crucial for success as academic instruction and support. Although there are varied accelerated approaches and designs, most accelerated models use one or more high-impact learning practices and noncognitive learning strategies to engage students and to facilitate their success. High-impact learning practices interwoven with noncognitive learning strategies used in accelerated learning include the following:

- cohorts;
- fostering a sense of belonging and connection;
- just-in-time instruction;

- teaching and emphasizing college knowledge and student-success behaviors (time management, grit, mindset, empowerment, metacognition); and
- contextualization to help students grow and succeed in college.

Although this list is by no means comprehensive, it provides a useful primer to help explain why accelerated learning is more effective than traditional developmental education modes, particularly with community college students.

Due to a confluence of internal and external factors, community college students often struggle to find their purpose and sense of belonging in college. Traditional developmental models, no matter how well intentioned or well taught, perpetuated the system that makes some students feel they do not belong in college. This is the messaging students receive from traditional developmental education: because you are not ready for real college courses, here are courses that do not count toward your degree, that you still must pay for, and that you must pass to get to the college courses you need to complete for your degree. Further, these English and math courses were not most students' favorite subjects in high school, and we seemingly punish students with extra English and math courses as soon as they arrive to college. Corequisites, although imperfect, help us more than any other recent developmental education intervention to break through that culture of segmentation and isolation. Students are able to immediately enroll in the college courses needed for their degrees with extra support to help them succeed. Students understand and appreciate that value proposition, especially when they see themselves excelling and often outperforming peers in their mainstreamed college composition courses. Accelerated composition destigmatizes developmental education and allows students to see the value and purpose of the corequisite course to their college coursework and to their lives (Daugherty et al. 2018).

VIRTUAL ACCELERATION

Virtual acceleration sounds like it could be the title of a virtual-reality game, which is apt since we all experienced distorted and upended realities and an explosion of virtual life as we lived through the pandemic. Prior to the pandemic, El Paso Community College (EPCC) did not offer any developmental education, including its accelerated corequisites, in online or hybrid modalities. However, the pandemic necessitated a quick pivot to these modalities, and ongoing shifts in students' attitudes and preferences towards online and hybrid modalities made it clear we needed to develop coherent, engaging, and effective online and hybrid course designs for our accelerated learning program (ALP) corequisites' sustainability postpandemic. In spring 2021, the EPCC English discipline embarked on its online corequisite-development project to meet this student and institutional need. The project's purpose was to redesign ALP corequisites to be seamlessly delivered and to fully support students in all learning modes: face to face, hybrid, and online. The team consisted of the core corequisite faculty group along with a full-time faculty member adept at the learning-management system and course design and nine adjunct faculty. All faculty received course-release time for the project, allowing full engagement with the design and development process.

The project's initial phase was brainstorming and research. Brainstorming included probing our current corequisite models' strengths and challenges, especially in online delivery. Guided questions for our online-delivery transition included the following:

- How could we effectively maintain contextualization, just-in-time support, and individualized instruction in the corequisite?
- How could we best maintain close collaboration between faculty team-teaching corequisites?
- What changes were needed in the corequisite syllabus, calendar, and course materials to sustain the fidelity of accelerated composition in asynchronous virtual learning environments?
- What kind of support and resources would be needed by students and faculty to support their online learning and teaching?
- What were the best practices in online-course design to help connect the two courses (corequisite and college composition)?

Each team member conducted research, and a robust literature review was constructed and shared. Although the research was varied and extensive, most team members gravitated towards research topics centered on best practices in online education and course design. Community college faculty rarely have time to conduct research like this, so the process itself was extremely productive, enriching, and professionalizing, especially for adjunct faculty. Specific research topics included

- embedding noncognitive learning in college writing and reading courses;
- engaging students with gamification theory;
- contextualizing reading and writing strategies;
- fostering a sense of belonging, affiliation, and community;
- using electronic textbooks;

- incorporating technology tools and apps;
- assigning and evaluating e-portfolios;
- innovative accelerated learning strategies in Texas;
- accelerated learning strategies in different states;
- asynchronous and synchronous online learning;
- antiracist pedagogy, practices, and assessments;
- prioritizing metacognition; and
- utilizing experiential learning and reflective writing.

The project's final outcomes included a revised, aligned course scope and sequence; a robust, drop-in corequisite curriculum on the college's learning-management system with interactive lessons, tech tools, and noncognitive learning resources; revamped faculty-training materials; and best practices for team-teaching corequisites. Special attention was paid to ensuring students understood they were enrolled in a corequisite and to delineating expectations and benefits for students through the syllabus and first-week course activities. In their study of corequisite implementation in Louisiana, researchers Emily Campbell and Rene Cintron (2018) emphasize the importance of student buy-in and understanding of corequisite program requirements and expectations. We strived to make no assumptions about what students knew before enrolling in the corequisite course and to ensure student-facing informational materials, such as syllabi statements and promotional flyers, clearly stated the who, what, when, where, why, and how of corequisites in jargon-free, benefits-focused language. For example, we emphasized the additional, individualized attention students would receive from their professor in their corequisite to help them succeed or the financial benefit of only having to buy one set of textbook and classroom materials since the first-year composition course and corequisite course use the same textbook and classroom materials.

As of fall 2022, most of our corequisites are now being offered face to face, although we still offer online or hybrid sections due to student demand. We are continually learning and improving our accelerated offerings based on student and faculty feedback. Our faculty-training materials were modified in January 2022 to address challenges in teaching accelerated composition virtually. Other challenges, like faculty recruitment, are being addressed through outreach and robust faculty and curricular resources provided by the online corequisite-development project. Corequisite faculty now have an overall better defined corequisite-course design and curriculum, including a scope and sequence aligned to accelerated learning and strategies and activities to develop noncognitive learning in students to maximize student retention and success. Noncognitive-learning/student-success behaviors are still emphasized in the online corequisite-course design and curriculum through readings, interactive videos, discussions, and low-stakes writing assignments such as journals, reflections, reader responses, summaries, and discussion questions.

FACULTY TRAINING

Ongoing faculty training and support is crucial to continuous improvement and sustainability. At EPCC, faculty are not required to teach corequisite courses. We must retain our current corequisite faculty and engage new faculty. All our efforts in curriculum design and professional development have made corequisites more attractive to faculty and have eased the transition to online teaching and learning.

From the beginning of our accelerated learning journey, it was clear faculty training was needed for effective implementation. Initially, we proposed and conducted a one-time, mandatory accelerated learning program (ALP) training session to educate faculty about the ALP approach and to teach them strategies and techniques. We felt this training was important for faculty to understand just how different the accelerated model was from traditional developmental courses, which were generally sequential and hierarchal and prerequisites to the next level of developmental courses or college-credit courses. Many of our faculty had been teaching traditional developmental courses for years or even decades, so an orientation was needed to get everyone on the same page. Since our corequisites were only a pilot at this stage, this type of limited-scope training was reasonable and appropriate.

After implementing corequisites at scale, however, it become clear that ongoing faculty training, not just the one-and-done initial training we had been doing, was necessary for effective implementation and sustained engagement from faculty (Daugherty et al. 2018). As we implemented at scale, we learned considerably and needed to modify our approach. We had to tweak curriculum, develop FAQs, develop focused training for different-instructor model corequisites, and adjust objectives. Our training was adapted, and we emphasized flexibility (with students, with each other, with the curriculum-design teams) in the corequisite model. This emphasis on flexibility ended up becoming extremely useful during the pandemic and the shift to online learning, as suddenly everyone had to become flexible and nimble. Training was also adjusted due to faculty feedback, curriculum changes, and the ever-evolving developmental education mandates from the state that sometimes affected our corequisite approach and content (Texas Higher Education 2018).

EQUITY AND ANTIRACISM IN ACCELERATED COMPOSITION

Accelerated models force us to reexamine our use and understanding of "underprepared" students, as we see that students bring with them a wealth of knowledge and experiences beyond the academic realm that can be used to help them succeed in college. This viewpoint aligns with equity and antiracism. When we do not acknowledge and address our students' backgrounds, cultures, and barriers when accessing and excelling in higher education, we are not fully seeing, serving, or educating our students. This paradigm shift does not mean we are eliminating standards or giving up teaching our students writing—instead, we are making an intentional change in our approach. We must see ourselves more as gardeners cultivating our students' intellectual growth than as doctors diagnosing and triaging students' perceived deficiencies. This shift in thinking has become even more urgent, as we now realize many of these perceived deficits are intrinsically tied into institutional racism and white supremacy.

At El Paso Community College (EPCC), corequisite composition reforms have grown and evolved while the country and academia have been undergoing an unprecedented pandemic and an urgent reckoning with racial and social justice. EPCC faculty have been attending antiracism training and professional development, learning how to use antiracist pedagogy and assessment to help address structural racism in educational institutions and writing classrooms. EPCC faculty have also been improving equity in classroom practices by participating in internal and external projects focused on this topic. Faculty from all disciplines are learning from each other how to make their classrooms more equitable and how to foster a stronger sense of belonging and connection in their students to their peers, to their professors, and to the college. Along with these national and institutional calls to incorporate antiracist pedagogy and equitable practices into teaching and learning, accelerated composition reforms have rightly prioritized noncognitive learning to advance student success.

The culturally relevant pedagogy and literature movement preceded this widespread antiracism awakening. The successful Puente programs of California and the nonprofit organization Catch the Next's campaign brought this highly effective and culturally affirming curriculum and pedagogy to Texas in the early 2010s. The foundation of culturally relevant pedagogy and literature shares many of the same understandings about white supremacy and racialized hierarchies that prominent antiracist scholars and authors Ibram X. Kendi and Asao B. Inoue have brought to the forefront of academic and societal discourse; however, this movement stopped short at intentionally addressing racism in the academy and the classroom and the power structures that continue to elevate and maintain white supremacy. Faculty were not asked or trained to engage in the crucial learning, self-reflections, inherent-biases recognition, and courageous conversations that can help make our institutions and classrooms more equitable to students of color and marginalized populations, such as student parents, first-generation students, and economically disadvantaged students.

As explained by Inoue (2015), ignoring, avoiding, or denying race will not get rid of racism or make an effective antiracist educator. Essentially, faculty, especially white faculty, must be willing to overcome their resistance to speaking about racism. Additionally, faculty must be able to face their discomfort in addressing their own privilege and transgenerational benefits from white supremacy. Without this personal and social awareness, writing faculty cannot possibly work to dismantle the racialized hierarchies that exist in their classrooms and assessments (24–30). Inoue asserts that scholar's avoidance of race in discussions of writing assessment with the "hopes that it withers and dies for lack of attention, which creates a nonracist world," will not help end racism. Inoue further describes the resistance he has faced in "explicitly thinking about race and racism in discussions of writing assessment" with the goal of getting "rid of racism, unfair racialized hierarchies" in writing assessment and our use of a Standardized Edited American English (SEAE) as "a hegemonic discourse." He points out that SEAE, although often "a racial marker," is not necessarily demonstrating racism "unless it is used against students in a writing assessment as the standard" (29). Many composition faculty have used and are currently using SEAE as an assessment benchmark. One of the next steps in our EPCC accelerated composition journey is understanding why using SEAE as the standard in writing assessment is problematic, opening a productive discussion among faculty, and tailoring professional development to help decolonize our writing classrooms.

Incorporating noncognitive learning in accelerated composition promotes equity in addition to improving student learning and outcomes. Further, antiracist practices and approaches complement noncognitive learning in corequisite models, creating a unique opportunity for writing educators to make their classrooms incubators of equity, justice, and social awareness and to empower students to assert their place in a society that often ignores, diminishes or attempts to erase them.

Accelerated teaching combines promising practices (Daugherty et al. 2021) for developmental education and bridges the academic content to the noncognitive learning we know is so important for students, yet we often do not have the time and space to teach noncognitive skills and habits to our students. The outcomes show accelerated learning is working, and the model is flexible enough to be adapted and tweaked to better serve students as we learn and grow with our students. Incorporating antiracist pedagogy and practices into accelerated learning is organic, effective, and imperative for its continued relevance and efficacy, especially among generations reaching adulthood while the US has and continues to wrestle with systemic racism, white supremacy, and institutionalized violence against people of color, especially Brown and Black men.

Our department is in its nascent stage of incorporating antiracist practices and antiracist writing assessments into our curriculum and professional development. Although I should note our English department has individual faculty who have already been deeply engaged in antiracism pedagogy and assessment in their courses, it has not been intentionally or broadly implemented throughout the department. At our next corequisite professional-development session, faculty will read excerpts and watch videos of Inoue's discussion of racialized writing assessment (Namubiru, Li, and Habib 2021). Then, we will guide faculty to conduct a hopefully eye-opening assessment about how we use Standardized Edited American English (SEAE) to evaluate first-year college students' writing. We will also dialogue and workshop ways we can adjust our syllabi and assessments accordingly and address more equitable ways to improve students' clarity and impact in their writing without diminishing their multilingual backgrounds. We will delve into recent advances in labor-based contract grading at this session, which is used in some individual faculty's courses, but is not widespread or at scale. We have bilingual students who speak multiple versions of English and Spanish depending on the situation, and this incredible wealth of linguistic diversity should be celebrated, honored, and incorporated into pedagogical practices and corequisite curriculum. We strive to learn more about leveraging our region's unique linguistic diversity in our accelerated composition courses. We see antiracist pedagogy and assessment as imperative in accelerated composition's continued evolution and growth.

I think this is an incredibly exciting and rapidly evolving time to teach college composition. Developing and teaching accelerated writing models has improved my teaching and enlightened my mind to all the noncognitive skills and support our students need to be successful academically and to the urgent need to address systemic racism ingrained in our educational institutions and academic departments. There are certainly challenges to the model, but the benefits are clear, as accelerated composition has the potential to continuously improve and adapt to best serve our students.

CONCLUSION

Our notions of academic preparedness and writing assessments can be problematic, steeped in societal inequities and institutional systems of inequity and privilege. Accelerated composition as a discipline and its practitioners must be flexible, holistic, openminded, and open to failure because not all ideas will succeed. As long as we keep student success—students' growth, development, achievement, momentum toward their goals—as the focus, accelerated composition, no matter the specific model, is more equitable and effective for students and is more fun and exciting for faculty to teach! Accelerated learning is more purposeful for students and for faculty—this attribute makes a compelling case for practitioners to keep trying to refine and improve it. El Paso Community College's (EPCC) accelerated composition journey likely has similarities to other community colleges and public universities' journeys. Community college faculty, with their heavy teaching loads and extensive noninstructional duties, may not have had the time to pause and reflect on just how much they have accomplished at their institutions individually and collectively to advance student success through the accelerated composition movement. I hope this chapter provides some helpful context and reflection along with stressing the importance of continuing to learn, grow, and evolve with our students.

REFERENCES

Campbell, Emily, and Rene Cintron. 2018. "Accelerating Remedial Education in Louisiana." *New Directions for Community Colleges* 2018 (182): 49–57. https://doi.org/10.1002/cc.20301.

Daugherty, Lindsay, Celia J. Gomez, Diana Gehlhaus Carew, Alexandra Mendoza-Graf, and Trey Miller. 2018. "Designing and Implementing Corequisite Models of Developmental Education: Findings from Texas Community Colleges." RAND Corporation. https://www.rand.org/content/dam/rand/pubs/research_reports/RR2300/RR2337/RAND_RR2337.pdf.

Daugherty, Lindsay, Alexandra Mendoza-Graf, Diana Gehlhaus, Trey Miller, and Russell Gerber. 2021. "Student Experiences in English Corequisite Remediation Versus a

Standalone Developmental Education Course: Findings from an Experimental Study in Texas Community Colleges." RAND Corporation. https://www.rand.org/pubs/research_reports/RRA810-1.html.

Elbow, Peter. 2002. "High Stakes and Low Stakes in Assigning and Responding to Writing." *New Directions for Teaching and Learning* 1997 (69): 5–13. https://doi.org/10.1002/tl.6901.

Golden, Paullett. 2018. "Contextualized Writing: Promoting Audience-Centered Writing through Scenario-Based Learning." *International Journal for the Scholarship of Teaching and Learning* 12 (1). https://doi.org/10.20429/ijsotl.2018.120106.

Goleman, Daniel. 2006. *Emotional Intelligence: Why It Can Matter More Than IQ.* New York: Bantam.

Holt, Svetlana. 2007. "Emotional Intelligence and Academic Achievement in Higher Education." *Dissertations Abstracts International Section A: Humanities and Social Sciences* 68 (3-A): 875.

Inoue, Asao B. 2015. *Antiracist Writing Assessment Ecologies: Teaching and Assessing Writing for a Socially Just Future.* Fort Collins, CO: WAC Clearinghouse.

Inoue, Asao B. 2021. *Above the Well: An Antiracist Literacy Argument from a Boy of Color.* Fort Collins, CO: WAC Clearinghouse.

Moss, Pamela A. 1994. "Validity in High Stakes Writing Assessment: Problems and Possibilities." *Assessing Writing* 1 (1): 109–28. https://deepblue.lib.umich.edu/bitstream/handle/2027.42/31885/0000837.pdf?sequence=1.

Namubiru, Esther, Weijia Li, and Anna Sophia Habib. 2021. "Asao Inoue on Writing Centers and Antiracist Pedagogies." *Connecting Writing Centers Across Borders: A Blog of WLN: A Journal of Writing Center Scholarship.* https://www.wlnjournal.org/blog/2021/03/asao-podcast-2/.

Perin, Dolores, and Rachel Hare. 2010. "A Contextualized Reading-Writing Intervention for Community College Students." *CCRC Brief* 44 (June). http://ccrc.tc.columbia.edu.

Texas Higher Education Coordinating Board. 2016. "Developmental Education: Updates and Progress for Underprepared Students." https://reportcenter.highered.texas.gov/reports/data/crs-de-tsi-developmental-education-updates-and-progress-for-underprepared-students-report/.

Texas Higher Education Coordinating Board. 2018. "Developmental Education Update and 2018–2023 Statewide Plan for Supporting Underprepared Students." https://reportcenter.highered.texas.gov/reports/data/report-on-developmental-education-rider-33/.

Texas Higher Education Coordinating Board. 2021a. "Developmental Education (DE)." Last modified 2021. https://reportcenter.highered.texas.gov/reports/data/crs-developmental-education-overview/.

Texas Higher Education Coordinating Board. 2021b. "Statewide Plan for Supporting Underprepared Students: Updates and Progress." https://reportcenter.highered.texas.gov/reports/legislative/statewide-plan-for-supporting-underprepared-students-updates-and-progress/.

Texas Higher Education Coordinating Board. 2021c. *2021 Texas Public Higher Education Almanac.* https://reportcenter.highered.texas.gov/agency-publication/almanac/2021-texas-public-higher-education-almanac/. Last modified 2020.

United States Census Bureau. 2020. "El Paso County, Texas." Last modified 2020. https://data.census.gov/all?q=el+paso,+texas.

United States Census Bureau. 2020. "Hudspeth County, Texas." Last modified 2020. https://data.census.gov/cedsci/all?q=hudspeth%20county,%20texas.

UTEP. 2021. "UTEP and EPCC Sign Partnership to Promote Student Success." Campus Newsfeed. Last modified November 15, 2021. https://www.utep.edu/newsfeed/campus/utep-and-epcc-sign-partnership-to-promote-student-success.html.

12
REVISITING DWECK'S GROWTH MINDSET IN THE FIRST-YEAR COREQUISITE CLASSROOM

Charlee Sterling

INTRODUCTION

I got ready to leave for school early one crisp Monday morning, prepandemic, with a feeling of dread in the pit of my stomach. My first class of the day was WRT 101-Writing Studies Studio, our college's corequisite composition class, and for reasons I couldn't entirely identify, my most difficult class of the week. I wasn't sure, at least at first, why I had such difficulty with this section; after all, I had taught 101 multiple times previously. Could it be the time of day? A class at 8:30 a.m. is always challenging, especially on Mondays; surely that had something to do with why I was struggling—somehow, we'd gotten to October and the class hadn't "gelled" yet. Several of the students in this section were diligent, pleasant, and polite, but they were a quiet bunch compared to the group of three friends who regularly trooped into the classroom five to ten minutes late (when they showed up at all), fresh from their morning practice, boisterous and with no small degree of ill-disguised resentment at having to be there. This resentment manifested itself in different ways, depending on their mood: some days, one or all three were simply sullen and nonparticipatory; other days, they laughed at in jokes or at something happening in class (other students? their work? me?). At best, their behavior shifted the generally friendly, supportive mood of the class to something awkward and uncertain; at worst, they were disruptive, and I began to despair.

At the beginning of the semester, I had explained to my students what this corequisite composition course was all about: supporting their writing with extra instruction and feedback, not only for the four-credit composition course most of them were taking but also for their coursework across the curriculum. Any writing task or project involving writing, big or small, I told them, was something they could share and get support for in our studio. This had not always been the case at my institution. Goucher College is a four-year liberal arts institution just north of Baltimore, and we have a strong history of emphasizing the importance of writing across the curriculum, but our previous iteration of academic writing (i.e., prior to 2014) was problematic for several reasons. Prior to implementing the corequisite composition curriculum we adapted from the accelerated learning program model created by Peter Adams and our neighbors down the road at the Community College of Baltimore County, our curriculum and course sequence were typical and conventional ("About ALP" 2023). Those who placed directly into first-year composition started their sequence with WRT 104-Composition in the fall, in which they'd focus on developing an academic voice, appropriate grammar and usage, and conducting academic research with proper source citation and documentation. Then in the spring, this cohort of students would select their second-semester composition course (105) from a list of fun, themed courses designed to reinforce the skills learned in their fall composition classes. Further, in the second semester of composition, students could earn college writing proficiency (CWP)—a college requirement necessary for graduation—at the end of 105 as determined by their 105 professors, indicating both to the college and to the student their ability to write successfully in Mainstream US English (or Standard English, as it was then called) with an academic voice, using and documenting sources appropriately to analyze or to make an argument. As CWP was a gateway prerequisite to several upper-level courses in writing and in other majors as well, the stakes were high: for some, not achieving CWP could shut them out of the courses they wanted or could keep them from progressing in their majors.

By contrast, the cohort of students who placed into the developmental level of composition began their college careers already behind: even the course number for developmental composition, WRT 103, reinforced the idea that they were considered lower or lesser every time they looked at their schedules or walked into their classrooms; students had to pass 103 in the fall before being allowed to progress to 104 in the spring, and an additional composition course, WRT 106, in the fall: they started their college careers needing an extra semester of composition, sometimes more than one if they didn't pass 103 the first time through. Further complicating matters was the problematic additional 106 course: a "catchall" comprising students who started in developmental composition (following the 103, 104, 106 sequence), as well as those who started with the regular sequence (104, 105) but who did not earn proficiency and were thus required to take 106 as many times as necessary to earn CWP. No one in 106—neither the students nor the faculty—was happy to be there, and when students frequently had to retake it because they failed to earn CWP, they were taking their fourth or fifth semester of composition.

That these kinds of developmental writing classes and curricula are generally not effective for underprepared, underserved students has been widely documented in this text and elsewhere; that they were incredibly challenging to teach cannot be overstated. How could we make the developmental class rigorous and interesting while meeting underprepared students where they were? How could we effectively reteach skills we thought they should already have upon entering college and do so without making them less rigorous? How could we address the multiplicity of issues and skill levels students brought with them into the classroom? How could we catch this cohort up to their peers while battling a lack of engagement and, often, outright resentment? Students often reported feeling demeaned by the class or by their professors who, they felt, talked down to them or who only focused on improving their grammar and usage. The cohort who regularly placed into developmental writing, it must be acknowledged, included many students of color, students who were economically disadvantaged, first-generation college students, students with learning differences, and students whose home language was not English, or sometimes a combination of all of these subgroups. And they were justifiably frustrated with us and with our curriculum, or downright angry about their placement: they started behind their peers in uninteresting classes often emphasizing grammar and usage, they were shut out of the engaging spring composition offerings, they had to take an extra semester or two of composition in their second year, and because they were delayed in meeting a necessary college requirement, they got behind in or were sometimes shut out of the majors they were interested in. That the previous composition curriculum was thus deeply flawed is obvious, and in 2014 we eagerly adopted a corequisite model as a keystone piece of a reinvented writing curriculum: all students now take a four-credit, 100-level writing studies class in either the fall or the spring of their first year at Goucher, followed by a four-credit 200-level *writing-enriched-curriculum* (WEC) course in their second or third year; CWP is now earned separately by portfolio submission to a committee of readers rather than being the purview of one potentially biased instructor. We offer an honors section of writing studies in the fall for students who apply—15–20 percent of the incoming first-year class—and between 15 and 20 percent, on average, need the support of the corequisite Writing Studies Studio, which they can take concurrently with (or in the opposite semester of) writing studies. We place our students into their classes based on a holistic reading of a brief placement essay and fine tune our placement after classes begin with a diagnostic writing sample administered during the first week of classes, so students needing more support find their way into the corequisite course.

The advantages of our curricular shift for our students were immediate, and I begin each semester with an explanation to students of this current curriculum and the role and aims of the corequisite course, expounding upon its benefits: it keeps them on track with their writing requirement rather than starting them from behind; it creates a community of writers with whom they can share both their work and other concerns, especially concerns about college-level learning; it allows us to customize their learning to their individual writing challenges and to provide real-time feedback on their writing throughout the semester. And, with this particular course section, as with others, I talked about how the studio course aligns with the idea of *mindset*, motivation psychologist Carol Dweck's popular buzzword about how effort and the stories we tell ourselves about our successes, failures, and intellectual risk-taking can positively or negatively affect our learning. On move-in day, our new first-year students arrive to campus with tons of stuff, often more than can fit in their dorm rooms, packed in an assortment of boxes, bins, and bags. But they also bring with them other baggage: what they've learned, or think they've learned, about themselves as students and as writers from their various high-school successes and challenges. In our classrooms and advising sessions with first-year students, we've all heard someone say, "I'm not good at writing" or "I always get Cs on my papers, so I probably won't do well in my writing class." Prior learning experiences often reinforce these attitudes by measuring "successful learning" with a letter or number: an A on a paper, a 93 percent on an exam, a 4 on an AP exam, a 650 on an SAT section. While we might concede that objective assessment of some sort might be necessary both for measuring student learning and for accountability, data points alone might not tell the entire story—they can't reveal how much or little effort a student put into the work, or how the student has improved over time. "Success" can't always be defined collectively, as each student's "baggage" is so individual; perhaps earning a B- on a paper *is* a success for a student who is used to getting Cs and Ds. Dweck, in her popular book *Mindset* (2007), names some of this baggage "mindset," discovering that when taught to perceive success and failure in relation to the effort made and persistence put into the task, not just as innate talent, students, even low-achieving ones, can *improve*; mindset, Dweck, argues, plays a pivotal role in all students' success and in how they perceive failure (219). I read about this idea when her book first came out and found it compelling: wouldn't it be great if all our students, but especially *these* students—those who may feel that they struggle with writing or that they are poor writers—could understand from the beginning that not only is there no shame or stigma in needing more support for their writing but that with the right mindset and right support, they can learn, improve, and grow into great writers?

So, motivated as I always am by this rationale, I asked this 101 section to take an internet-generated mindset quiz to discover whether they had a growth or a fixed mindset towards learning and towards writing; then I assigned two TED Talks, one on mindset, Dweck's "The Power of Believing That You Can Improve" (2014), and another on grit and the importance of perseverance (Duckworth 2013). We talked some about what we learned from the TED Talks and the quizzes and began to dig into their upcoming writing assignments. That's done, I thought; we're set. They've all begun thinking about their mindset, we've talked about it, we all are primed to have a growth mindset about writing: now we can get on with more important matters. This approach had seemed to work well enough in the past; the studio would then carry on with discussions of various relevant writing-related topics, some preplanned and some emerging organically throughout the semester. Several of the students in this particular section really did try to embrace the process: they submitted their exercises and drafts, they willingly engaged in every activity I assigned in class, they read their peers' work and offered their thoughts and opinions; they took every chance at extra help offered them. But that small subgroup just wouldn't buy what I was selling: they missed class frequently; they submitted assignments late or sometimes not at all; they reluctantly submitted their drafts for discussion and at times flat out refused. Merely *talking* about mindset, grit, and persistence was clearly not going to be enough: was this just defiance and poor behavior? Or was something else going on?

FIXED AND GROWTH MINDSETS

Mindset is what we believe about ourselves, our intelligence, and our motivation. Dweck first identified mindset when studying how children perceive success and failure. In one early study, Dweck gave children a round of challenging puzzles to complete; if they solved them, they were given harder ones (Blackwell, Trzesniewski, and Dweck 2007).

Dweck and her team observed and surveyed them: some children loved the challenge, even when they didn't get it right; they enjoyed learning from their mistakes. Some, on the other hand, got frustrated and some even gave up when they hit a puzzle they couldn't do (Dweck 2017, 42). How do people cope with failure? Trying to understand the answer to this question, and the children's differences in attitude, motivation, and effort towards a difficult task, became the basis for Dweck's work. People with a "fixed mindset," Dweck found, believe they were born with certain innate intelligences, talents, and abilities that are limited and "set in stone" or "fixed"; the implication here is that if someone believes their abilities are fixed, they also believe that if they need to make an effort to do or to learn something, they must not be smart or talented in that area and that they could never develop that talent. Further, if people believe their intelligence and ability is fixed, failure at a task means they must not have the innate ability to succeed at it. A fixed mindset can stymy both the struggling student and the successful student: the struggling student might believe no amount of effort will ever lead to a successful outcome, so why bother: "I'm a C- or D writer," one student in this class told me, his very identity defined by the low grade. Another student once remarked, "I'm smart and I do pretty well in all my other classes; I guess writing's just not my thing 'cause I have to work so hard at it." For this student, failure to complete a task, to understand material, or to do well on a test or an essay is personal, an external confirmation of that internal narrative about what they are innately good at and what they aren't.

A high-achieving student with a fixed mindset, however, might believe innate ability and a finite but discernable intelligence alone, not effort or persistence, are at the root of their success, so they might not put much effort into a more challenging new task if they were successful with earlier ones. I overheard one student in this section say to a friend about their writing studies professor, "I always got As and Bs on my papers before: she must not like me"—since their ability, as they saw it, was fixed and established, it wasn't their fault they didn't do well, so more effort towards it wouldn't change anything. Another commented, "I don't understand why I have to take this studio; I don't need help with my writing; they made a mistake making me take this class." This student often didn't bother to complete even the simplest of assignments and sat in the back of my classroom talking with their friends during almost every class instead of engaging with the day's activity.

As Dweck (2017) puts it, for high-achieving students with a fixed mindset, "effort is only for people with deficiencies. And when people already know they're deficient, maybe they have nothing to lose by trying. But if your claim to fame is not having any deficiencies. . . . effort can *reduce* you" (58). Dweck calls this phenomenon "low effort syndrome" (77).

Consider too the other implications of fixed-mindset narratives when they are encoded into and reinforced by our educational structures and institutions; what messages—about race, class or (dis)ability—do we perpetuate, unknowingly, as teachers, within the very structures in which we teach if we have fixed-mindset ideas about our students' intelligence and abilities? At a college where approximately half the student body overall is white, our corequisite composition students are often students of color; anecdotally our corequisite students might also be students who are poor, might be first-generation college students, might be students whose first language is not English, or might be students with learning differences or disabilities. For these first-year students, the combination of a fixed mindset and negative stereotypes can be deeply harmful, "hijack[ing] people's abilities . . . but also" making them "feel like they don't belong or 'fit in,'" creating social as well as academic challenges (Dweck 2010). Dweck (2010) claims that "teaching a growth mindset seems to decrease or even close achievement gaps." Why? Growth mindset challenges the negative labeling and stereotyping that can create or reinforce a fixed mindset. "When Black and Latino students adopt a growth mindset," Dweck notes, "their grades and achievement test scores look more similar to those of their non-stereotyped peers. . . . In these studies, every group seemed to benefit from holding a growth mindset, but the stereotyped groups gained the most" (2017, 76–77). In another study, African-American students were asked to write an essay for an essay contest that was judged by an Ivy League professor, a representative of the "white establishment," who gave them substantial feedback that was both highly critical and constructive. Those students identified as having a growth mindset acknowledged he might be too traditional, too old, or biased but also commented that they could learn something from his feedback even if he came across like "a pompous asshole" (76–77). Students with a fixed mindset, on the other hand, reacted negatively to this feedback, seeing it as a biased "threat, an insult or an attack" (7). Every student enters college with all sorts of pre-received notions about their abilities, successes, and failures, and what they experience in their K–12 education comes with them into their college classrooms. But we should acknowledge that a fixed mindset can have an even greater impact on those of our corequisite students who are affected by structural racism and bias: they suffer even more negative impact from fixed mindsets.

A growth mindset, on the other hand, is the idea that intelligence, talent, and ability can be learned; growth and improvement can happen through sustained effort: persistence, practice and help from others allow us to improve (Dweck 2017, 7). Students with a growth mindset believe grades are not as important as learning itself: they can be passionate about learning for its own sake, even if they struggle with it. Students with growth mindsets are willing to keep working at something, even if they're not very good at it when they start, because they enjoy the challenge; failure is not a referendum on their innate intelligence but rather an opportunity to learn something that will help them improve next time (16). "I love writing," one corequisite student told me. "I write all the time. I didn't get a very good grade on that last essay I was working on, but I met with my professor and now I see how I can rewrite it. That last draft was really good practice for our next assignment." This kind of love for the subject, or "passion," as Dweck puts it, "is the hallmark of the growth mindset. . . . The passion for stretching yourself and sticking to it, even (or especially) when it's not going well, is the hallmark of the growth mindset. This is the mindset that allows people to thrive during some of the most challenging things in their lives" (8). Imagine having a corequisite classroom full of passionate writers and empowering them to unlock their own potential, simply by shifting their self-narratives: those who previously thought or have been told they weren't as gifted as others could now learn and grow and achieve if they're passionate about learning and willing to put in sustained effort, and students who already thought of themselves as bright could work harder and achieve even more.

Mindset, Dweck (2017) claims, "permeates *every* part of your life. Much of what you think of as your personality actually grows out of this 'mindset'; much of what may be preventing you from fulfilling your potential grows out of it" (68). This is an enormously important claim, implying that once we understand how and why our mindset isn't working for us, we can change it and have control over how we fulfill our potential. As teachers, we want to help *every* student reach their full potential as writers, and as teachers of corequisite composition, we especially want to enable low-achieving writers to improve and to be successful. But how realistic is this goal? Will a corequisite writer ever reach the level those in, say, our honors classes achieve? Dweck addresses this objection head on, posing the question, "Does this mean that anyone with the right mindset can do well? Are all children created equal?" (64). Dweck doesn't answer the question directly but points to an underperforming school in Los Angeles, Garfield High School (of

Stand and Deliver fame), where teachers set out to teach calculus, and despite being told they'd never succeed, students not only passed AP calculus but went on to earn AP credit: "There's a lot of intelligence out there being wasted by underestimating students' potential to develop" (60, 33). Dweck's many years of studies with students ranging from four-year-olds to first-year college students provide much compelling evidence that, when taught to perceive success and failure in relation to the effort made and not just innate talent, students, even low-achieving ones, can significantly improve; mindset must play a pivotal role in all students' success and in how they perceive failure. Helping students succeed is what we all aspire to do as composition teachers, right? We want to believe that everyone can write well if they just try hard enough and that we *can* teach everyone to be strong writers if *we* just try hard enough. But we often have no idea what we're up against.

FIRST-YEAR-STUDENT CHALLENGES AND FIXED MINDSET

First-year students bring lots of baggage from their previous educational experiences to college, and the transition from high school to college offers new challenges on top of what they already bring with them: making new connections, both institutional and social, creating new social and academic habits, being responsible for managing their own time, setting priorities, maintaining physical and mental health, and adjusting to both their new social independence and, often, to new (and higher) academic expectations. The first-year experience, Dweck (2017) notes, often encompasses "the anxiety" of the "dethroned": students who thought of themselves as smart and able in high school and were repeatedly told so directly and through the grades and other achievements they earned, but who either didn't get into their top choice of school or who suddenly find themselves surrounded by people just as bright or brighter (58). Could this anxiety be part of what was going on with my small group of rebellious corequisite composition students? Perhaps their attitudes and behaviors were a direct manifestation of low-effort syndrome. Were they fixed-mindset students who needed to protect their identities as high achievers, and who wanted to look smart to new peers and professors but not have to work too hard because they saw the necessity for effort and persistence as a sign of a lack of intelligence and ability (60–61)?

Some of Dweck's work suggests this might have been exactly what was going on. She and her team conducted a study of first-year chemistry students, many of whom were premed, and many of whom had been very high achievers in high school but were now encountering a "weed-out" class that could be a determinant of their future career paths. Students in Chem I are often considered "cutthroat," but that's because the stakes of their success are so high. Dweck and her team surveyed the students to determine their mindsets at the beginning of the semester and took careful note of their grades and study habits throughout, and what they found is fascinating: many students did poorly on their first exam, and they were given the chance to look at the tests of those who scored better. Those identified with growth mindsets chose to look at higher-scoring tests, seeing a chance to learn and improve. Dweck found they were able to rebound after earning a poor first grade, and many in this group improved their grades significantly throughout the semester (33). These first-year chem students demonstrated important aspects of a growth mindset necessary for success in college: curiosity, persistence, the willingness to take risks by challenging oneself, and the importance of finding help when needed.

Those identified as having a fixed mindset, however, chose to look primarily at the tests of those with close-to-failing grades rather than the exams of those with higher grades. Dweck (2017) argues they did this to make themselves feel better: "Others did worse than I did" (36, 60–61). She further found that some of these fixed-mindset students' grades didn't improve on the next exam after that initial low score because they didn't try to learn why they had done poorly: they often assigned blame to others or found other excuses for their poor results (33). Perhaps this mindset was at the root of my "problem" studio students: if they saw themselves in the same light as Dweck's fixed-mindset Chem I students, it's no wonder they didn't want to participate in class because, fundamentally, they didn't think they belonged there and saw the results of their placement essays as a failure on their part that happened before they even arrived on campus: their very presence in the studio countered their own belief about their ability, intelligence, and potential for success; it reinforced a fixed mindset—not "I failed" but "I am a failure" (17–18).

In another study of first-year students at the University of Hong Kong, where everything is taught in English, Dweck (2017) measured the mindsets of students with weaker English skills and then asked them whether, if they were provided the opportunity to take a course to improve those skills, they would take it (17–18). The students who said they'd take this course if offered were those with a growth mindset: they thought the course would give them the chance to better their English-language skills and thus improve their potential for college success overall (18).

Those who were uninterested in taking such a course, however, were those with a fixed mindset: these first-year students, Dweck argues, needed to feel smart at the beginning of their college careers; to agree to take this course would be to reveal "deficiencies," and they were willing to trade future success as college-level learners for a short-term validation of their innate intelligence, ability, and the maintaining of their identities as smart kids: this, Dweck concludes, "is how the fixed mindset makes people into non-learners" (18).

A similar study conducted by Sisk et al. (2018) helps explain why some students register for our studio course even if they don't place into it: they come in with a growth mindset about writing and will take *any* opportunity to learn that they can get; it also explains, in part, why plenty of the students we do place into the corequisite studio might choose *not* to register for it, or to register and attend grudgingly. The consequences of a fixed mindset, though, are serious: I didn't want any of my corequisite students to be nonlearners right at the start of their college careers just because their placement indicated a need for more support; if my "problem students" had a fixed mindset, how could I turn this fixed-mindset narrative around and steer them towards success, not only in studio but also as writers and learners?

A GROWTH-MINDSET COREQUISITE CLASSROOM

One problem I identified was my own lack of initial follow-through: I had asked students to identify their mindsets towards the studio but never actually asked them directly to share their answers with me; a few did in our general discussion about mindset during the first week of class, but most kept the results of their mindset quizzes to themselves. Thus, I hadn't tried working with them to understand why they approached writing with a particular mindset, or how they might shift it, nor did I give them actual tools or strategies to do so: all I did was to give them another label to contend with, essentially signaling, "You should have a growth mindset—get working on that!" So, the first thing I did to try to turn this around was to conference individually with every one of the students in the studio: friendly and encouraging, I "invited" them—all of them—to my office at scheduled times for a (mandatory) conversation with me. For a class only scheduled to meet one hour a week, this process was somewhat laborious and time consuming, but well worth it. Because I required it of all students in the studio class, and not just the few problem ones, no one felt singled out, put on the spot, or reprimanded, plus having to meet me face to face feels much less anonymous, even in a small class of ten or twelve people, than sitting in the classroom; even the most resentful student finds it much harder to disengage. I took notes, asking each student about their previous writing experiences and their personal academic challenges, especially their writing challenges, and how they thought the studio was going. And, in passing, I also asked them what their mindset quiz revealed: while several of the engaged, amenable students expressed having a fixed, and not a growth, mindset, *all three* of the challenging students reported a fixed mindset.

Listening to these three students talk, I immediately began to discover the reasons: one student revealed he hadn't actually spent more than ten minutes on his placement essay, figuring some other factors—As and Bs in high-school English and some AP credit—would weigh into placement. As someone who saw himself as a strong writer who didn't need corequisite composition, he felt stuck because he didn't know he could have asked about or challenged his placement. The second of these three students revealed he had always hated writing because he was dyslexic and had always done poorly with writing in middle and high school. The third problem student was simply embarrassed, confessing he felt he was a bad writer who never put much effort into writing; he had wanted to make more of an effort to improve but felt a degree of social pressure to go along with his two new teammates and friends, which meant he should not seem to care too much about the class in front of them. The importance of these conversations become immediately obvious: I was able to better understand the root of these students' behavior and attitudes towards the class. By taking the time to listen, I gave them a chance to be and feel heard.

Some recent meta-analyses finding weak correlations between mindset and achievement have given critics reasons to push back against Dweck's mindset theory (Loper 2021); they frequently point out that she dismisses innate intelligence as something that doesn't matter while saying all we need to do is praise effort, not intelligence (Gross-Loh 2016). However, innate intelligence, talent, and ability *do* matter—it's not an either/or situation. Dweck notes, both in her most recent edition of *Mindset* in 2017 and in an interview in the *Atlantic* (2010), that everyone has fixed mindsets about some things and growth mindsets about others and that the important thing is to identify and try to understand our fixed-mindset triggers. Student success depends on many things, such as education and access, in addition to innate intelligence *and* effort (Hendrick 2019). In my conversation with the first student, I tried to model a growth mindset myself by acknowledging my error and what I had learned from it alongside an acknowledgment of both his fixed mindset and writing ability; I then encouraged him to share some of his writing with me, and when I agreed with him that it was certainly competent, he was reassured to have his idea of himself as a strong writer validated. While it was too late in the semester for him to drop the class, I encouraged him to share his skills and habits with his studio peers during workshops, which he began to do with growing confidence in his own skills.

As Carl Hendrick (2019) points out, a growth mindset alone is not enough for a struggling student; when they make an effort and still don't achieve, other factors beyond their control—racial bias, poverty, or learning differences, often unacknowledged—might be at play that no amount of effort can overcome; we can't just tell low-achieving students to "try harder": we must give them new strategies when the old ones are ineffective. By focusing on mindset and effort, are we then we giving false promises to students, especially those who underachieve, that they will be successful writers? In the 2017 edition of *Mindset* (published ten years after her original publication), Dweck is careful to note mindset is *not* the belief that "anyone can be anything . . . with proper motivation or education" but rather that we can't predict how far someone might go if they make a sustained effort and have help: "The Growth mindset is the belief that abilities can be cultivated" (50). But she concedes that mindset "doesn't tell you how much change is possible or how long change will take. And it doesn't mean that *everything*, like preferences or values, can be changed" (quoted in Gross-Loh 2016). Dweck concedes that her ideas are often oversimplified, that when we praise effort and only effort, we're more focused on students' self-esteem when we should be focusing on what was learned by making that effort, what strategies were working and not working, and what other resources might help someone find success (Gross-Loh 2016). In conversation with the second, dyslexic, student I discovered he hadn't documented his need for accommodations because he hadn't known how or that he could, so I put him in touch with the people, forms, and other resources he needed. The third student, seeing a shift in his comrades' attitudes and behaviors, began making more of an effort, and the problem in my studio eventually began to resolve itself. Relieved, I began thinking about what other classroom strategies I could use to actively and intentionally foster a growth mindset.

One strategy is to create opportunities for students to experience success in real time, bringing about a growth mindset by providing students with an effective strategy and praising them for using it successfully (Hendrick 2019; Loper 2021). For example, a student shared a draft of an analytical essay they were writing for a history class; the essay lacked a clear focus and purpose and also lacked a context for readers to understand it. Where in earlier iterations of the studio I might have simply shared the draft on the screen, asked students to talk through what was and wasn't working and offer their suggestions for improvement, this time I provided students with a strategy for refining the thesis: write your thesis as two clauses: in the first, state your opinion; in the second, state how and/or why you have that opinion by using the word *because* at the beginning of the second clause. I asked everyone—not just the student whose work it was—to work in pairs to write a new thesis for the introduction, recording their work in a collaborative document so we could directly compare their revisions to the original. Though varying in quality, all their revisions improved upon the original, and all the students had a real-time growth-mindset win: their effort led to success because they learned and applied a new, specific strategy.

Other ways we can foster growth mindsets in our classrooms, even if we never mention the term, are through our approaches to assignment design, assessment, collaboration, and metacognition. In our corequisite studio, we spend a great deal of time simply analyzing assignment prompts, probing their design: What is a particular instructor asking us to do in this assignment? What are its parameters? What must we do or include to be successful? What are some options for how this essay might look? We talk through questions like these whenever a student gets a new writing assignment. This process takes so much anxiety out of the writing process, especially for those with fixed mindsets who might not understand the assignment, let alone have strategies for approaching it. Then we might try some of the possible approaches we've identified by completing a part of the assignment together or in small groups to discover what works and what doesn't. Another consideration is the assignment design itself: creating assignments that allow students to experiment and try new approaches is crucial. One way of achieving this is to scaffold a larger high-stakes assignment by breaking it up into smaller, low-stakes assignments: an outline, introduction, conclusion, body paragraph; or a project proposal, an annotated bibliography of sources, for example, that will be graded along with the final draft. The high-stakes final-essay drafts or projects, I feel, are the purview of the composition class when it comes to grading an individual assignment; I tell students I won't be grading the final draft at all. Instead, I assess the low-stakes assignment steps, making the completion of these parts or steps, and not the quality of the work, the focus of the grade. Working with parts of a draft in the corequisite classroom, we emphasize multiple revisions, experimenting with new wording or new ways of organizing ideas and finding new ways of bringing evidence into the conversation. We further practice skills and habits by analyzing, revising, editing, and proofreading full rough drafts, both sample essays I provide and students' own work; assignment samples are crucial because they illustrate how an assignment might be approached, taking away much of the anxiety and clarifying what might be expected of them. Students do share final drafts of their writing assignments with the class and with me, not for a grade but rather so we can all see how much improvement they've made upon the original.

How we assess students in the course can also contribute to a growth mindset: do our assignments and approaches focus students' attention on the easiest way to earn an A in the course or rather on their curiosity, effort, and intellectual, academic growth? In previous iterations of the corequisite studio, I employed a grading contract in my corequisite composition course, modeling my approach after Asao Inoue's (2019): in my grading contract I specified exactly what students needed to do to pass the class with a B: how many classes they needed to attend, how many assignments they needed to complete, how much they needed to be engaged and participate (3, 16, 130). The grading contract was designed to emphasize effort and labor rather than to objectively measure the quality of students' work, taking a great deal of anxiety about grades off the table. More recently, I've been experimenting with "ungrading" my classroom completely: marking low-stakes activities, exercises, and steps or parts of larger high-stakes assignments as complete or incomplete and accompanying them with written and oral feedback only, without any letter grades whatsoever (Blum and Kohn 2020). Students are excited by this approach because it allows them to focus on improving their writing without the anxiety of earning that A or B and without worrying about earning a failing grade on a particular assignment: if they do poorly, they revise and resubmit it, and in fact, revision is a tremendously important part of student labor and effort. I give students the opportunity to tell me, honestly, how much effort they put into a particular assignment and its revisions and to discuss any mitigating factors that may have played a role in low effort, which helps me assess their work more meaningfully.

As I mention above, collaboration also plays an important role in the corequisite classroom: we write in community, completing writing exercises collaboratively; we share our individual work in pairs and small groups or workshop it with the whole class, supporting each other with constructive feedback and strategies for improvement; I share some of my work in progress as well so students can see the messiness of my own process and understand everyone has writing challenges. Another significant way I collaborate with students is by conferencing, either individually or in small groups. Conferencing allows us to work together on individual challenges and allows me to provide specific feedback and resources as needed, and most recently in my ungraded classroom, to collaborate with them to determine a midterm and final grade based on the effort they've made and the growth and improvement we discover together.

Perhaps the most interesting view of students' mindsets comes from reflective writing and metacognition and how metacognitive activities help with the collaborative process. One way I employ reflection is to ask students to identify the specific writing-related topics they would like me to cover in class: we thus collaborate on the actual course content while students also reflect on their own individual writing challenges and areas they might want to improve on. I also have students reflect on concerns or challenges with each new high-stakes writing assignment or project involving writing, especially after we complete an assignment-prompt analysis. They identify areas they might already know how to approach, areas where they might need help, and the challenges or other issues (curricular and extracurricular) that might impact their success. They then set a few specific goals for that assignment. When they've completed the high-stakes assignment or project, I ask them to write about their writing again, both to reflect on the process they used to complete it and to assess their own effort, learning, and growth: What did they feel they did successfully? What could be improved? What are their takeaways or goals for the next assignment? These reflections and self-assessments contribute greatly to conversations about grades and allow students to identify connections in their learning across the curriculum, crucial to gaining transferable skills (Scharff et al. 2017).

Shortly after Dweck first published *Mindset* in 2007, it seemed as if everyone, educators to coaches to leaders in corporate America, began talking about "leveraging" mindset. Despite the passing of this motivational psychology term into the popular zeitgeist, and despite the criticism Dweck has received (some of it justifiable) of her work, it cannot be denied that mindset can make a difference in our students' learning and success as writers. These ideas are particularly relevant in this moment as students enter college not only with the previously described educational baggage but also having suffered significant educational loss during the pandemic. What we say and do in the classroom, especially in the first year, matters: not just believing in our students' writing abilities but also believing in their potential to grow as writers and teaching them to believe it too. Implementing strategies that can help corequisite students to both achieve and meaningfully redefine for themselves what success in their writing can look like will contribute to their success in the composition classroom and across the curriculum.

REFERENCES

"About ALP." 2023. https://alp-deved.org/about-alp/.

Blackwell, Lisa S., Kali H. Trzesniewski, and Carol Sorich Dweck. 2007. "Implicit Theories of Intelligence Predict Achievement Across an Adolescent Transition: A Longitudinal Study and an Intervention." *Child Development* 78 (1): 246–63. https://doi.org/10.1111/j.1467-8624.2007.00995.x.

Blum, Susan, and Alfie Kohn, eds. 2020. *Ungrading* 2020. Morgantown: West Virginia University Press.

Duckworth, Angela. 2013. "Grit: The Power of Passion and Perseverance." Filmed May 6, 2013. TED video, 6:12. https://www.ted.com/talks/angela_lee_duckworth_grit_the_power_of_passion_and_perseverance?language=en.

Dweck, Carol S. 2010. *Mindset and Equitable Education*. National Association of Secondary School Principals. http://www.my-ecoach.com/online/resources/3865/Equitable_Mindsets.pdf.

Dweck, Carol S. 2014. "The Power of Believing that You Can Improve." *TED Talks*. https://www.ted.com/talks/carol_dweck_the_power_of_believing_that_you_can_improve/transcript.

Dweck, Carol S. 2017. *Mindset: Changing the Way You Think to Fulfill Your Potential*. New York: Ballantine Books.

Gross-Loh, Christine. 2016. "How Praise Became a Consolation Prize." *Atlantic*, December 16. https://www.theatlantic.com/education/archive/2016/12/how-praise-became-a-consolation-prize/510845/.

Hendrick, Carl. 2019. "The Growth Mindset Problem." Aeon, March 11. https://aeon.co/essays/schools-love-the-idea-of-a-growth-mindset-but-does-it-work.

Inoue, Asao B. 2019. *Labor-Based Grading Contracts: Building Equity and Inclusion in the Compassionate Writing Classroom*. Fort Collins, CO: WAC Clearinghouse. https://doi.org/10.37514/PER-B.2019.0216.0.

Loper, Chris. 2021. "Growth Mindsets Debunked? Not So Fast." Northwest Educational Service, May 16. https://www.nwtutoring.com/2021/05/16/growth-mindsets-debunked-not-so-fast/.

Scharff, Lauren F. V., John Draeger, Dominique Verpoorten, Marie Devlin, Lucie S. Dvorakova, Jason M. Lodge, and Susan V. Smith. 2017. "Exploring Metacognition as a Support for Learning Transfer." *Teaching and Learning Inquiry* 5 (1). https://pdfs.semanticscholar.org/b095/f5f82a6655311651dc69626699424e232e50.pdf.

Sisk, Victoria F., Alexander P. Burgoyne, Jingze Sun, Jennifer L. Butler, and Brooke N. Macnamara. 2018. "To What Extent and Under Which Circumstances Are Growth Mind-Sets Important to Academic Achievement? Two Meta-Analyses." *Psychological Science* 29 (4): 549. https://org/10.1177/0956797617739704.

"Study Finds Popular 'Growth Mindset' Educational Interventions Aren't Very Effective." 2018. Science Daily, May 22. https://www.sciencedaily.com/releases/2018/05/180522114523.htm.

PART V

Faculty Development

13
COREQUISITE COMPOSITION COURSES
A Need for Institutionalizing Professional Development for Programmatic Success

Haleh Azimi and Elsbeth Mantler

INTRODUCTION
Background

The accelerated learning program (ALP) is a corequisite model developed at the Community College of Baltimore County (CCBC) by Professor Emeritus Peter Adams over a decade ago. Students enrolled in ALP take credit-level college composition concurrently with a below-credit integrated reading and writing course (ACLT 053). At CCBC, the Composition I course includes twenty students, and then ten of those students also take ACLT 053 in the same semester with the same professor. There are variations of corequisite models across the country, but the overall adoption of corequisite models since ALP was developed has resulted in a significant developmental education reform. Taking both courses at the same time has improved student success rates tremendously compared to the stand-alone, traditional developmental sequence, in which students could be required take a number of below-credit writing and reading courses before ever entering their credit-level Composition I course.

A Community College Research Center (CCRC) study revealed that 74 percent of students who enrolled in ALP were successful in the first-year English composition course, more than double the success rate under the traditional program (Cho et al. 2012). While ALP originated at CCBC, there are now over three hundred ALP institutions across the nation, and seven states have made large-scale adoptions of some type of corequisite configuration for their composition courses. This adoption of ALP is largely due to years of longitudinal data that support its efficacy in raising success rates and lowering attrition rates for students placed in developmental reading and/or writing. English speakers of other languages (ESOL) programs have also reformed their course offerings: ESOL students are co-enrolled in Composition I and their highest level of ESOL writing and/or reading courses in the same semester and with the same professor for both courses.

The ALP model is successful in part because it ameliorates some of the stigmatizing effects experienced by students when they are placed in a section labeled completely *developmental*. An important feature of ALP is the relationship that develops among the students, who take the two courses together, and between the students and the instructor, who teaches both sections. The structure of this course removes a barrier for students who previously may have taken multiple levels of stand-alone developmental courses before ever reaching a credit-level course.

ALP has reached many postsecondary institutions across the country due to its positive contributions to student success, such as access to credit courses while taking below-credit work and significant gains in retention and course-completion rates. The work in ALP has influenced overall developmental education reform efforts not only in English composition but also in reading, ESOL, and math. The nature of this model also embraces the importance of and encourages instruction time for acknowledging student's nonacademic needs or noncognitive factors, which is the keystone of ALP. This corequisite developmental education reform effort is important to the field because it typically serves historically marginalized populations.

THE NEED FOR PROFESSIONAL DEVELOPMENT (PD) AND INSTITUTIONAL SUPPORT

The Problem

Developmental, or below-credit courses, were designed to "develop" the reading, writing, or math skills of students who have been historically marginalized, such as students of color. Historically marginalized students have typically placed into developmental reading, writing, and math courses, and these students are disproportionately students of color, continuing adults, first-generation students, and students from low-income backgrounds (Ganga, Mazzariello, and Edgecomb 2018, 2). The approach to placing students in developmental education courses is deficit oriented and further marginalizes student populations. The accelerated learning program and other corequisite offerings provide developmental education reform to assist with providing an equitable and accessible educational opportunity for students.

Therefore, faculty teaching students placed in ALP and other corequisite models need to engage in opportunities for quality professional development on an ongoing basis to ensure they are trained to work with their students, and professional-development opportunities are important for both full-time and part-time faculty (Azimi and Mantler 2020). These professional-development opportunities should be created with deep intentionality and must be grounded in national and institutional data.

This ongoing and meaningful professional development is required to sustain quality corequisite models and must be done with significant institutional support. Institutions across the board must put financial support behind what they think is important.

Postsecondary institutions rely heavily on adjunct-faculty employment, and in community colleges in particular, "about 67 percent of instructional faculty are part-time" (Bickerstaff and Chavarín 2018). According to Jennifer Datray, Patrick Saxon, and Nara Martirosyan (2014), the lack of PD "may be considered neglect on the part of administration as professional development is cited as a best practice that is essential for program success" (40). Achieving the Dream (ATD), a nonprofit organization that strengthens community colleges to promote student success, identified the need to develop large-scale efforts to connect adjunct faculty with student-success initiatives utilizing a thoughtful and specific approach. ATD developed the Engaging Adjunct Faculty in the Student Success Movement program in 2016 because adjunct-faculty engagement is essential in improving student success (Bickerstaff and Chavarín 2018).

Adjunct faculty are often hired at the last minute to teach below-credit courses, creating few opportunities for professional development. Datray, Saxon, and Martirosyan (2014) argue that adjunct faculty teaching below-credit courses are not provided enough meaningful professional-development opportunities, and withholding such professional development from adjunct faculty negatively impacts student-success outcomes and the experiences of faculty teaching the courses. Peter Adams (2019) contends that the students placed in below-credit courses are taught by the most marginalized faculty at the most underfunded institutions. With this dependency on this marginalized faculty group, there is an even greater need for institutions to provide funding to sustain high-quality corequisite programs such as ALP.

Likewise, faculty development for both full-time and part-time faculty is equally important when adopting corequisite programs. When implementing and institutionalizing a high-quality corequisite program such as ALP, leadership must think about professional-development needs in order to address various components of the program so it will continue to improve results for students placed in below-credit level courses. Because of the unique structure and focus of ALP courses (including extensive contact time with students, smaller classes sizes, and an emphasis on addressing noncognitive factors in students' lives), professional development is necessary to sustain a program that supports both faculty and student needs.

Along with an emphasis on professional development for faculty, institutions must view corequisite programs as only a small piece of the ecosystem of student success. The work is not completed once a corequisite program is established. Rather, institutions must evaluate a variety of developmental education reforms in conjunction with one another. Accelerated corequisite models must work with the institution's efforts to address curriculum reform and redesign, delivery of instruction through different modalities, and assessment and placement reforms. With these moving parts, it is imperative to institutionalize ongoing and quality professional-development opportunities so those teaching the courses truly understand the reform efforts, their connections with one another, and how to put into practice the work relating to corequisite composition while considering other related developmental education reforms. Without meaningful and ongoing professional development, those teaching the courses will understandably have a gap in their knowledge about how to approach their work, and this important professional development can only occur if institutions provide funding to ensure its ongoing success.

Addressing the Problem

Professional development is instrumental in the success of a long-term program like ALP, and such professional development requires significant institutional support. Institutional support is necessary both in terms of advocacy from senior leadership and financial support for programs.

At CCBC, it took holistic leadership support and financial support of the administration to provide Adams with the necessary means to identify ALP as the course option for students who placed one level below college composition. Support from the administration was critical in moving this program forward because it helped others—such as faculty in ESOL, math, and academic literacy—at the college to have a shared understanding of and commitment to offering below-credit courses

Table 13.1. Below credit and acceleration pre-IRW

Semester 1	Semester 2	Semester 3
RDNG 051	RDNG 052 4 billable hrs.	ENGL 101 3 credit hrs.
ENGL 051 4 billable hrs.	ALP ENGL 052 3 billable hrs. + ENGL 101 3 credit hrs.	

Table 13.2. Acceleration with IRW

Semester 1	Semester 2
ALP ACLT 053 + ENGL 101 3 credit hrs.	General education courses

within this new model. The support of administration has been essential throughout the institutionalization of ALP at CCBC. Grant funds were also secured from the William and Flora Hewlett Foundation through the Community College Research Center in 2010, and then in 2012 the Kresge Foundation also contributed significant funding for the program (Adams 2021).

In 2016, CCBC reconfigured its developmental education offerings. The stand-alone, below-credit English and reading courses were eliminated from the course catalogue, as was the upper-level developmental writing course, Advanced Writing II (ENGL 052). This was the three-billable-hour course paired with Composition I (ENGL 101) when Adams first configured ALP. The institution shifted from separate and sequential stand-alone developmental writing and reading courses to an academic literacy (ACLT) course, which is an integrated reading, writing, and critical-thinking, below-credit course. ACLT 053 is the integrated reading and writing (IRW) class that has been paired with ENGL 101 since 2016. With this change, the reading discipline shifted to academic literacy (ACLT), and English and ACLT faculty have taught ALP since this shift.

Prior to the implementation of IRW, students who placed at the lowest level of RDNG and ENGL had to take sixteen below-credit hours (billable hours) before entering Composition I (ENGL 101). If a student placed in RDNG 052 and ENGL 052, they still had to take four hours of

RDNG 052 plus the six hours of ALP. Since adopting ALP and its IRW model, students who have placed in ALP (ACLT 053 with ENGL 101) take three below-credit hours paired with ENGL 101.

The shift in how CCBC approached developmental education through the integration of developmental writing and reading required cross-collaboration among disciplines, departments, and offices at the college. ALP connected to the Office of Instruction and Student Services, which includes advising, testing, and registration. This cross-collaboration reached all areas of the college, and the collaborative work occurred because of the holistic-leadership support and financial support of the senior-level administration when ALP was first adopted. In any scaled change, such as the structural and pedagogical shift to an IRW course, it is important that all the participants in the student's experience are knowledgeable about this reform. Administrative support is very crucial during these times of transition because it can help bring together the many facets of the institution that serve the students' needs.

Since CCBC has shifted its approach to ALP with ACLT 053 as the integrated reading and writing (IRW) model as the support course, the leadership structure has also changed. Prior to this shift, Composition I was paired with Developmental Writing II as its support course. At this time, the structure included one ALP director from the English department. However, once ACLT 053 became a part of the model, the institution recognized a need for leadership representation from both the English and academic literacy disciplines; therefore, ALP is now led in a codirectorship model: one English and one academic literacy faculty work collaboratively to direct the work within this program. This codirectorship model reflects the shift in eliminating all below-credit levels at CCBC, aside from ACLT 053, the IRW below-credit course. Both codirectors teach one ALP course every semester, but they are also provided release time to lead the extensive professional-development efforts required to sustain a successful program at CCBC and professional development for external institutions.

The ALP student-success data helped justify to CCBC's senior leadership that providing significant financial support for the program would result in continued improvement in student-success outcomes. Therefore, through the years, ALP leadership has identified the need to allocate funding for ongoing professional development to support and sustain the success of ALP. Both the unique structure of the model and the interwoven nature of the program merit continued support to faculty. It was clear to the administration that ALP was meeting student needs in a way the traditional levels of developmental writing and reading CCBC used to offer did not. Because of this success, CCBC's administration provided financial backing to further its ongoing support for this program.

Since ALP's adoption, providing ongoing, relevant professional development has been essential in its successes, and the internal and external professional-development opportunities are outlined in the following sections. These sections provide an emphasis on various professional-development formats to address shifting from traditional developmental models to corequisite models and curricular-based professional-development offerings. These professional-development opportunities have a range of purposes and require different support from the administration, but primary to ALP's success is providing quality professional development to those involved with the program. The importance of consistent professional development is paramount for faculty teaching ALP. Oftentimes, the faculty teaching in this model do not receive any formal education or training regarding corequisite models of learning, so the onus then falls on the institution to help ensure faculty are able to support these particular students. Professional opportunities can only occur if there is both leadership and financial support.

PROFESSIONAL DEVELOPMENT AT THE NATIONAL LEVEL

ALP became an integral part of developmental education reform efforts at the national level once the Community College Research Center (CCRC) published its study, which demonstrated ALP's significant success (Cho et al. 2012; Jenkins et al. 2010). CCRC's research initially focused on the outcomes of ALP-enrolled students compared to those enrolled in developmental English and reading courses, along with ALP's cost-saving measures for institutions (Jenkins et al. 2010). CCRC continued to focus on the successes of ALP and found that ALP-enrolled students had higher attempt rates in Composition I, higher completion rates in Composition II, and increased persistence compared to their non-ALP counterparts (Cho et al. 2012). These positive results garnered ALP national attention because of the program's work toward improving outcomes for students placed in developmental courses.

Consequently, the need to provide professional development at the national level has been part of the ALP director's and now codirectors' job responsibilities. This national level professional development has included leading the National Conference on Acceleration in Developmental Education (CADE), regional conference opportunities, and external consultations for institutions adopting ALP and other corequisite models. CCBC supports the ALP codirectors in leading these national professional-development efforts by providing financial backing for their national-level work. This financial support has been delivered in a variety of formats, including assisting with payments for plenary speakers at CADE, providing funding to support faculty and staff attendance at some of the national events hosted by ALP, or allocating funds to help assist outside institutions to work on curricular changes.

The National Conference on Acceleration in Developmental Education (CADE)
While the Community College of Baltimore County (CCBC) is where ALP was initially adopted, other postsecondary institutions took the CCRC studies seriously and decided to reform their own developmental education programs to improve their student outcomes and experiences. As a result, there was a need to share CCBC's corequisite model at the national level. CCBC, under Peter Adams's leadership, decided to create the National Conference on Acceleration in Developmental Education (CADE) in 2009 to share information about ALP and create opportunities for scale-up at other institutions.

CADE 2009 was hosted in Baltimore, Maryland, and it included a rich offering of approximately twenty-five concurrent sessions that focused on a wide range of topics. Interestingly, the concurrent sessions offered at CADE 2009 were mainly presented by faculty and staff outside CCBC. It was very apparent that ALP as an approach was fully embraced by colleagues in the field who wanted to find ways to better serve students placed in below-credit-level courses. The focus of the concurrent sessions included approaches to corequisite coursework in English, reading, mathematics, and English speakers of other languages (ESOL). Faculty, administration, and staff also presented on ways their institutions had addressed noncognitive factors and had approached the scale-up of ALP and other corequisite models.

CCBC has since hosted CADE every June, and these conferences typically have rotated from Baltimore (or locations near Baltimore in close proximity to CCBC) to other states that have adopted corequisite models for any below-credit-level offerings. CADE has always included a day filled with preconference sessions to launch the conference festivities. These preconference sessions are half-day, hands-on, professional-development opportunities that facilitate in-depth work among the preconference facilitators and attendees. These preconference sessions are important because they help institutions plan for acceleration adoptions with their students and programs in mind. Since 2009, CADE has offered preconference sessions, working with seventy-five to one hundred preconference attendees each year.

Since its initial launch, CADE has functioned as a space for important professional-development opportunities for educators in the field of developmental education. As such, this national conference does not include conference themes—instead, we contextualize the purpose of the conference in the Call for Proposals (CFP) published each year in March. The CFP situates the conference in important work that connects directly with acceleration in postsecondary education while also focusing on the importance of concurrent sessions that connect with topics current and relevant to the field of developmental education reform and research. For example, some of the concurrent sessions at CADE 2021 and CADE 2022 addressed linguistic variations in the classroom, antiracist curricular approaches, equitable placement practices, and various corequisite models for all points of adoption, and many of the sessions included student presenters.

This approach to filling the program with timely and quality concurrent sessions has also helped meet the professional-development needs of faculty, staff, administrators, and institutions at various levels in their acceleration and developmental education reform efforts. The conference is a way to break down the academic silos present at many institutions and engage with many facets of the student experience connected to developmental education reform. The needs of both faculty and students in corequisite models of learning can be unique and specific, so a community of practice on the national level helps practitioners communicate about strengths and challenges of their particular reform movements. The range of offerings at CADE provides support for anyone who is interested in ALP or other acceleration models regardless of their knowledge level.

Mid-Atlantic Teaching and Learning Summit

While CADE is a national conference, there are regional gatherings that can serve as beneficial professional-development opportunities. In 2019, ALP hosted the first Mid-Atlantic Teaching and Learning Summit at CCBC. This gathering was for educators from Maryland, Delaware, West Virginia, Virginia, New Jersey, and Pennsylvania. Math, ESOL, and ALP were the topics covered during this one-day event. A number of states require that institutions offer below-credit coursework, and the mid-Atlantic region is widely representative of states that do not require corequisite courses; therefore, the corequisite and developmental education reforms vary from school to school across this region. The codirectors of ALP at CCBC identified a need for a regional gathering to provide an opportunity for educators within the region to connect in a professional setting.

The Mid-Atlantic Teaching and Learning Summit provided a space for educators to share practices and policies relating to corequisite work and developmental education reforms at the local level. This important professional-development opportunity featured Adams as the keynote speaker, along with a panel of educators who candidly talked about reforms at their institutions. Additionally, invited presenters provided hour-long sessions on topics ranging from linguistic diversity in teaching composition, to math, and ESOL in the corequisite model.

Working within regional and local consortiums is an opportune way to gather and conduct targeted professional-development opportunities that relate specifically to those within local communities. There are many groups that convene for regional sessions, such as the Houston Co-requisite Conference, CUNY's Innovative Teaching Academy, and the California Acceleration Project (CAP). CCBC's ALP leadership looks to other professional groups for insight on ways to localize opportunities for professional growth and development. Efforts among other groups across the country provide ALP with the inspiration to plan for future mid-Atlantic summits.

The Accelerated Learning Program Institute

Both CADE and the Mid-Atlantic Teaching and Learning Summit have served as large-scale professional-development offerings through the form of conferences, and both professional-development opportunities are geared toward a large-scale audience at all levels of corequisite adoptions. Another opportunity, the ALP Institute, was first offered in the summer of 2019, and the goal of the ALP Institute was to provide targeted professional-development opportunities for institutions in the beginning stages of offering ALP within their developmental education composition offerings. ALP leadership recognized a specific need regarding requests for faculty development from external institutions looking to accelerate their developmental education sequences. The goal was to provide three days of professional development for groups of faculty from the same institutions so they could return to their institutions prepared to scale up and institutionalize ALP.

The 2019 ALP Institute was a success. Nineteen faculty attended, representing six institutions from across the country. The ALP Institute offered full-day sessions that provided in-depth faculty professional development on topics that included belongingness and addressing noncognitive factors, integrated reading, writing and critical thinking in composition courses, scaling up ALP, aligning composition with the support (ALP) course, addressing grammar and skills in context, and developing a thematic approach to teaching composition. The ALP codirectors and other CCBC faculty facilitated the various sessions based on their expertise and knowledge of topics. This professional-development opportunity created a space for meaningful connections among colleagues from the same institutions and across institutions.

The ALP Institute was a unique professional-development opportunity because external institutions paid for their faculty to travel to Baltimore, Maryland, for this significant event hosted by CCBC's ALP codirectors. The ALP Institute will be offered again, and its goal will be to expand and continue focusing on institutionalizing acceleration in composition. The ALP codirectors will also address other important topics regarding developmental education reforms since the adoption of corequisite coursework is one piece of the acceleration puzzle. CCBC's dean of Developmental Education and Special Programs, Dr. Monica Walker, also offered financial support for the ALP Institute because she understood the value of the program. This is another example of how necessary administrative support is to ongoing reforms.

External Consultations

The ALP Institute brings faculty from external institutions to CCBC to learn from a variety of CCBC ALP faculty on approaches to institutionalizing ALP at their colleges, but the ALP codirectors also conduct external consultations, which are individualized based on organizational and program needs. These consultations began over a decade ago with external grant support. The first person to begin these traveling consultations for ALP was Adams, and then they were continued in a robust way by the previous ALP director, Susan Gabriel. External institutions reach out to the ALP codirectors to request consultation services, and the codirectors meet with the requesters to conduct an informal needs assessment. During the needs assessment, the codirectors listen to requests and consider the configuration of the institution's current below-credit composition courses to determine the best approach to tailor the consultation to meet the institution's needs. The ALP codirectors provide the group with personalized and specific agendas and workshop suggestions. The various types of external consultations range from introductory workshops about ALP and finding ways to institutionalize ALP at individual institutions to addressing curricular changes through an integrated model.

There is typically a strong emphasis on curricular work during these external consultations since shifting from a traditional developmental education model to an accelerated model requires course alignment between Composition I and the support course. These consultations ground curricular professional development in the Council of Writing Program Administrators' (CWPA) "WPA Outcomes Statement for First-Year Composition" (2022). The WPA outcomes statement endorses the integration of critical thinking, reading, and composing in first-year writing courses rather than separating reading and writing as discrete skills.

Addressing relevant curricular approaches during the consultations is a priority for the ALP codirectors. Along with working with institutions to refine their course outcomes using an integrated reading and writing (IRW) approach in Composition I and its companion course, the focus is always to also address shifting from a skills-based model to a thematic approach. Theme-based curricular approaches help cultivate a teaching-learning environment that brings together themes relevant to student's lives while addressing the course objectives. Ultimately, as part of the consultation process, the codirectors of ALP help support institutions in creating authentic curricula and course materials that meet the needs of their students through the development of theme-based teaching units. The impact of this professional-development offering is far reaching.

INTERNAL PROFESSIONAL DEVELOPMENT

The need for external professional development is extensive, and the approaches to meet those needs vary from event to event. Similarly, individual institutions who have adopted corequisite models require ongoing internal professional-development opportunities, which require just as much deliberate planning as external opportunities, along with significant support from the institution.

When planning internal professional development, institutions should look at data and best practices within the field of developmental education reforms and first-year writing courses to inform the types of professional development needed to support student-success initiatives. Internal professional-development work is designed to support brand-new faculty teaching ALP, ongoing training for those who have taught ALP for several years, and faculty and staff professional-development opportunities that relate to any internal institutional changes that impact ALP. For example, in 2016, when the approach to ALP shifted to an IRW approach at CCBC, the ALP leadership saw a need for significant professional development to address these curricular and structural changes. Such significant changes require ongoing professional development to ensure the success of the program.

Once again, funding is essential in ensuring the success of a corequisite program, and funding is equally important when devising a plan to address professional-development needs for internal purposes at any institution adopting an accelerated model such as ALP. Funding is needed to provide stipends for adjunct faculty to attend the mandatory training for new ALP faculty and for adjunct faculty who meet all the requirements outlined in the Certified ALP Instructor Workshop Series, both of which are outlined in the sections below. Additionally, institutional support to provide meals during internal professional-development sessions is incredibly useful in building community during the sessions. Likewise, the internal professional-development sessions also include the extensive ALP curriculum. Developing curricula for ALP requires a great deal of work; therefore, the ALP codirectors rely on the institution to offer financial support to faculty developing ALP curriculum.

New ALP Training

Any corequisite program is unique in its structure and course design, and this configuration requires the need for ongoing professional development. Even though ALP originated sixteen years ago, the program itself requires ongoing onboarding of faculty who are brand new to teaching ALP every semester—even at CCBC.

At CCBC, the ALP codirectors first provide context for why we approach below-credit courses at CCBC with a corequisite model. This historical view incorporates important longitudinal data to document the success of retention, persistence, and attempt rates in both Composition I and II. Our rationale for bringing ALP to full scale is grounded in the data, and a comparison is made to show new faculty that prior to ALP, students placed in the lowest levels of developmental English and reading were taking sixteen billable hours of coursework even before they ever entered their credit-level composition courses. The ALP codirectors also show that the previous developmental levels of English and reading created multiple exit points, so we stood to lose more than half our students who passed the course simply because they did not return the next semester.

Once the overview of developmental education reforms is shared, the remaining focus for those brand new to ALP is practical sessions on the topics most critical to teaching within the ALP model, and this approach is suggested for any institution providing internal professional development for ALP faculty. The most important and primary aspect of ALP to understand is how to approach belongingness and student's noncognitive needs, so a portion of the faculty-development workshop is devoted to this. The others address curriculum, including integrated reading and writing (IRW), aligning the two courses, theme-based teaching, active and collaborative assignments, low- and high-stakes learning opportunities, and feedback on high- and low-stakes assignments.

It is important to include ALP faculty and leadership in these professional-development opportunities. Attendance of ALP leadership is an important part of ALP's success so they stay up to date with the New ALP Training. Involvement from leadership helps provide support for ALP faculty in their teaching since they are the ones who staff and supervise the faculty teaching ALP courses.

Mentorship

The New ALP Training plays a critical role in setting new ALP faculty up for success, but it has become apparent that new ALP faculty also need ongoing one-on-one support from ALP mentors. CCBC has such a long history of offering ALP that there are many experienced ALP faculty members in the English and academic literacy disciplines.

Each person who is new to ALP is also assigned to work with an experienced ALP colleague in their first semester teaching the model. This mentor/mentee relationship is invaluable to the success of the program. The ALP codirectors ask for ALP mentor volunteers at the start of each semester. When pairing mentors with new ALP faculty, the ALP codirectors consider the new hire's expertise, their assigned ALP modality, and their campus location. For example, if there is a new ALP faculty member with a strong background in postsecondary literacy, the ALP codirectors would likely pair that person with an ALP mentor with a composition background.

This additional layer of support has served as a meaningful way to assist new ALP instructors in meeting the needs of their students. The ALP mentor conducts an observation of their mentee's ALP class, and this observation serves to offer ongoing assistance to new ALP colleagues. The mentor/mentee relationships continue beyond the assigned semester because this ALP mentorship opportunity helps cultivate professional relationships among colleagues.

The Certified ALP Instructor Workshop Series

Both the New ALP Training and mentorship opportunities support those new to teaching ALP, but the Certified ALP Instructor Workshop Series was designed to support more experienced ALP faculty. This series was codeveloped by ALP leadership and requires cross-collaboration between the English and academic literacy disciplines. Participation in this professional-development workshop series counts as one graduate-level credit for full-time faculty who complete the requirements of the optional workshop series for CCBC's promotion process. ALP leadership also asked their academic dean to provide a stipend for adjunct faculty who completed the certification requirements. Both the equivalency and stipend requests were approved by the college, and those who become certified ALP instructors are prioritized for ALP courses whenever possible. The Certified ALP Instructor Workshop Series requires attendance and participation in a total of four workshops, along with the development of an ALP teaching project that is shared with and made accessible to all faculty teaching ALP.

Since its launch in 2017, the Certified ALP Instructor Workshop Series has served as an important, ongoing, and relevant optional professional-development opportunity for all English, academic literacy, and English speakers of other languages faculty at CCBC. Extending this robust professional-development series to those with and without ALP experience plays a significant role in filling the need for providing quality professional-development opportunities at the college. Extending the series to non-ALP faculty has increasingly become a need since so many faculty teach Composition I, even if they do not teach it within the ALP context.

The workshops are each 1.5 hours in duration. Some faculty attend workshops spanning multiple semesters, and others attend all the sessions in an academic year. The goal is for faculty to have the flexibility to interface with this professional-development opportunity at their own pace so they can get what they want from the series. Each of these workshops is designed to delve into specific curricular topics important to ALP, and the workshops vary year to year based on need and current issues at CCBC and within the fields of composition, integrated reading and writing, and overall developmental education reform. For example, in 2019, the College Composition I Common Course Outline was revamped to follow a holistic and IRW approach informed in part by the Council of Writing Program Administrators' "Framework for Success in Postsecondary Writing" (2019). The Certified ALP Workshop Series that corresponded with this change in course outcomes engendered a lively debate about the goals of a composition classroom and new ways to assess with the new common course outline in place. Because of the COVID-19 pandemic, the series also included sessions on teaching ALP in synchronous and asynchronous modalities. Each session is facilitated by different ALP faculty depending on their background and expertise relating to workshop offerings. These workshops have been adaptive and responsive, and this flexibility is crucial for all professional-development opportunities.

Once a faculty member attends the four required sessions (three fall; one spring), they develop or revise materials for ALP. The ALP codirectors work closely with faculty involved in ALP curriculum development to provide ongoing support for their work on their projects. Once faculty submit their materials to the ALP office, they are given a certificate to document they are a certified ALP instructor, and depending on their status, they either qualify for equivalency or for the adjunct stipend for completing the requirements outlined in becoming a certified ALP instructor, as previously noted.

Curriculum

The New ALP Training, mentorship support, and the Certified ALP Instructor Workshop Series are all professional-development offerings that address ways ALP faculty can successfully implement and/or create ALP curriculum for their classes. Since ALP's changes in 2016, when ALP transformed from pairing Composition I with Academic Literacy 053 instead of Developmental Writing II, the program eliminated skills-based textbooks to address both composition and reading skills. Prior to those changes, developmental English and reading courses addressed writing and reading in a skill-and-drill-based approach. The leadership that shifted its approach to serving ALP students by adopting an integrated model with Composition I (ENGL 101) and Academic Literacy 053 (ACLT 053) decided to fully eliminate the use of textbooks and readers. Instead, ALP at CCBC decided to fully support the use of authentic course materials developed in-house by faculty teaching ALP.

This initial curriculum development was supported by full-time ALP faculty, including ALP leadership. However, it was important for ALP leadership to include the involvement of English and ACLT faculty to develop ALP curriculum to amass a thoughtful collection of fully developed teaching materials for all ALP faculty to access.

Eliminating the use of costly and, for the most part, ineffective textbooks, aligned strongly with ALP's mission to eliminate student barriers. The vast majority of ALP classes had been taught by adjunct faculty, so ALP leadership knew eliminating textbooks and readers in ALP classes required the development of authentic course materials that offer entire units of study to help support faculty in teaching their classes.

A large number of these authentic teaching materials have been developed since 2016, and they are now referred to as ready-to-use ALP curriculum. The ready-to-use curricular materials include everything from lesson plans, to assigned college-level reading materials for Composition I and Academic Literacy 053, to low- and high-stakes assignments, to quizzes, and to essay prompts. The ready-to-use materials are created so the assignments are fully developed for both ENGL 101 and ACLT 053. All readings are free and open educational resources (OER) as well. These materials are invaluable to the success of the program, and a significant number of the ready-to-use materials are developed by those who engage in the Certified ALP Instructor Workshop Series.

Since the ready-to-use curriculum was developed, the ALP leadership has offered ongoing professional-development opportunities each semester to help faculty access and understand the curricular options available for their use. The ready-to-use curriculum is stored on the learning-management system (LMS) so all ALP faculty can access the extensive materials, and part of professional development includes an in-depth and hands-on look at the curriculum to provide faculty an opportunity to see how the ready-to-use materials can work within their courses. For example, many faculty employ labor-based grading in their courses, and ways to adjust the assignments to fit a labor-based grading system are shared with faculty in professional-development opportunities.

Along with administrative support, grant funding secured by the ALP codirectors has also played a strong role in curriculum development. The curricular work involved the creation of units based on themes related to financial literacy that directly connected with students' lives. Topics such as cost of living, saving, and investing were embedded in thematic units, which focused on students' financial-literacy experiences in their day-to-day lives. Additionally, curricular work has involved the development of new learning opportunities to enhance connections to antiracist curricula. For example, one adjunct faculty member created a theme-based teaching unit titled "Players and Protests: Examining the Socio-Political Power of American Sports." This unit contains a plethora of open-access readings, activity prompts, and multimodal resources. This curriculum provides a window into complex topics with the entry point of sports. The ALP students then write an editorial based on one of the issues they connected with in the unit. Students take a critical look as issues such as Native American team names and mascots, the commodification of Black bodies, and institutionalized racism in sports leagues. This unit has been very popular with students, and it is one strong example of a way to address antiracist teaching by analyzing a facet of society.

Ongoing and regular updates to the materials play an important role in ensuring the materials are never outdated, and faculty can modify materials for their courses if they choose to. ALP leadership regularly provides professional development on the ready-to-use materials offered in the various course modalities, and the ready-to-use curriculum is also shared prior to the start of the semester to give faculty ample time to select the resources they are interested in using.

The Accelerated Learning Program Action Committee

Since its inception, the accelerated learning program has relied on faculty to make decisions in support of the program. The Accelerated Learning Program Action Committee (ALPAC) is an advisory committee that meets monthly in the fall and spring semesters. Membership of ALPAC requires that faculty teach ALP at least once each academic year, and members are comprised of English, academic literacy, English speakers of other languages faculty, and the ALP administrative assistant. The ALP codirectors are the cochairs of the advisory body, and the work completed by ALPAC pertains to curriculum development, research and best practices, and professional development.

While ALPAC has existed since 2009, the ALP codirectors more recently led members of this advisory body to codevelop a shared mission and vision, and this collective practice resulted in the following:

> The Accelerated Learning Program Action Committee's (ALPAC) mission is to promote student success by fostering anti-deficit teaching and learning approaches that embrace academic and non-cognitive needs. ALPAC envisions itself as a leader in developmental education reform efforts at the institutional, local, regional, and national levels. Its vision includes reducing academic and non-academic barriers by supporting faculty through professional development opportunities through ongoing curricular and non-curricular decisions that are anchored in the use and analysis of ongoing qualitative and quantitative data to address

student success through accessible and equitable educational opportunities. (Accelerated Learning 2020)

The ALPAC vision captures especially the value the advisory body places on leading and developing professional-development opportunities within the field.

ALPAC members serve as an integral part of ALP's success. They typically serve as ALP mentors and are the faculty who provide work that reaches across the college to assist with and lead developmental education reforms. Additionally, ALPAC members frequently serve as professional-development facilitators for the Certified ALP Instructor Workshop Series, and they also help to support CADE as conference volunteers.

CONCLUSION

Cultivating and Maintaining Professional-Development Opportunities

Professional-development opportunities should be conceived in a variety of formats available and accessible to a wide audience with varying degrees of experience. There should be varying professional-development opportunities depending on experience with ALP, and the range of opportunities should be developed with absolute intention. For example, the focus for CADE differs from that of the Certified ALP Instructor Workshop Series. Both professional-development opportunities cultivate opportunities for growth and learning about ALP. However, the national conference highlights topics relating to all corequisite programs, disciplines outside composition, and work relating to developmental education reforms, while the Certified ALP Instructor Workshop Series provides targeted professional-development sessions specifically for a CCBC ALP faculty member teaching Composition I and Academic Literacy 053.

It is important that those planning professional-development opportunities identify their purpose to ensure the experiences of participants are met or exceeded. Likewise, the professional-development opportunities should align with the program's areas of expertise and overall vision and mission.

The Importance of Funding

There are so many moving parts and items of consideration when planning thoughtful professional-development opportunities for corequisite programs, but the most consistent piece to the puzzle is that allocation of funding is essential to ensure professional-development opportunities are a mainstay within institutions.

Funding professional-development opportunities is often a challenge. It is always critical to prioritize professional development, but in doing so, those designing the professional-development opportunities must substantiate the need and relevance of this work to garner support from internal and external funding sources.

ALP professional development is possible at CCBC because the college supports the ALP codirectors' leadership roles through reassigned time. The ALP codirectorship job description outlines significant duties relating to internal and external professional development as part of the basic job responsibilities. The college understands that continued learning is one of the most important aspects of ensuring student success, so it supports ongoing, relevant professional-development opportunities for all ALP stakeholders. CCBC supports a codirectorship instead of a directorship model so those leading ALP also teach it every single semester. The inclusion of teaching responsibilities for the ALP codirectors allows them to lead with a very practical, hands-on perspective as true practitioners, and the college's commitment to providing reassigned time to two faculty members for an ALP codirectorship serves as a funding source to support ongoing internal and external professional-development needs.

While the structure for the codirectorship is invaluable, the work relating to professional-development needs cannot be addressed through this means alone. There is an ever-growing demand for teaching corequisite courses in both asynchronous and synchronous modalities. It is important that institutions allocate funding resources so those with experience in online teaching and curriculum development are provided with financial support to assist with quality online professional-development opportunities.

Additionally, the success of ALP could not be measured without the support of the Institutional Research (IR) Office. This office tracks student-success rates of those enrolled in ALP, which is essential in ensuring ALP is meeting student needs. The data that come from IR help inform professional-development needs, among other items that fall within the scope of the ALP office's work. It is important that institutions prioritize Institutional Research's involvement in tracking ALP's success, completion, and retention rates. While this tracking uses IR's time and funds, the prioritization of data-tracking efforts for ALP is critical to its ability to serve its students—especially since ALP serves historically marginalized populations.

Though first-hand financial support from individual institutions is imperative, it is also important for corequisite programs to look to external funding sources in the form of grants to support their professional-development efforts.

At CCBC, curriculum development and updates are ongoing. Since CCBC approaches ALP with ready-to-use, authentic course materials, updating and maintaining current and relevant curriculum is critical to its success. Ongoing maintenance of and updates to curriculum is a significant time commitment. The ALP codirectors have secured funds through external grants to assist with curriculum development, which has become even more critical since ALP is offered in face-to-face, asynchronous, and synchronous modalities. Whenever applying for external funding for curriculum development, the ALP codirectors directly tie the need for curriculum development to the need to help support the integration and costs of including professional development to familiarize faculty with the new curriculum.

Looking Ahead

Without robust and ongoing faculty professional development, corequisite composition runs the risk of becoming ineffective because of the unique nature of the program. If corequisite work is new to an organization, collaboration between the Office of Instruction and the Office of Planning, Research, and Evaluation should be one of the first partnerships developed. This collaboration will ensure data-tracking measures are in place. ALP has longitudinal data to document its successes, and external organizations also have collected longitudinal data on how ALP has served its students. Individual institutions should continue to collect their own data, as this evidence helps support a path for administrators to offer their financial support. The partnership with IR will also tease out data about areas that require work, and with this data, faculty involved with corequisite work can plan thoughtful professional-development sessions.

It has often been said that organizations demonstrate a true level of support when they designate a portion of their budget toward a program. Advancing the work to best serve students cannot occur unless institutions willingly open their pockets. Senior leadership must take seriously the increases in student-success rates since the adoption of corequisite education, and the leaders of programs such as ALP must substantiate the need for ongoing professional development so institutions find value in the allocation of funds for this work.

REFERENCES

Accelerated Learning Program Action Committee. 2020. "Item 1: Developing ALPAC Vision and Mission." ALPAC Meeting Minutes, November 30. Community College of Baltimore County: ALP OneDrive.

Adams, Peter. 2019. "Strong Developmental Education Is Critical to Students and Society." Center for Analysis of Postsecondary Readiness. https://postsecondaryreadiness.org/strong-developmental-education-critical.

Adams, Peter. 2021. "Recognition." Peter Adams. https://peteradamsalp.com/recognition/.

Azimi, Haleh, and Elsbeth Mantler. 2020. "Supporting Adjunct Faculty Through Quality Professional Development: A Holistic Approach." *Learning Abstracts* 23 (8).

Bickerstaff, Susan, and Octaviano Chavarín. 2018. "Understanding the Needs of Part-Time Faculty at Six Community Colleges." Community College Research Center, Teachers College, Columbia University NY. https://ccrc.tc.columbia.edu/media/k2/attachments/understanding-part-time-faculty-community-colleges.pdf.

Cho, Sung-Woo, Elizabeth Kopko, Davis Jenkins, and Shanna Smith Jaggars. 2012. "New Evidence of Success for Community College Remedial Students: Tracking the Outcomes of Students in the Accelerated Learning Program (ALP)." *CCRC Working Paper* 53. Community College Research Center, Teachers College, Columbia University, NY.

Council of Writing Program Administrators. 2019. "Framework for Success in Postsecondary Writing." https://wpacouncil.org/aws/cwpa/pt/sd/news_article/242845/_parent/layout_details/false.

Council of Writing Program Administrators. 2022. "WPA Outcomes Statement for First-Year Composition (3.0)." https://wpacouncil.org/aws/CWPA/pt/sd/news_article/242845/_PARENT/layout_details/false.

Datray, Jennifer, Patrick Saxon, and Nara Martirosyan. 2014. "Adjunct Faculty in Developmental Education: Best Practices, Challenges, and Recommendations." *Community College Enterprise* 20 (1): 34–48.

Ganga, Elizabeth, Amy Mazzariello, and Nilli Edgecomb. 2018. "Developmental Education: An Introduction for Policymakers." Center of Analysis for Postsecondary Readiness. https://postsecondaryreadiness.org/developmental-education-introduction-policymakers.

Jenkins, Davis, Clive Belfield, Cecilia Speroni, Shanna Smith Jaggars, and Nikki Edgecombe. 2010. "A Model for Accelerating Academic Success of Community College Remedial English Students: Is the Accelerated Learning Program (ALP) Effective and Affordable?" *Community College Research Center Working Paper No. 21*.

INDEX

Accelerated Learning Program (ALP), 4, 8–10, 12, 19, 22–24, 39, 41, 49–51, 66–77, 80–97, 102, 104–106, 113, 127, 131, 165, 207, 209–216, 218, 223, 225, 232, 251–271
"Accelerated Learning Program, The: Throwing Open the Gates" (Adams et al.), 5, 19, 51
Accuplacer, 21, 52, 191. *See also* assessment
Adams, Peter, 5, 9, 12, 19, 20, 23–24, 36, 49, 51, 52, 60, 65, 69, 86, 120, 130, 161–173, 209, 232, 251, 253–255, 258, 260, 261
adjunct faculty, 223, 253, 263, 265–267
administration (college), 20, 39, 53–55, 67, 71, 91, 127, 177, 212, 253–258, 267–268
America's Unmet Promise: The Imperative for Equity in Higher Education (Witham et al.), 7
antiracism, 26, 57, 71, 80, 104, 125, 185, 207–208, 210, 224, 226–228
Assembly Bill 705 (AB 705), 18, 24, 25, 39, 40, 166, 190
assessment, 3, 9, 22, 25, 26, 29, 37–38, 51, 67, 70–71, 76, 78, 80, 83, 104, 121–133, 146, 148, 154–155, 161, 186, 198, 202, 207–208, 210, 213–216, 224, 226–229, 234, 244, 246, 254, 261. *See also* Accuplacer; labor-based grading
asynchronous learning, 8, 71–74, 89, 200, 223–224, 266, 270–271. *See also* modality; online education; technology
attendance, 30–31, 68, 76, 88, 94–95, 130
attrition, 3, 68, 165, 251

Bahr, Peter, 21, 52
Bartholmae, David, 47, 163, 168–169
basic writing, 5–6, 10, 12, 37, 46–51, 53, 123, 128, 131, 140, 202
Berthoff, Anne E., 169, 182
Bickerstaff, Susan, 175, 253
Blaauw-Hara, Mark, 33, 123, 126, 178
Butte College, 4

California Acceleration Project (CAP), 4, 7, 10, 18, 20, 24, 39, 41, 190, 196, 207, 260

California Community College System, 4, 8, 17, 18, 20, 30
Chabot College, 3, 4
choice boards, 68, 70–76
Community College of Baltimore County (CCBC), 4, 5, 6, 12, 18, 19, 52, 65, 69, 77, 131, 166–167, 207, 209, 232, 251–271
Community College Research Center (CCRC), 4, 6, 69, 77, 164, 220, 250, 251, 257, 258
Complete College America, 6, 121, 161
Conference on Acceleration in Developmental Education (CADE), 20, 49–50, 257–260, 269
COVID-19 pandemic, 8, 36, 55–56, 61, 67–68, 71, 72, 78, 80–97, 192, 213, 218, 221, 222, 225, 226, 246, 266

developmental education, 3–8, 9–11, 23, 30, 33, 37, 41, 45–47, 50, 53–55, 57, 61–62, 65–67, 69–70, 77, 83, 121–126, 161, 164–165, 173, 175–179, 184, 187, 190, 202, 209–216, 219–222, 225–226, 228, 232–233, 251–252, 254–266, 268–269. *See also* basic writing
digital divide, 61
Duckworth, Angela, 29, 235
Dweck, Carol, 7, 28, 231, 234–246

Elbow, Peter, 31, 124, 127, 172, 202, 213
El Paso Community College (EPCC), 208–212, 215, 222–223, 225–227, 229
equity, 7, 8, 11, 12, 17, 19, 22, 26, 37, 39, 53, 65, 67–68, 70–71, 76, 80, 93, 106, 122, 132, 154, 191, 202, 226, 227–228, 229,
Express to Success Program (ESP), 17–18, 24, 25, 29, 34–35, 39–40

faculty development. *See* professional development
first-generation college students, 12, 27, 36–37, 83, 145, 207, 209, 218, 227, 233, 237, 252
first-year composition (FYC), 3, 4, 102, 180, 183; and journals 190, 191, 193, 196, 198, 199, 200, 202

fixed mindset. *See* mindset
funding, 20–21, 41, 166, 253–258, 263, 267, 269–271

Gates Foundation, The Bill and Melinda, 6
Goucher College, 232, 234
grading. *See* assessment
grit, 27, 29, 30, 32, 40, 214, 217, 219, 222, 235
growth mindset. *See* mindset

Henson, Leslie, 3, 19
Hern, Katie, 7, 10, 18, 19, 20, 33, 40

Inoue, Asao B., 22, 71, 78, 80, 103, 104, 116, 123–125, 128, 185–186, 197, 210, 227, 228, 245
internet. *See* online education; technology

Journal of Basic Writing, 5, 12

Kendi, Ibram X., 26, 53, 227
Kingsborough Community College (KBCC), 6, 65–66, 68, 70
Ko, Melissa, 22

labor-based grading, 78, 121–133, 210, 228, 267
Lamott, Anne, 180
Las Positas College, 3, 4
leaky pipeline, 25
library, 36, 152, 149, 153
Lin, Yuxin, 11
Liou, Stephanie, 7

Madera Community College (MCC), 190–191, 200
math, 8, 18–21, 39, 41, 65, 86, 106, 143, 147, 161, 167, 190, 191, 208–209, 222, 252, 254, 258, 259, 260
metacognition, 26, 29, 105, 125–126, 129, 154–155, 176, 178, 180, 181, 183–185, 193, 196, 198, 210–211, 216, 219, 222, 224, 244, 246
Mid-Atlantic Teaching and Learning Summit, 259–260
mindset, 7, 9–10, 27–28, 29, 32, 33, 40, 110, 199, 210, 214, 217, 219, 222, 234–246. *See also* Dweck, Carol
modality, 56, 58, 80–82, 84–85, 88–89. *See also* online education; technology
Molloy, Kathy, 3, 10–11, 17–18, 24–25, 29, 34, 35, 39–40

National Organization for Student Success (NOSS), 11
noncognitive skills, 9–10, 27–30, 32, 54, 105, 125, 207–212, 214, 216–219, 221, 223–229, 252, 254, 258, 261, 264

online education, 8, 19, 38, 56, 61, 68, 71–73, 80–85, 87–95, 97, 130, 138, 192, 200, 219, 221–225, 270. *See also* technology

Ran, Florence Xiaotao, 11
Reading Apprenticeship, 105, 178, 180–182, 190
Redesigning America's Community Colleges: A Clearer Path to Student Success (Bailey et al.), 6
remediation, 4, 5, 7, 8, 11, 27, 49, 50, 54, 67, 70, 71, 106, 135, 146, 161, 164, 190, 200, 202
Research and Planning Group, 4, 30
research paper, 27, 136–155

pass rates, 3, 9, 67, 69
pandemic. *See* COVID-19 pandemic
Porterville College, 18, 136, 144
professional development, 10, 12, 39, 77, 96–97, 165–167, 173, 202, 208, 210, 213, 215, 218, 225, 226–228, 251–271

Queensborough Community College, 69–70

Santa Barbara City College (SBCC), 17–18, 24–25, 34
Snell, Myra, 7, 20
standards, 4, 22, 124–125, 137, 139, 153, 226
stretch model, 23, 88
studio model, 23, 24, 231–236, 240–245
Suffolk County Community College (SCCC), 46–48, 51–53, 55, 57, 61
Sullivan, Patrick, 4, 176, 181, 182
syllabus, 22, 26, 36, 128–130, 167, 171, 183, 210, 213, 219, 223, 224, 228

technology, 22, 36–37, 61, 78, 85, 87, 93–96, 153, 224, 235; *See also* online education
"This Ain't Another Statement! This is a DEMAND for Black Linguistic Justice!" (CCC), 38, 57
threshold concepts, 101–102, 104, 109, 110, 142, 146, 177
throughput, 25, 39, 40, 41, 190

Tinberg, Howard, 102, 103, 105, 106, 113, 153, 176
transfer (from two- to four-year college), 3, 6, 8, 25, 39, 40, 66, 99–117, 126, 135–137, 140, 141, 147, 155, 177, 183–184, 190, 202, 219
tutoring, 23–24, 35–36, 40, 87, 121, 219–220,

University of Alaska Anchorage, 81–82, 84

Wardle, Elizabeth, 101, 139–141, 177
white language supremacy, 38
Wood, J. Luke, 26,
Wood, Tara, 22
writing about writing, 33, 100, 103, 141, 143–144, 177–178, 180, 183
writing centers, 23–24, 35–36, 217–219

Yancey, Kathleen Blake, 101–102

Zoom, 73–75, 85, 87, 90–92, 94, 95, 113, *See also* online education; technology

ABOUT THE AUTHORS

Peter Adams taught English, mostly basic writing, at the Community College of Baltimore County for thirty-four years, retiring in 2014. During those years, he led the development of the accelerated learning program, the earliest version of the corequisite approach to developmental education. Since retiring, he has consulted with more than two hundred colleges as they developed versions of corequisite developmental education and as they grappled with the challenges of integrating reading and writing. Adams has authored four writing textbooks, including, most recently, *The Hub: A Place for Reading and Writing*.

Carrie Aldrich earned a PhD in language, literacy, and culture from the University of Iowa, a master's degree in applied linguistics from the University of Alaska Fairbanks, and bachelor's degrees in English education and sociology from Indiana University. She teaches a variety of writing courses, coordinates writing placement, is faculty liaison to the writing center, and serves as a member of the Faculty Senate Diversity Committee at the University of Alaska Anchorage. Her research focuses on sociocultural approaches to retention and success in first-year writing. In all of her work, she strives to develop a healthy culture of literacy in homes, classrooms, and communities.

Haleh Azimi is codirector of ALP at CCBC. She has eleven years' experience teaching academic literacy and composition courses at CCBC. She is committed to her work with ALP and develops and leads initiatives to further the student-success efforts. She has a BS in English writing from Towson University, an MAT in secondary education English, and her EdD in educational leadership and management with a policy concentration from Drexel University.

Jami Blaauw-Hara is the writing program coordinator and a professor of English and communication at North Central Michigan College, a rural community college. She and a colleague brought the corequisite model of developmental writing to North Central, and the resultant program won the 2019 Diana Hacker TYCA Outstanding Program Award. For years, she led the Reading Apprenticeship program at North Central, helping faculty members across the curriculum better support student reading. Her recent work has appeared in *Composition Studies* and the edited collection *(Re)Considering What We Know: Learning Thresholds in Writing, Composition, Rhetoric, and Literacy*.

Mark Blaauw-Hara is an assistant professor, teaching stream, at the University of Toronto Mississauga. Before that, he was the WPA at North Central Michigan College, a rural community college, where he codeveloped and taught in a corequisite model of developmental writing. North Central's corequisite program won the 2019 Diana Hacker TYCA Outstanding Program Award. Mark's book *From Military to Academy*, published in 2021, focuses on the writing and learning experiences of student military veterans; he also coedited a collection titled *Understanding WPA Readiness and Renewal* with Joe Janangelo, which was published in 2022. Mark has been the president of the Council of Writing Program Administrators, and his writing has appeared in several journals and edited collections.

ABOUT THE AUTHORS

Lesley Broder joined the English Department of CUNY's Kingsborough Community College in Brooklyn in 2008, shortly before receiving her doctorate in English from Stony Brook University. She began her career as a middle- and high-school teacher and later taught at Suffolk County Community College and Stony Brook University, where she also served as assistant director of the writing center. At Kingsborough, she coordinated the accelerated learning program for nearly a decade. Professor Broder's research focuses on gender and sexuality, popular theater trends in New York City, and writing placement and assessment. Her essays have appeared in *Modern Drama* and *The English Record* in addition to several edited collections, including the fourth volume *of New Perspectives in Edward Albee Studies*.

Jill Darley-Vanis has been teaching at Clark College since 2000. Her research, conference presentations, and published works focus on assignment design, transfer theory, and more equitable classroom practices. For the past ten years she has been teaching in two different acceleration models, I-BEST and ALP. She has been published in the journal *Teaching English in the Two-Year College* (*TETYC*) and the book *Transparent Design in Higher Education Teaching and Leadership*; and she has presented at the Conference on College Composition and Communication (CCCC), the First-Year Experience (FYE), the Two-Year College Association (TYCA), and the State of Washington's Assessment in Teaching and Learning (ATL) conference. Jill has served on the board of *TETYC* and in English Department leadership and is now serving on the MLA's Higher Education Practices (HEP) Community College Forum Executive Committee.

Melissa Favara began teaching at Clark College in 2007 and holds a BA in English with a creative writing emphasis from Western Michigan University and an MA in English literature from Pennsylvania State University, where she studied Victorian and modernist literature with a critical focus on queer theory. For the past decade, her teaching has focused on accelerated composition, both in the Integrated Basic Education and Skills Training (I-BEST) program and in ALP. She has presented on learning communities at the National Learning Communities Conference (NLCC) and on creating vulnerability spaces in the ALP classroom at the Modern Language Association (MLA) conference. Melissa writes creative nonfiction that has been published in *street roots*, *Metro Parent*, *McSweeney's Internet Tendency*, and elsewhere.

Meridith Leo is a graduate of a two-year community college and joined the English faculty of Suffolk County Community College's Ammerman Campus in 2010. She earned her PhD at St. John's University, where she focused on narratives of difference and belonging along with culturally responsive literacy narratives. Her research at St. John's University led to work in corequisite (ALP) coursework, which is detailed in her dissertation "Integrating Emerging Writers into the Post-Remedial College: A Consideration of Accelerated Learning Programs." She teaches courses in composition and rhetoric as well as creative nonfiction.

Melissa Long is an English professor at Porterville College. Though her focus is in the classroom teaching college composition (both with and without a corequisite) and British literature, she also works as the campus outcomes coordinator, facilitates a community of practice for student-centered teaching, and oversees the college's implementation of AB 705. She lives in Visalia, California, with her husband, four kids, two dogs, and an impressive collection of 118 nutcrackers.

Elsbeth Mantler is codirector of the accelerated learning program (ALP) at the Community College of Baltimore County. She has twelve years' experience teaching developmental writing and composition at CCBC. Elsbeth has been teaching ALP since 2010, and she considers it the most important part of her teaching career. She has a BA in

English literature from Salisbury University, as well as an MA in American studies from the University of Southern Maine.

Sarah Prielipp has a PhD in rhetoric and writing from Michigan State University. As a community-engaged, cultural rhetorics scholar, she focuses on writing in a variety of contexts both in and out of the classroom. Her current research projects include a collaborative, longitudinal project with University of Alaska Anchorage colleague Carrie Aldrich to study students' experiences during and after the ALP model. She is also researching participatory assessment as antiracist pedagogy and praxis.

Gregory Ramírez has taught at Madera Community College since 2008. He earned his bachelor's and master's degrees from California State University, Fresno, then earned his DA in English pedagogy from Murray State University. He has presented (or copresented) at conferences in Portland, Atlanta, San Diego, and Sacramento, and virtually for the Southwest Popular/American Culture Association (SWPACA) Conference, for the Conference on College Composition and Communication (CCCC), and for the Kentucky Organization for Student Success (KOSS). His poetry has appeared in journals throughout the United States and in anthologies, including Heyday Books' reprinting of *Highway 99: A Literary Journey Through California's Great Central Valley* and *Corners of the Mouth: A Celebration of Thirty Years at the Annual San Luis Obispo Poetry Festival*. He lives in Clovis, California, with his wife, Stephanie, and their two children.

Margaret Nelson Rodríguez, professor of English at El Paso Community College, teaches composition and corequisite composition and operates from deep knowledge of the corequisite/ALP movement. At EPCC, she leads the English corequisite working group and the online development effort for the English discipline, all while serving as curriculum committee chair and special projects assistant to the vice president of instruction and workforce education. She has expertise in teaching writing, in course redesign, in curriculum development, and in faculty development; she is also a fierce advocate for developing writers and two-year college students. As a grant writer, Margie has secured more than $1 million in funding for EPCC initiatives and projects, including funding for the Humanities Collaborative, which supports students as they study humanities at EPCC and transition to the University of Texas at El Paso. Margie holds a master's degree from UTEP.

David Starkey is Emeritus Professor of English, founding director of the creative writing program, and a former director of the composition program at Santa Barbara City College. A frequent collaborator with the late Wendy Bishop, Starkey helped develop a pedagogy focused on the cross-pollination of composition and creative writing. In addition to his work with Bishop, which includes the coauthored *Keywords in Creative Writing* (2006), he is the editor of two collections of essays on pedagogy, *Teaching Writing Creatively* (1998) and *Genre by Example: Writing What We Teach* (2001), and a special issue of *Teaching English in the Two-Year College* (Dec. 2014). His writing on corequisite composition is informed by his participation in SBCC's Express to Success program, an early adopter of the ALP/corequisite model.

Charlee Sterling earned her PhD in English and American literature from New York University in 2003 and currently teaches writing and literature at Goucher College in Baltimore, Maryland. Charlee's scholarly focus includes twentieth-century and contemporary American literature and Anglo-American modernism. She has previously written on the work of Edith Wharton and William Faulkner and on the ups and downs of teaching online; her current work focuses on composition pedagogy and comics and the important role comics, multimodality, and popular literature and culture can play in the writing studies classroom.

www.ingramcontent.com/pod-product-compliance
Lightning Source LLC
Chambersburg PA
CBHW020520080526
44583CB00013B/669